*The Civil War and the Transformation of
American Citizenship*

CONFLICTING WORLDS
New Dimensions of the American Civil War

T. Michael Parrish, Series Editor

THE CIVIL WAR
AND THE
TRANSFORMATION
OF AMERICAN
CITIZENSHIP

EDITED BY
PAUL QUIGLEY

LOUISIANA STATE UNIVERSITY PRESS   BATON ROUGE

Published by Louisiana State University Press
Copyright © 2018 by Louisiana State University Press
All rights reserved
Manufactured in the United States of America
First printing

DESIGNER: Barbara Neely Bourgoyne
TYPEFACE: Ingeborg
PRINTER AND BINDER: TK

Library of Congress Cataloging-in-Publication Data are
available at the Library of Congress.

ISBN 978-0-8071-6863-9 (cloth: alk. paper)—ISBN 978-0-8071-6864-6 (pdf)—
ISBN 978-0-8071-6865-3 (epub)

CONTENTS

ACKNOWLEDGMENTS

This volume began to germinate at a conference in Blacksburg in April 2015. The Civil War–era history of citizenship had long intrigued me, developing into a scholarly itch I couldn't quite figure out how to scratch. I found it difficult to imagine a single research project doing justice to such a complex, multifaceted subject. Collaboration was the obvious answer. The best way to scratch the itch, it turned out, was to assemble a group of experts who could bring a variety of perspectives and methods to bear on the knotty problem of what citizenship meant and how it changed during the Civil War era.

Twenty-four speakers from across the United States and Europe participated in the conference, and for three days we explored our subject from a rich assortment of angles. I take great pleasure in thanking everyone who made the conference such a success: the panel chairs and the presenters, who ranged from graduate students to senior professors in both law and history; keynote lecturers Laura Edwards and Steven Hahn; graduate assistant Kristin Carlson; the staff at the Inn at Virginia Tech; and donors to the Virginia Center for Civil War Studies, which sponsored the event.

It's been a privilege to work with LSU Press to turn the project into a book. I especially appreciate the support and encouragement of Mike Parrish and Rand Dotson. An anonymous reviewer made a number of thoughtful suggestions that have improved the final product, while editor Lee Sioles did a fine job taking the manuscript through the final stages.

Most of all, I am grateful to the essay authors, who cheerfully met deadlines, made multiple rounds of edits, and worked hard to ensure that their disparate topics engaged with common themes. Thanks to you all for making this such a rewarding experience.

The Civil War and the Transformation of
American Citizenship

Introduction

PAUL QUIGLEY

What is citizenship? It is a concept we are all familiar with, but one that can be maddeningly difficult to define neatly. Across the modern world, citizenship has become central to the formation and the operation of the democratic nation-state. At its most simple, it is a fixed legal status that we acquire through birth or naturalization. It provides access to a clearly defined set of rights and obligations—the right to enter certain territory or to claim certain resources, the obligation to pay particular taxes or perform national service. We either possess it or we do not. Yet for all its apparent specificity and rigidity, in practice citizenship can be a remarkably capacious, fluid concept. It encompasses not only legal and political but also social and economic rights and obligations. It frequently involves a sense of cultural belonging to a bounded community. Citizenship changes over time and space, and it overlaps with other forms of loyalty and status. And so, the question remains: What *is* citizenship?

If citizenship is complex today, it was still more so in the era of the American Civil War. In 1862 even US Attorney General Edward Bates found it impossible to provide a precise definition of US citizenship, which was, as he put it, "now as little understood in its details and elements, and the question as open to argument and speculative criticism as it was at the beginning of the Government."[1] If even the attorney general was confused by the elusiveness of the concept, what hope did ordinary Americans have?

The concept of citizenship would become somewhat clearer with the constitutional amendments that followed the Civil War, particularly with the adoption of the Fourteenth Amendment in 1868. Previously, citizenship had been defined at the state level, except in the case of naturalized immigrants. The original Constitution and the Bill of Rights had delineated rights and obligations of "the people" and had rested, largely implicitly, on the Founders' vision of a nation-state operated by citizens. Now, the Fourteenth Amendment explicitly established a new category of national citizenship with these words: "All persons born or naturalized in the United States, and subject to the jurisdiction thereof, are citizens of the United States and of the state wherein they reside." This new definition pointedly included African Americans, reversing the racial exclusiveness of prewar American citizenship that had been exemplified by the Supreme Court's 1857 *Dred Scott* decision. It also reflected the immense sacrifice of human life between 1861 and 1865, a sacrifice that began by threatening the very survival of emerging notions of citizenship and ended in refining the concept and making it more relevant than ever. Clearly, the crises of the Civil War and emancipation drove Americans to define citizenship with greater inclusivity and greater precision.

Yet we must look well beyond the Fourteenth Amendment to understand this process fully. The development of new concepts of citizenship involved Americans far from Washington, DC: Americans northern and southern, male and female, black and white, immigrant and native-born. This was not simply the top-down imposition of new legal rules. Instead, it was a collaborative and wide-ranging reassessment of the many meanings of citizenship in the United States. Constitutional law was important, but it was just one dimension among many.

The essays in this book explore many dimensions of this expansive process from a wide range of perspectives. What the essays share is the aim of understanding how Civil War Americans used citizenship to articulate and contest different visions of what America was and what it ought to be; who belonged and who did not. Together, they reveal deep connections among the central problems of the Civil War: the place of white southerners within the Union and the place of African Americans within American society and politics. We often separate these two issues, but of course they were tightly intertwined. The debate over citizenship—what it meant, who could claim it, who ultimately arbitrated it—was a common thread running through Civil War Americans' otherwise disparate experiences and agendas. To be sure, they used the concept in different ways and to different ends. But for everyone, citizenship provided a capacious, flexible language with which to advance their own priorities—whether they were black women using the law to secure ownership of their own bodies or Confederate POWs agonizing over whether to take the oath of allegiance; whether they were Confederate veterans reimagining citizenship along economic lines or black firemen claiming new political rights and new access to public space. Ultimately, this volume clarifies the fundamental issue that all Americans fought over throughout the Civil War and Reconstruction years: What did citizenship mean and who got to define it?

At the time of the American Civil War, citizenship was a relatively new idea. Although its roots lie in the ancient world, the distinctively modern notion of the citizen emerged from the age of revolutions in the late eighteenth century. In France and the United States, revolution brought with it new claims of equal status and rights that flowed into the idea of the citizen. The creators of modern citizenship defined it in contrast to the monarchical system of subjecthood. Instead of a vertical hierarchy in which power and status flowed down from the monarch, citizens operated on a horizontal plane. Citizens were loyal to the polity, not to an individual monarch. In theory, at least, all were equal.

No serious commentator would claim that the universalist ideals of citizenship were immediately realized. Yet it is common to assume that those ideals were progressively implemented over time, with the boundaries of the citizenry gradually expanding over the course of the long nineteenth century (1789–1914), incrementally including social groups that had initially been left out. In the case of the United States, it can seem as though the Founders defined citizenship and all that remained to be done was expand the boundaries of the fixed category so that it embraced all Americans regardless of race, gender, or class. Jacksonian democracy brought non-property-holding white men, previously excluded from full citizenship rights (notably the right to vote), into the citizenry; the post–Civil War amendments did the same thing for African American men. Women were fully incorporated when they secured the vote in the wake of World War I. The United States is often taken to be the supreme example, but by no means the only example, of the liberal narrative of citizenship.[2]

Many scholars of citizenship have questioned the liberal framework, observing that in the United States and elsewhere the boundaries of citizenship have contracted as well as expanded; that "progress" is not always forward-moving or linear. Furthermore, they have argued that inequalities of race, class, and gender have been inherent to citizen-

ship—not aberrations from its lofty ideals—even in countries such as
the United States and France that are normally seen as exemplars of
open, inclusive citizenship.[3]

Experts on citizenship in a range of times and places have also expanded the meaning of the term to include much more than formal
political status, much more than the right to vote or hold a passport. An
especially important contribution came from British sociologist T. H.
Marshall, who differentiated between three forms of citizenship: civic,
political, and social. Although his schema has been criticized—among
other things for the overly neat association of these three forms with the
eighteenth, nineteenth, and twentieth centuries, respectively—the core
ideas that citizenship involves more than legal status, and that it has
evolved, continue to be widely influential. Scholars of citizenship around
the world now view citizenship as an unstable process, the result of ongoing negotiations between many actors, a process in which power can
flow up as well as down. They have studied military service, labor move-
ments, the public sphere, gender relations—all facets of the wide-ranging
concept of citizenship. Their insights are already beginning to enrich
the investigation of citizenship in the era of the American Civil War.[4]

The most common approach to Civil War era citizenship has been to
explore the expansion of the category to include new groups—particularly African American or immigrant men, who relied on military service to assert citizenship. Such studies traditionally advanced an overly
straightforward narrative of outsider groups acquiring the fixed status
of citizenship. Yet the most useful recent works have moved toward critical interrogation of the concept itself, asking how the extended crises of
war and emancipation gave rise to new ideas of what citizenship meant
and what it ought to mean.[5]

As historians such as Laura Edwards, William J. Novak, and Michael
Vorenberg have argued, the Civil War era was a crucial stage in the development of ideas of citizenship in the United States. Before, the concept simply did not exist in the way we understand it today. But as a
result of the war's dislocations, new claims for rights emerged—often
welling up from below rather than being imposed from above—and
formed part of the new framework of national citizenship.[6] In an en-
lightening study of southern loyalists, Susanna Lee presents "vernacular
citizenship" as a fluctuating negotiation between Federal commissioners and loyalists claiming compensation for wartime incidents.[7] Other
valuable insights have come from scholars of African American women

during the Civil War era. Building on important 1990s scholarship that rooted citizenship within the household, more recent work by Elizabeth Regosin, Hannah Rosen, Chandra Manning, and others has drawn our attention to the importance of African American women in the reformulation of citizenship during and after the Civil War.[8] This volume brings together and moves forward emerging strands of this new scholarship of citizenship in the Civil War–era United States.

It was the condition of war, more than anything else, that stimulated change by enabling central governments in Washington, DC, and Richmond to drastically expand their reach into individuals' lives. The war demanded an all-out mobilization of societies, economies, and populations on both sides. In the Union, the Republican-dominated Congress implemented a new economic vision that made public land available to homesteaders, supported a cross-country railroad, promoted public colleges, created a national income tax, and introduced a national currency system.[9] In the Confederacy, despite the powerful myth of southern states' rights ideology, wartime exigencies called forth an unprecedented expansion of government authority. By 1864, the Richmond government exercised extensive control over the physical movement of those within Confederate territory, over economic pursuits and foreign trade (most of it via blockade runners), and over much else besides. In the judgment of historian Emory Thomas, this was "the nearest thing to state socialism to appear in the nineteenth century."[10] Both the Confederacy and the Union fit into a long pattern of war stimulating state formation, a pattern that stretches back to the French and American Revolutionary wars and forward to the world wars of the twentieth century. Just as, in Charles Tilly's pithy formulation, "War made the state, and the state made war," we might say that war made the citizen and the citizen made war.[11]

In the American Civil War as in other conflicts, conscription was the centerpiece. Although both sides used conscription, it worked differently in the Confederacy than in the Union. Most notably, the Confederacy's greater need for manpower necessitated a national draft almost a year earlier than in the Union (April 1862 versus March 1863), and also meant that a greater percentage of the Confederate military was comprised of conscripts and substitutes than was the case in the Union (20 percent versus 8 percent).[12] As recent scholarship on this subject has emphasized, this was not simply the imposition of a new model of citizenship by central governments. Rather, conscription policy was an evolving, cooperative effort between national, state, and local authorities. It built on the foundation of state- and local-level militia service in the early stages of the Civil War, and indeed throughout US history. And, as was the case in other parts of the world, coerced conscription was often overshadowed by the idea and the practice of voluntary enlistment, refracted through the ideology of nationalism. Wars have modified citizenship not merely through the fiats of central governments, but by the actions and ideas of ordinary citizens as well.[13]

There was often a more instrumentalist dimension to citizens' willingness to fight. Just as governments used war to expand central power, so too did individuals use war to advance new claims on government—to renegotiate the framework of citizenship. The classic paradigm here is of previously disfranchised groups relying on their contributions to their country's war effort in order to strengthen their claims to equal citizenship, often in the form of a claim on suffrage rights. Witness British and American women's successes in the wake of World War I. And witness African Americans' claims to citizenship as a result of their Union service during the Civil War. Frederick Douglass articulated precisely this agenda in 1863, writing, "Once let the black man get upon his person the brass letters U.S.; let him get an eagle on his button, and a musket on his shoulder, and bullets in his pocket, and there is no power on the earth or under the earth which can deny that he has earned the right of citizenship in the United States." As Christian Samito has shown, both African Americans and Irish Americans—albeit in different ways— embraced Union military service as a path to citizenship.[14] Across the world during the long nineteenth century, from France and Prussia to the United States and various parts of Latin America, citizenship was becoming connected to universal military service, each requiring the other in an increasingly symbiotic relationship.

In the United States and elsewhere, the tightening link with military service strengthened the existing nexus of masculinity and citizenship.[15] If being a citizen meant serving as a soldier, and being a soldier meant being male, what did that mean for women? Although war and conscription undeniably masculinized the formal category of citizenship, the extensive mobilization of "people's wars" in the long nineteenth century created opportunities for women to renegotiate their roles in other dimensions of citizenship. During the Civil War, as government made expansive new demands on Union and Confederate women alike, women in turn demanded new things of government. In the Confederacy, for example, white women wrote countless letters to government officials, complaining about the material hardships of war, protesting government policies, and demanding that government do something for them in return. In writing those letters, Confederate women drove forward the war's redefinitions of citizenship, often in ways that went against prevailing norms.[16] There were also opportunities for African American women to forge new relationships with government as a result of the Civil War. Rhetoric at the time and scholarship ever since has focused on black men's wartime citizenship claims, but as they escaped slavery black women, too, effected changes in the very concept of citizenship: who was included and what it meant.[17]

Wartime debates over citizenship persisted long after 1865. To be sure, Union victory settled some of the biggest questions raised by the war. The Union was preserved and slavery would, soon, be gone. Yet many issues remained in the summer of 1865 and beyond, among them fundamental questions about the nature of American citizenship. Would former slaves be treated as equal citizens? What about former Confederates? Should the wartime expansion of governmental authority be considered temporary or permanent? Did national citizenship now completely override state citizenship? Was citizenship about political status, civil rights, or economic activities? Perhaps all three? Partial answers to these questions were provided by the constitutional amendments and other statutes. But the details were contested and evolving, taking shape in countless struggles far from the halls of power in Washington, DC.

Recent studies of the postwar period have emphasized that African Americans advanced their own definitions of citizenship. They demanded certain rights and defined the concept in novel ways, albeit typically without explicitly aiming to do so. As Gregory Downs has put it, post–Civil War "freedpeople's politics were, like many people's politics, deeply practical." Former slaves continued to use their military service, among other arguments, to push for new rights and access to additional resources. They demanded not only that they be included in the existing category of citizenship—that they deserved the right to vote, for instance—but also that citizenship ought to be expanded to include social equality, access to public education, and economic opportunity.[18] Material advancement, most often economic independence through landholding, sat at the very top of former slaves' priorities. This economic agenda was part of, not separate from, their transition to citizenship.

Former slaves in various parts of the world navigated the transition from slavery into freedom and citizenship not only as individuals, but also as groups—most often family groups.[19] In the postwar United States, political authorities and former slaves alike—albeit in different ways and for different reasons—viewed the family as a bridge to citizenship. After all, slavery had excluded slaves from meaningful membership in the national community in part by denying them the ability to form families with the same legal and political status as white families. For this reason, legalizing marriage became a priority for former slaves and for white northern Republicans in the aftermath of the Civil War—a way to assimilate freedpeople not just into mainstream patterns of private behavior, but into public life as well. Freedmen's Bureau officials like Davis Tillson viewed men's authority over their wives and children as being a crucial element of equal citizenship with white men: "the husband," as he put it, "has the same right to control his wife and children that a white man has." Whether white or black, northern or southern, male or female, postwar Americans renegotiated citizenship in its social, economic, and familial as well as its political and legal dimensions.[20]

The first three essays in this volume address the complicated rearrangement of race and citizenship during the Civil War era, opening up new perspectives that take us far beyond the Fourteenth Amendment. We begin with the microhistory of one individual's evolving relationship to citizenship. Elizabeth Regosin tells the fascinating story of Huldah Gordon, a formerly enslaved black woman who navigated her own path through the challenges of Civil War and emancipation. In relating Gordon's journey, Regosin raises some of the central questions and themes of the volume as a whole: What did citizenship actually mean in the lives of people who lived through the Civil War era? Was it an unalloyed good? How decisive were the constitutional changes dictated from Washington, DC? Who adjudicated citizenship claims? How important was cultural belonging? Although direct evidence is lacking, Regosin carefully builds up a picture of Huldah Gordon's vantage point on the transformation of citizenship. Far from being an unalloyed good, it could contain strands of subjugation as well as empowerment for former slaves. Regosin's essay also reminds us that citizenship involved economic welfare, family relationships, and even sexual morality, rather than being a straightforward political connection between the individual and the central government.

Tamika Nunley takes up some of the same issues in her essay, which examines black women's claims to freedom in wartime Washington, DC. Before the Thirteenth Amendment, even before the Emancipation Proclamation, the US Congress instituted compulsory but compensated emancipation in the District of Columbia with the Emancipation Act of April 1862. Because of the disruptions of war, and because slavery was still legal in Maryland and other areas around the capital city, implementation of emancipation was difficult. As Nunley demonstrates, enslaved women were at the forefront of the struggle to make their freedom meaningful, while slavery continued to exist elsewhere. Using the law among other resources, they challenged white southerners' longstanding belief that white supremacy and the right to own slaves were core elements of American citizenship. That belief—that definition of citizenship—had been under attack from the very beginning of the Civil War, but for all the efforts of the African American women studied by Nunley it was not yet clear what the outcome would be. The only certainty was that the stakes of their struggle were staggeringly high. In wartime Washington, DC, as would eventually be the case across the US South, emancipation and the incorporation of African Americans as citizens was a fraught, indeterminate process.

In thinking about the changing relationship of race and citizenship during the Civil War era, we tend to think first of African Americans. After all, the abolition of racial slavery was one central result of the Civil War, and its consequences formed the central problems of Reconstruction. Yet, as Earl Maltz shows in his essay, legal debates over racialized citizenship following 1865 did not only encompass African Americans. These debates also involved the contested status of other minority groups such as Native Americans and Chinese immigrants. As Republican lawmakers incorporated African American men into the citizenry, they faced the problem of what to do about Native Americans, many of whom had long been defined as "subjects" rather than "citizens" in American law. Chinese immigrants, meanwhile, could seem even more alien—even more culturally and religiously different—than either Native Americans or African Americans. Maltz follows the debates over Native Americans and the Chinese through the constitutional amendments of the late 1860s and into the 1870s. As these two groups remind us, determining the racial boundaries of American citizenship continued to be problematical even after the Fourteenth Amendment.

Furthermore, changes in American citizenship did not all concern

race. The unprecedented trials of modern war forced Americans to redefine the very concept of citizenship: its boundaries, its membership,
its constellation of rights and obligations, the way one acquired or lost
it, its cultural meanings, and its economic implications. Neither the
Confederacy nor the Union explicitly codified the terms and membership of national citizenship—other than for immigrants who were naturalizing. Rather, what we see on both sides during the war years are
renewed efforts to define citizenship in a piecemeal fashion, in response
to the particular exigencies of war. There was no blueprint. These new
articulations of citizenship came from all directions, not just the central
government; from soldiers and civilians on the ground as much as from
political and legal officials.

In the context of war, citizenship status became more consequential
than ever. Previously, the question of whether one was defined as a citizen had not mattered directly to most Americans, particularly white
Americans, on a day-to-day basis. But once the conflict got under way,
being able to identify who was who—which side a given individual belonged to—assumed vital importance. Both the Union and the Confederacy became increasingly interested in drawing a firm line between
citizens and noncitizens. By August 1861, the Confederacy was defining
US citizens as "alien enemies" and demanding that they depart from
Confederate territory within forty days. Property owned by such persons could be confiscated—"sequestered"—by the Confederate authorities. Citizenship status mattered deeply. Because this was a civil conflict,
with indeterminate and often fluctuating borders between the two sides,
and with two populations that looked, spoke, and acted very much like
one another, it was difficult to know who was an enemy and who was
a friend. Hence what historian Stephen Neff has described as wartime
America's "extraordinary obsession with oaths of loyalty."[21] Hence the
new importance of passports, oaths, and other means of documenting
individual allegiance.

The three essays in the second section address the role of loyalty
oaths in adjudicating citizenship during the Civil War. Jonathan Berkey focuses on Winchester, the Virginia town that repeatedly changed
hands. Here as in so many other places, the territorial border between
Union and Confederacy fluctuated throughout the war. The population
border—the line between the Confederate and the Union citizenries—
was no more stable. Residents of Winchester found themselves in
a tricky situation, pressured to swear allegiance to the United States

during periods of occupation but knowing that such an act would have negative consequences if and when the Confederates returned. Their affective bonds with Virginia and the Confederacy conflicted with the tangible benefits of affirming US citizenship. As Berkey shows, citizenship was no abstraction. Accepting US citizenship afforded permission to travel and to trade in occupied Virginia—extremely consequential privileges amid the economic and security crises of the Civil War. For the Confederate prisoners of war studied by Angela Zombek, the implications of taking the oath were even graver. Having been captured and imprisoned, Confederate soldiers could be given the chance to affirm their allegiance to the United States, in return for improved conditions and perhaps even release. Zombek's POWs remind us that individual decisions about citizenship status can be based on the most pragmatic of considerations, and that in the context of internecine war, defining another individual as a citizen could be a highly coercive act. The final essay related to oaths begins with a June 1862 conflict between future president Andrew Johnson and the minister William Wharton. Johnson, at that point Tennessee's military governor, was attempting to persuade Wharton to take the oath of loyalty to the Union, but Wharton refused, citing his allegiances both to God and to the state of Tennessee. Lucius Wedge uses this episode to dig deeply into Johnson's and Wharton's opposing definitions of what citizenship was and where religious beliefs fit in. In this case as in so many others, the crisis of war forced clarification of long-standing uncertainties.

The final section of this volume contains three essays examining different visions of citizenship that emerged after 1865. The first, by Caitlin Verboon, uncovers a little-studied means of fashioning citizenship that was employed by black men in postwar southern cities: serving as volunteer firefighters. Although there had been black firefighters even before the war, emancipation changed the context in which they operated, destabilizing the old certainties about black exclusion from public life and raising unsettling questions about African American citizenship on the local level. By performing a valuable service in public space, Verboon shows, black firemen both claimed and redefined citizen status. Like black male service in the Union military, serving as volunteer firefighters displayed masculine strength that had clear implications not only for the specific activity of fighting fires, but also for the citizenship status of black men. Reinforcing one of the volume's major themes, Verboon also highlights that citizenship could be coercive and constraining as

well as empowering, obligating African American men to protect local
communities.

The final two essays turn to ex-Confederates, asking how their views
on citizenship changed after defeat. As with any other group of Americans, their conceptualizations and practices of citizenship varied widely.
The Confederate veterans studied by David Williard confronted a sort
of existential crisis following Appomattox. For many of them, disillu-
sionment with the public world of war and politics prompted a turning
inward, toward a new ethos of hard work as the rightful means of practicing citizenship. Instead of political participation, it was now work
that differentiated citizen from noncitizen—and by defining white men
as the only real workers, ex-Confederates strove to maintain white
supremacy in new ways. As Williard argues, this ultimately became a
variation on the old theme of white southern men resting their claims
for public power on their authority in the domestic sphere. Because it
so easily traversed the realms of the household, the economy, and formal politics, the language of citizenship was a uniquely effective means
to achieve their new goals. For other white southerners, however, defeat and emancipation were so disruptive that they emigrated to Latin
American countries and other parts of the world. As Claire Wolnisty
reveals, Confederate migrants to Latin America may have left behind
the political trappings of their former citizenship, but they continued
to view themselves as citizens of the Confederate South even after the
demise of the Confederacy. They practiced this citizenship-as-belonging
by maintaining familial and economic ties across national borders.
Clearly, this entire generation of white southerners failed to find easy
answers to the problems of citizenship generated by the Civil War and
Reconstruction.

The volume concludes with an afterword by Laura Edwards, the pio-
neering historian of law, gender, and society in the nineteenth-century
South. As Edwards reminds us, for large periods of American history
citizenship was much more about shared governance than it was about
individual rights claims. And while the Federal government was certainly part of the picture, most governance was carried out by state
or local governments, and even by churches, civic organizations, and
households. Americans were more likely to define themselves as citizens of local communities or states than as citizens of the United States.
These definitions were shaped more by local conflicts and ad hoc nego-

tiations—"the stuff of citizenship," as Edwards describes it—than by a predefined blueprint imposed by Washington, DC. It was only after the Civil War, as a result of the conflict and its aftermath, that our modern conception of an individual rights–based and national-level American citizenship began gradually to form.

There was no clear end point to the crisis of citizenship unleashed by the Civil War and emancipation. The short-term expansion of the racial boundaries of the citizenry was followed by a long period of contraction as the promise of Reconstruction gave way to Jim Crow segregation. The political dimension of American women's citizenship was uncertain until the ratification of the Nineteenth Amendment in 1920—and its economic and social dimensions have continued to be disputed to the present day. Even now, well over two centuries into the history of the United States, citizenship is a contested category in many aspects of American life. Doubtless, this will continue to be the case. It always has. But there is no question that the decades of the Civil War, emancipation, and Reconstruction constituted a singularly significant phase in the development of American citizenship. Not only did this period give rise to the new legal category of national citizenship. Not only did it incorporate African Americans, albeit imperfectly, into the status and privileges of legal citizenship. It also forced all Americans to rethink the fundamental meanings of citizenship in many aspects of their lives. The results have reverberated through American society, politics, and culture ever since.

NOTES

1. Bates quoted in Hannah Rosen, *Terror in the Heart of Freedom: Citizenship, Sexual Violence, and the Meaning of Race in the Postemancipation South* (Chapel Hill: University of North Carolina Press, 2009), 13. Michael Novak has also emphasized the lack of clarity of citizenship in the mid-nineteenth-century United States, and warned of the perils of assuming that it meant the same thing then as it does now: Novak, "The Legal Transformation of Citizenship in Nineteenth-Century America," in *The Democratic Experiment: New Directions in American Political History,* ed. Meg Jacobs, William J. Novak, and Julian E. Zelizer (Princeton, NJ: Princeton University Press, 2003), 85–119.

2. For a classic statement of this interpretation, see James H. Kettner, *The Development of American Citizenship, 1608–1870* (Chapel Hill: University of North Carolina Press, 1978).

3. Influential critical studies of American citizenship include Rogers M. Smith, "The 'American Creed' and American Identity: The Limits of Liberal Citizenship in the United States," *Western Political Quarterly* 41 (1988): 225–51; Rogers M. Smith, *Civic Ideals: Conflicting Visions of Citizenship in U.S. History* (New Haven, CT: Yale University Press, 1997);

Linda K. Kerber, "The Meanings of Citizenship," *The Journal of American History* 84, no. 3 (December 1997): 833–54; Douglas Bradburn, *The Citizenship Revolution: Politics and the Creation of the American Union, 1774–1804* (Charlottesville: University of Virginia Press, 2009); Stephanie McCurry, *Confederate Reckoning: Power and Politics in the Civil War South* (Cambridge, MA: Harvard University Press, 2010); Barbara Young Welke, *Law and the Borders of Belonging in the Long Nineteenth Century United States* (New York: Cambridge University Press, 2010); George M. Fredrickson, "The Historical Construction of Race and Citizenship in the United States," in *Diverse Nations: Explorations in the History of Racial and Ethnic Pluralism* (Boulder, CO: Paradigm Publishers, 2009), 21–38; William Link and David Brown, eds., *Creating Citizenship in the Nineteenth-Century South* (Gainesville: University Press of Florida, 2013).

4. T. H. Marshall, "Citizenship and Social Class," in *Sociology at the Crossroads: And Other Essays* (London: Heinemann, 1963), 67–127; Hilda Sabato, "On Political Citizenship in Nineteenth-Century Latin America," *The American Historical Review* 106, no. 4 (October 1, 2001): 1290–1315; Derek Benjamin Heater, *Citizenship in Britain: A History* (Edinburgh: Edinburgh University Press, 2006); Laura E. Nym Mayhall, *The Militant Suffrage Movement: Citizenship and Resistance in Britain, 1860–1930* (Oxford: Oxford University Press, 2003); Andreas Fahrmeir, *Citizenship: The Rise and Fall of a Modern Concept* (New Haven, CT: Yale University Press, 2008); Peter Guardino, *Peasants, Politics, and the Formation of Mexico's National State: Guerrero, 1800–1857* (Stanford, CA: Stanford University Press, 2002); Immanuel Wallerstein, "Citizens All? Citizens Some! The Making of the Citizen," *Comparative Studies in Society and History* 45, no. 4 (October 1, 2003): 650–79; Engin F. Isin and Bryan S. Turner, eds., *Handbook of Citizenship Studies* (London: SAGE, 2002).

5. Susannah J. Ural, ed., *Civil War Citizens: Race, Ethnicity, and Identity in America's Bloodiest Conflict* (New York: New York University Press, 2010); Christian Samito, *Becoming American under Fire: Irish Americans, African Americans, and the Politics of Citizenship during the Civil War Era* (Ithaca, NY: Cornell University Press, 2009); Stephen Kantrowitz, *More than Freedom: Fighting for Black Citizenship in a White Republic, 1829–1889* (New York: Penguin Press, 2012); McCurry, *Confederate Reckoning*. Though it has little to say about the Civil War specifically, Link and Brown, eds., *Creating Citizenship in the Nineteenth-Century South*, particularly the fine introduction, is very helpful in suggesting new ways for historians of the nineteenth-century United States to conceptualize citizenship.

6. Laura F. Edwards, *A Legal History of the Civil War and Reconstruction: A Nation of Rights* (New York: Cambridge University Press, 2015); Novak, "The Legal Transformation of Citizenship in Nineteenth-Century America"; Michael Vorenberg, "Citizenship and the Thirteenth Amendment: Understanding the Deafening Silence," in *The Promises of Liberty: The History and Contemporary Relevance of the Thirteenth Amendment,* ed. Alexander Tsesis (New York: Columbia University Press, 2010).

7. Susanna Michele Lee, *Claiming the Union: Citizenship in the Post–Civil War South* (Cambridge and New York: Cambridge University Press, 2014).

8. Stephanie McCurry, *Masters of Small Worlds: Yeoman Households, Gender Relations, & The Political Culture of the Antebellum South Carolina Low Country* (New York: Oxford University Press, 1995); Laura Edwards, *Gendered Strife and Confusion: The Political Culture of Reconstruction* (Urbana and Chicago: University of Illinois Press, 1997); Elizabeth Ann Regosin, *Freedom's Promise: Ex-Slave Families and Citizenship in the Age of Emancipation* (Charlottesville: University Press of Virginia, 2002); Rosen, *Terror in the Heart of*

Freedom; Chandra Manning, "Working for Citizenship in Civil War Contraband Camps," *The Journal of the Civil War Era* 4, no. 2 (2014): 172–204.

9. Richard Franklin Bensel, *Yankee Leviathan: The Origins of Central State Authority in America, 1859–1877* (Cambridge: Cambridge University Press, 1990); Edwards, *A Legal History of the Civil War and Reconstruction;* Heather Cox Richardson, *The Greatest Nation of the Earth: Republican Economic Policies during the Civil War* (Cambridge, MA: Harvard University Press, 1997).

10. Emory M. Thomas, *The Confederate Nation, 1861–1865* (New York: Harper & Row, 1979), 264–65; Paul Quigley, "State, Nation, and Citizen in the Confederate Crucible of War," in *State and Citizen: British America and the Early United States,* ed. Peter Onuf and Peter Thompson (Charlottesville: University of Virginia Press, 2013); Michael Brem Bonner, *Confederate Political Economy: Creating and Managing a Southern Corporatist Nation* (Baton Rouge: Louisiana State University Press, 2016).

11. Tilly quoted in Bruce D. Porter, *War and the Rise of the State: The Military Foundations of Modern Politics* (New York: Free Press, 1994), xix; C. A. Bayly, *The Birth of the Modern World, 1780–1914: Global Connections and Comparisons* (Malden, MA: Blackwell Publishing, 2004), 199–243; Thomas Bender, *A Nation Among Nations: America's Place in World History* (New York: Hill and Wang, 2006), 116–81; Miguel Angel Centeno, *Blood and Debt: War and the Nation-State in Latin America* (University Park: Pennsylvania State University Press, 2002); John Brewer, *The Sinews of Power: War, Money, and the English State, 1688–1783* (New York: Knopf, 1989); Linda Colley, *Britons: Forging the Nation: 1707–1837* (New Haven, CT: Yale University Press, 1992); Barbara Ehrenreich, *Blood Rites: Origins and History of the Passions of War* (New York: Metropolitan Books, 1997); John L. Comaroff and Paul C. Stern, eds., *Perspectives on Nationalism and War* (Amsterdam: Gordon and Breach, 1995); George L. Mosse, *Fallen Soldiers: Reshaping the Memory of the World Wars* (New York: Oxford University Press, 1991); Don Higginbotham, "War and State Formation in Revolutionary America," in *Empire and Nation: The American Revolution in the Atlantic World,* ed. Elija H. Gould and Peter S. Onuf (Baltimore: Johns Hopkins University Press, 2005), 54–71; Charles Royster, "Founding a Nation in Blood: Military Conflict and American Nationality," in *Arms and Independence: The Military Character of the American Revolution,* ed. Ronald Hoffman and Peter J. Albert (Charlottesville: University Press of Virginia, 1984), 25–49; Jörg Nagler and Stig Förster, eds., *On the Road to Total War: The American Civil War and the German Wars of Unification, 1861–1871* (Washington, DC: German Historical Institute, 1997), esp. introduction.

12. James M. McPherson, *Ordeal by Fire: The Civil War and Reconstruction,* 3rd ed. (Boston: McGraw Hill, 2001), 204; Albert Burton Moore, *Conscription and Conflict in the Confederacy* (New York: Macmillan, 1924); Curtis Arthur Amlund, *Federalism in the Southern Confederacy* (Washington: Public Affairs Press, 1966), 68–73; Emory M. Thomas, *The Confederacy as a Revolutionary Experience* (Englewood Cliffs, NJ: Prentice-Hall, 1971).

13. James Geary, *We Need Men: The Union Draft in the Civil War* (DeKalb: Northern Illinois University Press, 1991); Robert D. Carlson, "Breach of Faith: Conscription in Confederate Georgia" (PhD diss., Emory University, 2009); Rachel A. Shelden, "Measures for a 'Speedy Conclusion': A Reexamination of Conscription and Civil War Federalism," *Civil War History* (December 2009); Vitor Izecksohn, *Slavery and War in the Americas: Race, Citizenship, and State Building in the United States and Brazil, 1861–1870* (Charlottesville: University of Virginia Press, 2014); Daniel Moran and Arthur Waldron, eds., *The People in*

Arms: Military Myth and National Mobilization since the French Revolution (Cambridge: Cambridge University Press, 2003).

14. Samito, *Becoming American under Fire,* Douglass quotation at p. 6. See also Ural, ed., *Civil War Citizens.*

15. Ida Blom, "Gender and Nation in International Comparison," and Karen Hagemann, "A Valorous *Volk* Family: The Nation, the Military, and the Gender Order in Prussia in the Time of the Anti-Napoleonic Wars, 1806–15," both in *Gendered Nations: Nationalisms and Gender Order in the Long Nineteenth Century,* ed. Ida Blom, Catherine Hall, and Karen Hagemann (Oxford: Berg, 2000). See also Karen Hagemann, "Of 'Manly Valor' and 'German Honor': Nation, War, and Masculinity in the Age of the Russian Uprising Against Napoleon," *Central European History* 30 (1997): 187–220; Linda Kerber, "May All Our Citizens be Soldiers and All Our Soldiers Citizens: The Ambiguities of Female Citizenship in the New Nation," in *Women, Militarism, and War: Essays in History, Politics, and Social Theory,* ed. Jean Bethke Elshtain and Sheila Tobias (Savage, MD: Rowman and Littlefield, 1990), 89–103.

16. Laura F. Edwards, *Scarlett Doesn't Live Here Anymore: Southern Women in the Civil War Era* (Urbana: University of Illinois Press, 2000), 93; George C. Rable, *Civil Wars: Women and the Crisis of Southern Nationalism* (Urbana: University of Illinois Press, 1989), 73–90; McCurry, *Confederate Reckoning.* In other conflicts, too, war presented opportunities for women to connect their purportedly private activities to the public sphere. For example, nineteenth-century Prussian women's "wartime involvement in expanded charity placed the national leadership in a morally strong position to enter a debate about the state's future obligations to its disabled soldiers, veterans, war widows, and orphans." See Jean H. Quataert, "German Patriotic Women's Work in War and Peace Time, 1864–1890," in *On the Road to Total War,* ed. Forster and Nagler, 462. Along similar lines, compare American women's experiences with the British feminists studied by Laura Mayhall. These activists did not simply demand inclusion into the liberal category of citizenship as it already existed; rather, they tried to change the category itself, which in turn propelled a shift in the nature of the central state from "night watchman" to an institution concerned with implementing "social liberalism." Mayhall, *The Militant Suffrage Movement: Citizenship and Resistance in Britain, 1860–1930.*

17. See the essays in this volume by Elizabeth Regosin and Tamika Nunley.

18. Gregory P. Downs, "Anarchy at the Circumference: Statelessness and the Reconstruction of Authority in Emancipation North Carolina," in *After Slavery: Race, Labor, and Citizenship in the Reconstruction South,* ed. Bruce E. Baker and Brian Kelly (Gainesville: University Press of Florida, 2013), 98–121; Gregory P. Downs, *Declarations of Dependence: The Long Reconstruction of Popular Politics in the South, 1861–1898* (Chapel Hill: University of North Carolina Press, 2011); Edwards, *A Legal History of the Civil War and Reconstruction.*

19. O. Nigel Bolland, "The Politics of Freedom in the British Caribbean," in *The Meaning of Freedom: Economics, Politics, and Culture After Slavery,* Pitt Latin American series (Pittsburgh: University of Pittsburgh Press, 1992), 141–43.

20. Paul A. Cimbala, *Under the Guardianship of the Nation: The Freedmen's Bureau and the Reconstruction of Georgia* (Athens: University of Georgia Press, 1997), 195. See also Regosin, *Freedom's Promise;* Edwards, *Gendered Strife and Confusion.* In the 1790s, the French government had adopted a similar tactic, offering male slaves freedom in exchange for fighting against Haitian rebels, and offering freedom for their wives and children on

condition that their marriages were legally ratified. The same principle guided French policy following emancipation in the French West Indies in 1848. See Carolyn E. Fick, "The Haitian Revolution and the Limits of Freedom: Defining Citizenship in the Revolutionary Era," *Social History* 32, no. 4 (November 2007): 394–414; Myriam Cottias, "Gender and Republican Citizenship in the French West Indies, 1848–1945," *Slavery & Abolition* 26, no. 2 (2005): 233–45.

21. Stephen C. Neff, *Justice in Blue and Gray: A Legal History of the Civil War* (Cambridge, MA: Harvard University Press, 2010), 154. On loyalty and oaths, see also William A. Blair, *With Malice toward Some: Treason and Loyalty in the Civil War Era* (Chapel Hill: University of North Carolina Press, 2014); Anne Sarah Rubin, *A Shattered Nation: The Rise and Fall of the Confederacy, 1861–1868* (Chapel Hill: University of North Carolina Press, 2005).

RACE AND THE REDEFINITION OF CITIZENSHIP

Toward the Temple of American Liberty

Huldah Gordon and the Question of Former Slaves' Citizenship

ELIZABETH REGOSIN

It is true that we are no longer slaves, but it is equally true that we are not yet quite free. We have been turned out of the house of bondage, but we have not yet been fully admitted to the glorious temple of American liberty. We are still in a transition state and the future is shrouded in doubt and danger. Some of our friends seem to think our emancipation complete and our claims upon them at an end. A greater mistake could hardly be made. The colored people of the United States are still the victims of special and peculiar hardships, abuses and oppressions, and we still need time, labor and favorable events to work out our perfect deliverance.

—FREDERICK DOUGLASS, August 3, 1869

In an address delivered in 1869, four years after the ratification of the Thirteenth Amendment abolishing slavery, former slave and abolitionist Frederick Douglass declared that African Americans were in a "transition state," freed but not yet completely delivered from slavery. By contrasting the "house of bondage" with the "temple of American liberty," Douglass offered a notion of freedom that was tied up with the achievement of equal citizenship, asserting that without it, African Americans could never fully be free. The ratification of the Fourteenth Amendment in 1868 affirmed the provision of the Civil Rights Act of 1866 that made African Americans citizens of the United States and the states in which they lived, repudiating the 1857 *Dred Scott v. Sandford* decision. With this status came the promise of protection by the Federal government from efforts by states to trample the privileges and immunities guaranteed to all citizens. Significantly, too, the Fourteenth Amendment guaranteed to all citizens due process of law and the equal protection of the laws. Further, the imminent ratification of the Fifteenth Amendment, passed in Congress earlier in 1869, would equip African American men with the vote, widely regarded as the essential tool of citizenship.

Douglass's notion that the formerly enslaved were "not yet quite free," that they had not yet entered "the glorious temple of American liberty," suggested that the existence of the Fourteenth Amendment was not enough to guarantee equal citizenship or full inclusion in American society.[1] When Douglass called African Americans the "victims of special and peculiar hardships, abuses and oppressions," clearly he was referring to the day-to-day experiences of African Americans in the North and South in the aftermath of emancipation, even in the face of the Fourteenth Amendment's promise of citizenship and the equal protection of the law. Douglass's speech pointed to the specific incident of the Columbia Typographical Union barring his son's admission on the basis of his race, but the more general notion of hardships, abuses, and oppressions conjured up numerous situations with which his audience would have been familiar.[2] The denial of civil and legal rights at the local level, the use of violence and intimidation by whites to subordinate African Americans, the failure on the part of the Federal government to redistribute land to former slaves or even to make land accessible, the subsequent dependence upon former owners (one's own or others') for work—all of these conditions conspired to undermine the gains promised in the name of citizenship. These were not simply the hardships, abuses, and oppressions of those in the South; African Americans in the North struggled in many similar ways, fighting political exclusion, segregation, poverty, lack of access to a number of professions and to trade unions, and other daily trials that belied the notion that the North was ever the lodestar of freedom.

In spite of such limitations, Douglass expressed hope in the ultimate achievement of full freedom. The language of "transition," a process of crossing over from one condition to another, implied momentum toward a particular destination, a sense of linear progression toward full freedom. Later in his speech, Douglass highlighted such momentum: "The negro can nevermore be a slave. . . . Though now assailed by violence and oppression, he steadily gains and will continue to gain upon opposing forces."[3] Here Douglass seemed confident in the inevitability of the eventual full realization of freedom.

Clearly, rightly, what Douglass wanted was the achievement of a level of citizenship equal to that of the most privileged citizens. But perhaps

Douglass's notion of being "in a transition state," of casting freedom or citizenship in terms of a distant but reachable destination, misdirects our attention by forcing our gaze ever forward—emphasizing that which had yet to be gained—rather than downward to contemplate that which existed in the present moment. Historian Gregory Downs has warned historians against falling prey to such metaphors, arguing that their "teleology" makes them unhelpful if we are interested in substantive, or even clear, definitions of terms like freedom or citizenship.[4] Accordingly, the notion that former slaves had not yet entered the "glorious temple of American liberty" not only reminds us that former slaves did not possess equal citizenship to those most privileged citizens, it also prompts reflection on the citizenship of former slaves, how they experienced it, what it meant to them, on the ground in that moment.

Douglass does offer us a means to examine former slaves' citizenship in his expression of freedom's limitations. The notion of being "admitted" to the temple of liberty suggested that some other gatekeepers— legislators, public officials at all levels of government, even ordinary free-born citizens—would have to take action or would have to agree, at least, to the notion that African Americans were citizens. The public or collective nature of citizenship, defined by membership in a social and political community, dictates that legislation alone could never make it so. According to Douglass, full inclusion required recognition by other members, those comfortably ensconced within the temple of liberty.

We might examine this idea about necessity of admission to the temple of liberty through the lens of legal scholar Kenneth Karst's notion of equal citizenship as "belonging." In its broadest terms, Karst's idea of citizenship is relational; the substance of citizenship is rooted in one's belonging to the "national community," both in the external condition of being included by those already belonging and the parallel internal condition of feeling included.[5] In this vein, historian Stephen Kantrowitz argues specifically that early black activists, among them Frederick Douglass, understood that they needed something beyond legal citizenship, that they sought "a deeply, universally felt citizenship," an "emotional, spiritual, and intuitive sense of kinship" that superseded the bounds of race.[6] Douglass's use of the personal example of his son's exclusion from the Typographical Union illustrates precisely this idea that in spite of the abolition of slavery and of formal inclusion in the legal definition of citizenship, his actual citizenship could not be fully realized unless others recognized and treated him as a citizen.

This notion of citizenship as relational thus compels us to consider how citizenship *felt*, to examine it as not solely a fixed legal status, a mantle worn across the shoulders, but as a palpable condition, one that was fluid, shifting. We can imagine that in the post–Civil War, postemancipation era when the concept of citizenship was part of regular discussion and debate, people—especially, though not exclusively, former slaves—thought frequently about what citizenship felt like; that they evaluated it, assessed its weight, and measured it in everyday interactions and experiences. We can imagine as well that just as Douglass measured the progress of freedom in terms of distance from the house of bondage, former slaves used the conditions of slavery as a point of reference for giving meaning to their citizenship. In this way, too, we can talk about citizenship as relational.

Ex-slave Huldah Gordon's story presents a unique opportunity to explore the substance of former slaves' citizenship in the era of the Civil War because she can be traced through the historical record from the time of her birth as a slave until her death in 1894. As a slave, Huldah had only partially existed in the historical record—that body of evidence left behind among personal papers and public documents—her visibility obscured by the refusal on the part of the record keepers to acknowledge her humanity or her individuality. As she was inscribed into the public record after slavery—as an inhabitant of the state of Virginia, as a beneficiary of the Bureau of Refugees, Freedmen, and Abandoned Lands (Freedmen's Bureau), as a depositor in the Freedman's Bank, as a Civil War pension claimant, as a pensioner—Huldah became a visible historical subject, a someone rather than a something, a person in her own right rather than a slave.

This visibility, by its very nature, offers a means by which to consider what citizenship might have looked like for Huldah since it resulted from her various interactions with agencies and agents of the Federal government. Most certainly, such interactions do not guarantee that a person acted in the context of legal citizenship—whether considering oneself as a citizen, or being considered as such—since government agencies and agents regularly worked with noncitizens. For example, former slaves received aid from the Freedmen's Bureau not because they were citizens, since their place in society at the time of the Bureau's creation was unclear, but because of their status as former slaves. However, if we are thinking about how citizenship felt and thinking about citizenship as a sense of belonging, then we can imagine that engagement with these surrogates for the government might signal, beyond personhood, external recognition of Huldah's membership in the national community. The historical record does not reveal how Huldah herself assessed her citizenship, but it is reasonable to assume that her sense of citizenship and belonging, was shaped, at least in part, by such interactions.

Ultimately, Huldah's story suggests that a person might feel like a citizen before the legal contours of citizenship were fully defined, and alternately, might be considered a legal citizen but feel excluded from its benefits. Her experiences highlight the fact that beyond her race and status as a former slave, Huldah's womanhood—the ways in which it determined her place in the family and the workplace as well as broader societal expectations of her behavior—could both positively and negatively affect her citizenship. And as it illustrates concretely the benefits of citizenship, Huldah's story also raises questions about the price of inclusion and its ultimate desirability as one becomes a subject of, and therefore subject to, the state.

～

As a slave on John C. Cohoon Jr.'s Cedar Vale plantation in Nansemond County, Virginia, Huldah appears in the plantation's record book, in which Cohoon listed births and deaths, information about acquiring his slaves, and other miscellaneous facts about them.[7] Although the slaves in this "scarified, water-stained" ledger are identified by name (usually given name only), their status as Cohoon's property is unmistakable.[8] For example, Cohoon's use of the possessive in some of the list titles shows that he saw the people within as his possessions, as do the notations about which people were bought, sold, and given from and to whom. And as such, the men, women, and children who comprised the slave population of Cedar Vale plantation were inscribed into the historical record, one that did not capture or convey their humanity or their subjectivity. Accordingly, Huldah has no voice in the plantation record, neither the opportunity nor the means to author her own story, nor even the basic building blocks of identity to do so, at least in the traditional manner by which we establish identity. It is telling that we onlookers know more about Huldah than she knew of herself at that time. As we shall see, Huldah had no idea what date she was born, nor the dates and times of her children's births.

Among other lists in Cohoon's record, Huldah's name appears under "Names of My Negroes (Now living) and how I came by them," where she is simply counted as one of Cohoon's slaves and identified as the mother of a number of children. The record identifies Huldah's mother and three brothers as well as their prior owner. One brother, Elijah, was listed as "Born my property." Under "Ages of Negroes . . . Bob & Jennys Children," Huldah's date of birth is recorded as Saturday, November 27, 1825. In that same section, under the heading "Little Bob and Huldah [Junior's] Children" we see that Huldah had either mothered eight children with, or was married to, Little Bob, another of Cohoon's slaves. The dates and times of birth of their children are listed with notations of two deaths. The record ends in 1863, the year Cohoon died.[9] At that time, Huldah was thirty-eight years old and Little Bob was dead. Huldah's living children ranged in age from six to twenty.[10]

Because there was another woman named Huldah among Cohoon's slaves, Huldah Gordon appears alternately as "Little Huldah" or "Huldah Junior." Cohoon's record never refers to her as "Huldah Gordon." Generally, the Cedar Vale slaves were not assigned surnames in Cohoon's records, as was typical during slavery. Surnames signified family lines and the human connections associated with them. Slave owners often believed that their slaves did not have surnames or did not need them. Sometimes they called slaves after their own surnames, signifying for them property rather than family ties.[11] Southern slave-holding society ignored slaves' surnames, as it ignored slaves' family lines and ties, by refusing to give legal recognition and protection to slave marriages and familial relationships according to their own economic interests. Acknowledging that slaves had family ties or protecting those ties by law would interfere with the business of slavery and undermine the ideology undergirding the institution by recognizing slaves as individuals with fundamental rights to family relationships.

In contrast to the records of slavery, Huldah appears by her full name in the records of the Freedmen's Bureau. As early as 1866, Huldah worked with Freedmen's Bureau agents both to secure rations for herself and her children and to obtain the bounty and back pay belonging to her deceased son, Miles Gordon, a soldier killed while serving in the United States Colored Cavalry (USCC) during the Civil War, which will be addressed below. Huldah's name appears in three separate entries of the Norfolk, Virginia Freedmen's Bureau records regarding the provision of rations to freedpeople from the years 1865 to 1868. The Freedmen's Bureau records list Huldah and three of her children, "Ned" (Edward), "Logie" (Elijah), and Adeline as receiving aid. Although there is little detail in the register as to the amount and kind of rations Huldah received, in one entry she is listed among "Freedpeople who are unable to support themselves and have no Relatives able to assist them."[12]

We can surmise that this engagement with Federal agents, which may even have occurred prior to the establishment of the fact of her citizenship by the Civil Rights Act of 1866, played some role in shaping Huldah's sense of her place in the national community, although we cannot know with any certainty what that felt like. Given the dire circumstances under which the Freedmen's Bureau gave out provisions, it is possible that Huldah felt as if these agents of the government were looking out for her well-being. She may have felt included in that sense, perhaps grateful, even entitled or empowered by the support of the government and her access to it. On the other hand, Huldah may also have felt dependent, even belittled in proportion to the degree to which agents expressed the Freedmen's Bureau's firm message that freedpeople should not become too dependent upon charity. Too, in light of the fact that the Freedmen's Bureau in Virginia significantly reduced the amount of relief it provided during 1866 and 1867, it is possible that Huldah also felt neglected by the very agency created to help facilitate the transition from slavery to freedom.[13]

The same shift of Huldah's status, marked by the character of her appearance in the historical record, can be seen in the case of the Federal census. Although prior censuses had counted the number of slaves, a separate schedule for slaves was new to the seventh census (1850) and used again in the eighth (1860). The Slave Schedule was a subset of the census that counted slaves of individual owners in slave-holding states. Whereas instructions to marshals and assistant marshals (those who collected data) indicated that they take the names of free inhabitants, for the Slave Schedule they were instructed simply to take the names of owners, that "In the case of slaves, numbers are to be substituted for names."[14] The resulting record is stark and silent, featuring rows of blank lines interrupted only by the occasional name of a white slave owner. Each line represents a single slave, identified only by color, sex, age, and infirmity. Huldah was likely present in the 1860 schedule listed under Cohoon's name, a nameless female slave.[15] The absence of any names at all in this record, and the clear message it sends that slaves' names did not matter, underscores the slaves' invisibility in the antebellum state. Slaves were objects to be counted; they did not count.

Conversely, the 1870 census brought Huldah into public light, formally recognizing her as an "inhabitant" of Nansemond County, Virginia,

one who was a household member, not simply being counted, but ac-
counted for, meriting consideration not as one belonging to someone
else but as a person in her own right. Mandated in the Constitution as
the means by which to apportion representation, the census took on new
significance in 1870. For the first time since the creation of the republic,
the census counted fully the members of the African American population because the abolition of slavery and provisions in the second section
of the Fourteenth Amendment rendered the Three-fifths Compromise
null and void. As Robert Scott Davis thus noted of the 1870 census, "For
hundreds of thousands of African Americans, this document became
their first public record."[16] Although this document was not Huldah's
first public record and did not mark her status as a citizen—since noncitizens were included in the census—it did mark yet another moment
of interaction with an agent of the Federal government.

Assistant marshals, those who did the legwork of gathering census
data, were drawn from local populations, likely from among the white,
male inhabitants. Their written instructions counseled them to "approach
every individual in a conciliatory manner" and cited that "Anything like
an overbearing disposition should be an absolute disqualification for the
position."[17] Although the warning against overbearingness was new to
instructions for assistant marshals in 1870, previous census takers had
been urged to use "civil and conciliatory manners."[18] While it is likely
that the warning was issued in response to the behavior of assistant
marshals from previous censuses, we can imagine the significance of
such instructions in areas of the country where slavery had only recently ceased to exist. Perhaps Huldah would have known what to expect as the assistant marshal moved from dwelling to dwelling, asking
about the members of each household, their age, sex, color, profession/
occupation/trade, the value of their real estate, their place of birth, par-
entage, level of education, and any disabilities (physical, economic, or
legal). She might have heard about such encounters in her neighborhood, whether the assistant marshal was indeed conciliatory or whether
he treated those former slaves he interviewed with contempt. Perhaps
Huldah would have resented the intrusiveness of the census process,
that this man might come into her home, asking questions of Huldah
and her children. On the other hand, Huldah might well have welcomed
the recognition from the national government implicit in the encounter,
regardless of its nature.

For us, the 1870 census offers a compellingly detailed snapshot of

Huldah's life in that moment. Still living in Nansemond County, Huldah is listed as forty-five years old and as a member of a household that included her sons Edward and Elijah, ages twenty and fourteen respectively; daughter Adeline, age thirteen; and a young son of seven named Miles, who had not been listed in the Freedmen's Bureau documents. Since Edward is listed in the position of head of household, we can surmise that Huldah had not been formally remarried at that time.[19] Edward's occupation was that of laborer, while both Huldah and son Elijah are listed as working "in the fields," suggesting that Edward performed some work other than field labor. Since those doing fieldwork include a much younger male and an older woman, we can imagine that Edward's labor earned the greatest remuneration of those in the household, though likely not enough money to support the family on his own. Huldah's daughter Adeline is listed as "at home," a designation made of "children too young to take part in any production."[20] The census reveals that Adeline was blind, offering some sense of why she was at home but not "keeping house" or assisting in the material support of the family. Edward, Huldah, Elijah, and Adeline are all designated as "cannot read" and "cannot write," clearly a vestige of slavery for the first three. Young Miles had no occupation, as is the case with other children listed on the same page. Finally, the census indicates that Huldah's older daughter, Jenny, and oldest son, Samuel, lived with their own families nearby.[21]

The census data also offer those points of reference by which Huldah might have measured her citizenship. The most striking change from slavery revealed in the census is the fact that Huldah's children lived either with her or nearby. The census shows that her older daughter, Jenny Smith, lived in the area with her husband and children, as did Huldah's son, Samuel Gordon, and his family. As Samuel explained to a pension examiner in 1883, during slavery, Huldah's three older children were hired out to other farms and their mother saw them only once a year. Here all lived either in the same household or in close proximity. Also significant was that those working could contribute their earnings toward their own family economy rather than working to support their owner's family.

That process of measurement also may have included ways in which Huldah felt her status as a citizen challenged. In its attribution of Edward Gordon as head of the household, the census reminds us that Huldah's status was shaped as much by her gender as by her race, since her womanhood relegated her to the status of dependent rather than household head regardless of her position as the sole parent in the family. What did that relegation to dependent status feel like, especially in the face of seeing her sons win the right to vote by ratification of the Fifteenth Amendment when her womanhood assured that she could not? Further, to what extent did her inability to earn a living wage to support her family deprive her of a sense of the independence of citizenship, of, as Judith Shklar put it, "the right to earn" as a marker of her status as a citizen?[22] As he discussed the fact that his son was barred from the Typographical Union in Washington, DC, Douglass noted, "There the right to labor is on trial, the question is: Whether this newly emancipated race shall be allowed to work in any other than menial occupations."[23] Perhaps Huldah was asking the same question, though as David Williard reminds us in his essay herein on Confederate veterans, the relationship between work and citizenship, broadly conceived, was rooted in notions of masculinity, leaving little room to imagine that this badge of citizenship was one that Huldah might have easily worn.[24]

A more explicit indication of Huldah's sense of inclusion or belonging as a citizen can be seen in her initiation of a Civil War pension on behalf of her son's service in the USCC. The granting of military pensions to soldiers was a significant marker of citizenship, and the pursuit of a pension was a marker of one's sense of one's own right to just compensation, a return on the performance of the citizen's duty to his country. Caitlin Verboon's essay on black firemen in this volume raises precisely this notion of the "reciprocal nature of citizenship," that one might "act out" one's citizenship by laying claim to the government's obligation to a service rendered.[25] In the event of a soldier's death, this compensation was passed on to eligible surviving family members, which we might interpret as both an extension of the soldier's citizenship rights beyond his death and a sign of family members' own citizenship rights as well. The inclusion of African Americans in the Civil War pension system anticipated and then affirmed the principle of the Fourteenth Amendment that saw all citizens as equal and thus equally eligible to such citizenship rights.[26] As Theda Skocpol's work on the Civil War pension system suggests, in this instance Huldah was recognized not so much as a former slave but, like any dependent of a soldier killed in the service of the Union, as deserving of the special benefits awarded to those who made such sacrifices for the nation.[27]

Through her contact with the Freedmen's Bureau, Huldah acquired her son Miles's bounty, the money promised to him in return for his service in the USCC. Huldah made her application in April of 1866 and received payment of over $260 in October of 1869. The Freedmen's Bureau records indicate that the process was lengthy because some back and forth between Huldah, agents of the Bureau, and other Federal agencies dealing with the payment of bounties was required to assure Huldah's identity and the fact of her son's service.[28] As was the practice in that era, the payment was deposited for Huldah in the Freedman's Savings and Trust Company, also known as the Freedman's Bank, an institution created to "provide African American soldiers with a secure place to save their money and at the same time encourage 'thrift and industry' in the African American community."[29] When asked about this payment later on during her pension case, Huldah reported that she "received Bounty through Mr. Percy of Freedmans Bank, don't know how much she got, thinks Mr. Percy told her she was entitled to $300, he gave her a Bank Book on which she drew money at different times untill Mr. Percy took the Book in and informed her that she had drawn all the money."[30]

Huldah's experiences with H. C. Percy offer further opportunity to consider her own sense of citizenship in relation to her interactions with a man who was employed in a variety of organizations, both public and private, local and national. Percy initially worked with former slaves in Virginia in his capacity as an agent of the American Missionary Association (AMA); he served as the superintendent of AMA schools in Norfolk and Portsmouth. When the Norfolk branch of the Freedman's Bank was created, Percy became its cashier.[31] By the late 1860s, Percy appears to have become an agent of the Freedmen's Bureau as well. Percy was also the notary public who filled out Huldah's application for arrears of pay and bounty in April 1866.[32] His name appeared on numerous documents in her pension claim, including a statement in 1872 in which he offered her a character reference as "a worthy old lady," based on his "long acquaintance" with her.[33] Huldah's description of his handling of her money in the Freedman's Bank coupled with the sense that Percy had devoted himself to the progress of former slaves suggests that he was a trusted figure to whom she could turn for help. At the same time, we know that because of her illiteracy, noted in the census and highlighted in the fact that she did not know the amount of money she had, Huldah was dependent upon Percy, especially upon his trustworthiness. Her experience suggests that one might feel pride as a depositor in the Freedmen's Bank, especially in light of the fact that the funds deposited were earned in service to the Union, and at the same time, one might feel vulnerable or patronized.

Huldah's pension file reveals that in March of 1870, she filled out an application for a Mother's Civil War pension under the Act of July 14, 1862, that, among other provisions, authorized pensions to dependent mothers of soldiers who died without leaving a widow or legitimate children.[34] As the mother of a soldier killed while in the service of the USCC, Huldah had the right to a pension if she could prove that she had been dependent upon her son for her material survival prior to his death and that she was currently unmarried, thus unsupported by a male breadwinner.[35] Huldah likely learned of her right to a pension from Freedmen's Bureau agents who helped her with her claim for Miles's bounty. It is also possible that her pension attorney solicited the application, a typical practice in the era.[36]

Ultimately, it took Huldah fourteen long years to win her bid for a pension, which was not necessarily all that unusual given her lack of access to documentary evidence and other such factors. Huldah's case appears to have been filed and reopened in three instances between 1872 and 1884. The frequent reopening of the case, which meant that the facts were called into question, led the Pension Bureau to conduct several detailed investigations into her claims, later called "special examination," a procedure conducted when agents suspected fraud or when they required more information to make a decision than was provided in a claim. Under these circumstances, a special agent from the Bureau would travel to interview the claimant and the various witnesses as well as to seek out pertinent documentary evidence and delve even deeper into the issues of the case. It's not at all surprising that Huldah's case was subject to investigation several times. The pension process was by its nature one rooted in suspicion, given the Bureau's task of awarding pensions only to those who were deemed worthy. The amount of suspicion with which the Bureau viewed a case increased proportionately to a claimant's lack of ability to provide material evidence, to his or her poverty and illiteracy, and finally, to the fact of a claimant being identified as African American and formerly enslaved. In his work on Civil War pensions, Donald Shaffer has found that although the offering of pensions might have been race-neutral, the process of pursuing a pension was not. Shaffer concludes that "In the intensely racist atmosphere of the late nineteenth and early twentieth century, African Americans found their worthiness was suspect in the minds of many white bureaucrats from the beginning."[37]

If we think about visibility as a measure of inclusion, it is crucial to note that the pension process served to create a record of Huldah's life, both during slavery and after, in the kind of intimate detail completely lacking in any of the previous records. The pension process was one of determining a claimant's ability to meet particular criteria. In that process, claimants were often asked to tell their stories to Pension Bureau and local government officials. Thus, the process itself afforded Huldah some opportunity to author her own story and to shape, to some degree, the way the record revealed her, although clearly this process was not one over which she had much control. Huldah's pension file will not be fully examined here, but the stories that unfold within serve to flesh out what were merely the bare bones of her story in the previous records, and indicate how far she had progressed from having been considered a piece of property recorded in her master's slave ledger to giving her own account of herself in the pension process.

Also, the corollary to this greater degree of inclusion was a greater degree of intrusion into Huldah's life by the state. Where the census, designed for enumeration, demanded routine answers to rote questions, the pension system engaged each citizen individually, often in much greater depth as officials probed claimants' lives to ensure that the claim to pension was just. In order to assess Huldah's worthiness as a dependent upon her son, Pension Bureau agents would ask questions about her marriage, her other children, her work, her sexual relationships, and her material situation, among other questions. If Huldah wanted a pension, she had no choice but to answer. And getting that pension was often contingent upon presenting her life, even living her life, in a way that the state dictated. Further, Huldah's story was not hers alone to tell. To weigh her claims, the process allowed others to contribute to the story, including her children, fellow former slaves from Cohoon's plantation, neighbors, veterans, and even her former young master. As with the census or her interactions with Freedmen's Bureau agents, we cannot know how Huldah experienced or interpreted these particular encounters with these representatives of the state, whether they affirmed her sense of herself as an equal citizen in the eyes of the state or whether she felt herself to be the object of special scrutiny precisely because of her race, gender, and former status.

The 1883 special examination recorded in the first person marks the first time that we actually "hear" Huldah's voice in the record. She reported: "I was born on Capt. John Cahoon's farm in Nansemond Co. Va . . . and belonged to said Cahoon; lived on said farm till Suffolk was

evacuated."[38] Huldah's words underscore the significant distance between this moment of proclaiming her own origins—"I was born"—and
the experience of having her origins recorded by her master in the context of an economic transaction: "Huldah (from Geo. Bevans)." Whether
what was recorded was what Huldah actually said we cannot know. But
the opportunity for Huldah to speak for herself, nonetheless, matters in
that she does so in her capacity as a citizen claiming her due from a government that has acknowledged its debt to a special group of its citizens.

Yet we are also compelled to consider the significance of the fact that
Huldah signed the record of her first person interview with an "x" rather
than her signature, indicating that although she could speak for herself,
she could neither read that which she had just spoken nor write for
herself. In addition, we must consider that even all these years after
slavery, Huldah had to rely upon her former young master, William
Cohoon, for basic information and affirmation of her own identity. The
Pension Bureau solicited information from Cohoon, as well as from his
brother and one of their cousins, on numerous occasions throughout
the process; William wrote letters or testified on such subjects as the
origins of Huldah's surname, the fact of her marriage and her identity
as Miles's mother, and the question of her dependence upon Miles. As
noted above, in most cases the Pension Bureau sought corroboration
of claimants' stories. In this instance, however, as was typical in the
cases of former slaves, those assessing the case accorded the former
owner greater weight and reliability as a witness. Striking too is the
fact that Huldah herself did not know her own date of birth or those of
her children and that, as he was in possession of his father's records
from slavery, Cohoon did. And because she had neither birth certificates
nor baptismal records, the plantation record was given authority. An
1876 deposition noted: "Affiant [Huldah] presents the following list of
children with dates of birth as furnished by her former Master's oldest
son."[39] Here we see remnants of slavery in the government's granting of
legitimacy to the records of slavery and in the fact that ownership still
echoed in the relationship between former slave and former master.

Although the possibility of gaining a pension underscores the benefits
of citizenship, the story that unfolds in the record points to the imposing
challenges of basic survival, of pursuing the right to earn, that Huldah
encountered as a former slave, limited as she was to agricultural or
domestic labor and dependent for employment upon the very class of
people who wished to see her remain permanently subordinate. How sig-

nificantly different was her material situation in relation to her days as a slave? The process's emphasis on the question of Huldah's dependence upon the soldier, especially in its first phase between 1870 and 1876, brings her economic situation in that era into sharper focus, revealing, not surprisingly, that like some four million other former slaves living in the South, Huldah's subsistence in the tumultuous years after the war was hard won. Special Agent James H. Clements reported that "Affiant [now 51 years old] has been compelled to support herself since Miles death, her son Edward helped her some untill his marriage last winter, none of her other children ever helped her, has two daughters living one of them is married, and has four children, her other daughter is living with Affiant, the daughter living at home is not married, she is totally blind and requires constant attention."[40] Testimony from Huldah's sons reveals that it was a combination of her own field labor and financial contributions from each oldest, unmarried son that enabled her and the younger children to survive.

The claim that "none of her other children ever helped her" wasn't quite accurate: perhaps she was misquoted or perhaps Huldah simply lied to make herself appear more sympathetic. Like his older brother, Samuel Gordon, the second oldest son after Miles, left the plantation to follow the Union army. Samuel testified that he "was not at home when Miles enlisted, was following the Army round, waiting on Officers, was about sixteen years old, received about ten dollars per month from the Officers he waited on. . . . [Samuel] went with the 67th Ohio soon after leaving Old Master's farm."[41] Samuel was away two years before returning home. During that time, he sent his mother about $25 or $30, which likely helped Huldah and her younger children get settled after leaving the plantation. Following his return home, Samuel lived with his mother for two years and gave her about half of the $250 he earned during that time. Samuel explained that after he married, he stopped making regular contributions to his mother's support, "but helped her a little now and then as he could spare it." He noted, however, that what he had given Huldah "since [his] marriage would not be sufficient to support his blind sister who resides with his mother." Samuel's testimony highlights the incredibly difficult economic times former slaves experienced. He claimed that he "is hardly able to support his wife and children, but he is willing to help his mother whenever he can. [He] earns less than one dollar per day, works for the R.R. Co."[42] Here it is clear that Samuel had enough trouble supporting his own immediate family, and although he gave his mother money, clearly he could not help her nearly as much as she needed.

After Samuel left home to be married, the next oldest son, Edward, took over contributing to the family economy. Recall that the 1870 census designated twenty-year-old Edward as the head of the household. At that time, Edward was earning "about twelve dollars per month the year round, above his board, out of which he gave his mother about six dollars per month." Edward married sometime in 1874 or 1875 and, as was the case with his older brother, the occasion of his marriage marked the end of his regular financial contributions to his mother's support. At the time he gave his testimony in 1876, Edward explained that his younger brother, Elijah, now twenty years old himself and living out of the house, was the one who contributed to their mother's support. Elijah earned twenty dollars a month working at a sawmill, but paid for his board out of that and helped his mother from the money left over. Edward explained that his fifty-one-year-old mother "works out whenever she can get anything to do."[43]

Huldah's dire situation gives substance to Douglass's more general expression of the "doubt and danger" that threatened the future of all those formerly enslaved. How would Huldah maintain such a grueling and precarious means of subsistence? At twenty years old, Elijah might soon marry and have his own family to support. Would young Miles take up the responsibility of her support as his brothers had? As she aged, Huldah would be less and less able to work to support herself and her daughter Adeline. In this moment, Huldah found no relief from this economic uncertainty in the pension system. Her extreme poverty offered no guarantee of a pension. In fact, in 1876, the Pension Bureau rejected her claim "on the ground that the claimant was not dependent upon the soldier for support during his lifetime, neither did he materially aid in her support."[44]

Huldah's pension file also illuminates the gendered nature of citizenship, how her identity as a woman shaped her pursuit of a pension. For reasons unclear in the record, the Pension Bureau reopened Huldah's case in 1882.[45] Between March 1882 and April 1883, the second phase of the claim, the Pension Bureau reexamined the question of Huldah's dependence, but more importantly, it focused on the conditions of the birth of the second Miles Gordon, Huldah's youngest son, and in doing so, unearthed details of her relationship to a man who was not her husband. Up until 1883, no mention was made of the boy in Huldah's pension file.

But during the special examination, Samuel Gordon and another witness both mentioned that Huldah had another son named Miles Gordon, born during the war. When pension agent Brown asked Huldah about "the second Miles Gordon," Huldah acknowledged his existence and named his father as Henry Holland. Holland, called Henry Cohoon by another witness, appears to have been a slave on the Cohoon plantation as well.[46]

Huldah's sexual behavior—her brief relationship with the father of the second Miles Gordon—became the sticking point of this phase of her pension quest. When Brown asked Huldah how long she and Henry had cohabited, she replied, "I had a home of my own and he came off and on for 2 months."[47] In spite of the fact that the two had known each other most of their lives, theirs was not a lasting relationship. Yet here, as was often the case among female pension claimants, we see Huldah's personal choices about her intimate relationships bump up against the sense of moral propriety that often informed the assessment of widows' and mothers' pensions. As mentioned earlier, were Huldah to have been remarried, she would lose her eligibility for a pension since she would be dependent upon her husband and wouldn't need support from the state. In this instance, it's clear that Huldah had neither remarried nor entered into a significant relationship with Holland. However, when her claim was rejected a month after the special examination, the Pension Bureau rejected it on the grounds that Huldah had "lived in open and notorious adultery" with Holland.[48]

The language of the rejection came directly from the Act of August 7, 1882. Among the provisions of this Act, which revised the existing conditions under which widow and minor children would receive their pensions, was one that terminated the pension of widows living in "open and notorious adulterous cohabitation."[49] Explicitly created as a means to protect the government from those widows attempting to cheat the system by not remarrying but simply cohabitating with a man, the law also had the effect of policing the morals of female pensioners. As historian Megan J. McClintock explained, "With approval of the 1882 law, the Bureau of Pensions no longer had to determine that a widow had remarried before terminating her pension, but merely that she lived with a man. After 1882, maintaining virtuous conduct was the price women paid for receiving government support."[50] The Act made no mention of mothers' pensions, what were referred to as "dependent" pensions. Yet Huldah's pension claim was rejected on the grounds of this Act nonetheless because the Pension Bureau found her behavior objectionable.

Ironically, in its concern with her sexual propriety, the state treated
Huldah like any other female citizen in pursuit of a pension claim. If
these were hardly conditions that might produce a positive sense of
belonging, they indicated a kind of belonging nonetheless. Yet we know
that in general, whites held up the intimate relationships of African
American women, especially former slaves, to special scrutiny. As
Brandi Brimmer has shown in her work on black women's Civil War pension claims, "racialized constructions of gender" within and beyond the
pension system left black women particularly vulnerable to accusations
of immorality and fraud. Huldah's brief affair with Henry Holland and
the fact that it produced a child would likely have been acceptable within
the community of former slaves.[51] By its own standards of morality or
propriety, the Pension Bureau found Huldah's relationship lacking, and
she suffered for it.

In an interesting turn of events, the final phase of Huldah's pension
quest, 1883–1885, was characterized by a kind of humanity in a government bureaucracy that might have offered Huldah a clear sense that her
citizenship provided her with value and standing in society. Documents
from this last phase are scarce in the file, but enough exists to piece
together the last bit of the story. What prompted her is unclear, but in
December of 1883, months after the Pension Bureau rejected her claim,
Huldah took action on her own behalf, making a plea to the commissioner of pensions to reopen her case. In a letter penned for her by a
notary public for the city of Norfolk, Huldah made her case: "knowing
as I do if reopen and a fair examination it will be found to be a just claim
My claim was rejected upon the grounds that I had live and cohabited
with a man since the death of my son Miles Gordon this I can prove to
the contrary by quite a number of my neighbors."[52]

In her desire for fair treatment and the opportunity to show that
her claim was creditable, Huldah directed the commissioner's attention
away from the problematic issue of her relationship with Henry Holland and pointed it toward what was the crux of her claim all along, the
issue of her dependence. Huldah made her situation clear in an appeal
recorded by a notary public: "my son as a slave did all he could for m[e]
and since the war I had no one to depent on for surpote and have had to
surporte myself and a blind girl child with no one to assist me."[53] Here
we might consider Huldah's assessment of her situation in relation to
the fact that she never remarried and thus was never wholly depen-

dent upon anyone in the way a wife would be expected to be dependent upon her husband. Instead, as she noted numerous times in her claim, she relied upon herself, ultimately, and had the added responsibility of Adeline's care. That she might have expected more significant financial support from her eldest son, the proclaimed head of the family in the absence of a husband, seems to be a likely implication of her statement.

The file is frustratingly silent as to its impetus, but ultimately, the Pension Bureau allowed for the resubmission of Huldah's claim, and approved it on November 8, 1884. The Pension Bureau awarded Huldah the standing $8 per month available to dependent mothers dating back to August 29, 1864, the date of Miles's death. Her file tells us nothing of how Huldah used the money, a significant sum for a former slave or for most Americans in the post-Reconstruction era. We can guess, though, that the money offered Huldah a measure of security in an otherwise insecure world, an opportunity, perhaps, to buy a home and care for herself in her old age as well as care for her blind daughter. After having sought help from her male children, perhaps Huldah had the opportunity to help them or her grandchildren. It also seems likely that receiving a pension from the government cast her citizenship in an overwhelmingly positive light, affirming her belonging and her agency as a citizen, and highlighting citizenship as a means to a better life. Whether Huldah conceived of the pension in those terms, we cannot know. Huldah's last pension payment was made September 4, 1894. Visible to the moment of her death, records from Virginia's Death and Burial Index show that Huldah died in November of 1894 at the age of 69.[54]

What was the nature of citizenship in the era of the Civil War from the perspective of one who had been enslaved? The historical record does not tell us what Huldah Gordon thought, but it does allow us to speculate about what citizenship might have meant to her. Regardless of what the Fourteenth Amendment bestowed, we can imagine that for Huldah, citizenship meant being treated fairly by the state, with kindness and concern, but also unfairly, with suspicion, contempt, and condescension. Citizenship offered the opportunity to demand what one was owed for service to the state and at the same time, it compelled one to behave in particular ways according to what the state demanded. As Huldah's experiences suggest, citizenship could make one feel simultaneously included in and excluded from the national community. Rather than a particular status one achieved and maintained or a nebulous state of being, Huldah's story brings to light a notion of citizenship as an experience one lived in specific moments, defined by one's interactions and encounters, tangible, measurable, variable.

NOTES

1. Douglass calls for the ratification of the Fifteenth Amendment as "a necessity . . . to the future peace and safety of the Republic." See Frederick Douglass, "We are not yet quite free: An address delivered at Medina, New York, on 3 August 1869," in *The Frederick Douglass Papers,* series one, vol. 4, ed. John W. Blassingame and John R. McKivigan (New Haven, CT and London: Yale University Press, 1991), 240.

2. Ibid., 232–33n19; 233.

3. Ibid., 240.

4. Gregory P. Downs, "Force, Freedom, and the Making of Emancipation," in *Rethinking American Emancipation: Legacies of Slavery and the Quest for Black Freedom,* ed. William A. Link and James J. Broomall (New York: Cambridge University Press, 2016), 44–45. Downs makes this case about "freedom," but his argument can also be applied to "citizenship."

5. Kenneth L. Karst, *Belonging to America: Equal Citizenship and the Constitution* (New Haven, CT: Yale University Press, 1989).

6. Stephen Kantrowitz, *More than Freedom: Fighting for Black Citizenship in a White Republic, 1829–1889* (New York: Penguin Press, 2012), 427.

7. The original record can be found in the Special Collections at the University of Virginia Library. The record has also been reproduced in the series *Records of ante-bellum southern plantations from the Revolution through the Civil War,* Series E, Selections from the University of Virginia Library; pt. 1, Virginia Plantations, reel 39. Herbert Gutman examines this record in detail in *The Black Family in Slavery and Freedom, 1750–1925* (New York: Pantheon Books, 1976), 123–43. Gutman reconstructed the family lines of Cedar Vale slaves, offering invaluable, comprehensible information about their family ties and connections. For a description of the record book and its contents, see C. G. Holland, "The Slave Population of John C. Cohoon, Jr. Nansemond County, Virginia, 1811–1863. Selected Demographic Characteristics," *The Virginia Magazine of History and Biography* 80, no. 3, part 1 (July 1972): 333–40.

8. Holland, "The Slave Population," 333.

9. Ibid., 332, 337.

10. Under "Deaths of My servants since 1st June 1813 the time of myself & wife's marriage," Robert is recorded as having died "4th May 1861 at ½ past 4." *Records of ante-bellum southern plantations from the Revolution through the Civil War.*

11. I address the subject of slaves' surnames in *Freedom's Promise,* chapter 2, "'We all Have Two Names': Surnames and Familial Identity." See Elizabeth Regosin, *Freedom's Promise: Ex-Slave Families and Citizenship in the Age of Emancipation* (Charlottesville: University Press of Virginia, 2002), 54–78. On Huldah's surname, see 62–65.

12. "Virginia, Freedmen's Bureau Field Office Records, 1865–1872," database with images, *FamilySearch* (familysearch.org/ark:/61903/3:1:S3HY-D1NY-BK?cc=1596147&wc=9LMG-T3 D%3A1078519902%2C1078525201 : 25 June 2014), Norfolk (subassistant commissioner, 1st district) > image 76 of 498; citing NARA microfilm publication M1913 (College Park, MD:

National Archives and Records Administration, n.d.); "Virginia, Freedmen's Bureau Field Office Records, 1865–1872," database with images, *FamilySearch* (familysearch.org/ark:/ 61903/3:1:S3HY-D1NT-CW?cc=1596147&wc=9LMG-T3D%3A1078519902%2C1078525201 : 25 June 2014), Norfolk (subassistant commissioner, 1st district) > image 164 of 498; citing NARA microfilm publication M1913 (College Park, MD: National Archives and Records Administration, n.d.); "Virginia, Freedmen's Bureau Field Office Records, 1865–1872," database with images, *FamilySearch* (familysearch.org/ark:/61903/3:1:S3HT-6QKW-C79?cc=1596147&wc=9LM2-6TL%3A1078519902%2C1078520701 : 25 June 2014), Norfolk (subassistant commissioner, 1st district) > image 543 of 721; citing NARA microfilm publication M1913 (College Park, MD: National Archives and Records Administration, n.d.), accessed March 29, 2017.

13. NARA Pamphlet M1913, "Records of the Field Offices for the State of Virginia, Bureau of Refugees, Freedmen, and Abandoned Lands, 1865–1872," United States Congress and National Archives and Records Administration, Washington, DC, 4, www.archives.gov/ research/microfilm/m1913.pdf, accessed July 18, 2016.

14. Carroll D. Wright, Commissioner of Labor, *The History and Growth of the United States Census* (Washington, DC: Government Printing Office, 1900), 153.

15. 1860 Census, Slave Schedule, Nansemond County, Virginia, John C. Cohoon, NARA Microfilm publication, M653, roll 1394.

16. Robert Scott Davis, "New Ideas from New Sources: Modern Research in Reconstruction 1865–1876," *Georgia Historical Quarterly* 93, no. 3 (Fall 2009): 292.

17. Wright, *History and Growth of the United States Census*, 156.

18. Ibid., 149, from the 1850 census, instructions "to the assistant marshals."

19. Instructions for the ninth census (1870) require that the marshals and assistants (census takers) list the head of household before any other family members. Ibid., 157.

20. Ibid., 159.

21. 1870 U.S. Census, Norfolk County, Virginia, population schedule, Western Branch Township, Portsmouth, Virginia post office, page 48, dwelling 367, family 429, Edward Gordon household; digital images, Ancestry.com (www.ancestry.com), accessed February 19, 2008. For Huldah's son Samuel and daughter Jenny, see page 49, dwelling 374, family 436, Samuel Gordon household, and dwelling 378, family 440, Martin Smith household.

22. Shklar argues that citizens saw themselves distinguished from slaves and servants precisely by the right to vote and the right to earn. Judith Shklar, *American Citizenship: The Quest for Inclusion* (Cambridge, MA: Harvard University Press, 1991), 1, 15.

23. Douglass, "We are Not Yet Quite Free," 231.

24. David Williard, "An Ideology beyond Defeat: Confederate Visions of Work and Citizenship in the Reconstruction South," in this volume.

25. Caitlin Verboon, "The 'Fire Fiend,' Black Firemen, and Citizenship in the Postwar Urban South," in this volume.

26. Akhil Reed Amar makes a convincing case for a reading of the Fourteenth Amendment that assumes the equality of all citizens born under the flag. See Akhil Reed Amar, *America's Constitution: A Biography* (2005; repr., New York: Random House, 2006), 382–83.

27. Theda Skocpol, *Protecting Soldiers and Mothers: The Political Origins of Social Policy in the United States* (Cambridge, MA: Belknap Press of Harvard University Press, 1992), 149.

28. "Virginia, Freedmen's Bureau Field Office Records, 1865–1872," database with images, *FamilySearch* (familysearch.org/ark:/61903/3:1:S3HT-DTGS-LLL?cc=1596147&wc= 9LMK-HZ9%3A1078519902%2C1078521301 : 25 June 2014), Norfolk (subassistant com-

missioner, 1st district) > image 276–277 of 1081; citing NARA microfilm publication M1913 (College Park, MD: National Archives and Records Administration, n.d.); "Virginia, Freedmen's Bureau Field Office Records, 1865–1872," database with images, *FamilySearch* (familysearch.org/ark:/61903/3:1:S3HT-DZ5W-PPG?cc=1596147&wc=9LMV-K68% 3A1078519902%2C1078522001 : 25 June 2014), Norfolk (subassistant commissioner, 1st district) > image 706 of 1030; citing NARA microfilm publication M1913 (College Park, MD: National Archives and Records Administration, n.d.); "Virginia, Freedmen's Bureau Field Office Records, 1865–1872," database with images, *FamilySearch* (familysearch .org/ark:/61903/3:1:S3HT-DTGS-P3X?cc=1596147&wc=9LMK-HZ9%3A1078519902 %2C1078521301 : 25 June 2014), Norfolk (subassistant commissioner, 1st district) > image 265 of 1081; citing NARA microfilm publication M1913 (College Park, MD: National Archives and Records Administration, n.d.); "Virginia, Freedmen's Bureau Field Office Records, 1865–1872," database with images, *FamilySearch* (familysearch.org/ark:/61903/3:1: S3HT-DZ5W-GKT?cc=1596147&wc=9LMV-K68%3A1078519902%2C1078522001 : 25 June 2014), Norfolk (subassistant commissioner, 1st district) > image 688 of 1030; citing NARA microfilm publication M1913 (College Park, MD: National Archives and Records Administration, n.d.); "Virginia, Freedmen's Bureau Field Office Records, 1865–1872," database with images, *FamilySearch* (familysearch.org/ark:/61903/3:1:S3HY-63BQ-7KT?cc=1596147&w- c=9LMP-4WL%3A1078519902%2C1078520506 : 25 June 2014), Norfolk (subassistant com- missioner, 1st district) > image 37 of 54; citing NARA microfilm publication M1913 (College Park, MD: National Archives and Records Administration, n.d.), accessed March 29, 2017.

29. Reginald Washington, "The Freedman's Savings and Trust Company and African American Genealogical Research," *Prologue Magazine* (Summer 1997), vol. 29, no. 2, ar- chives.gov (www.archives.gov/publications/prologue/1997/summer/freedmans-savings- and-trust.html), accessed July 1, 2016.

30. Pension Claim of Huldah Gordon, mother of Miles Gordon, Co H, 1st USCC, Records of the Veterans Administration, Record Group 15, National Archives, Washington, DC.; Huldah Gordon affidavit, June 21, 1876.

31. Joe M. Richardson, *Christian Reconstruction: The American Missionary Association and Southern Blacks, 1861–1890* (Tuscaloosa: University of Alabama Press, 1986), 280n16.

32. "Virginia, Freedmen's Bureau Field Office Records, 1865–1872," database with im- ages, *FamilySearch* (familysearch.org/ark:/61903/3:1:S3HT-DTGS-LLL?cc=1596147&wc= 9LMK-HZ9%3A1078519902%2C1078521301 : 25 June 2014), Norfolk (subassistant commis- sioner, 1st district) > image 276-277 of 1081; citing NARA microfilm publication M1913 (Col- lege Park, MD: National Archives and Records Administration, n.d.), accessed March 29, 2017.

33. Huldah Gordon pension file, H. C. Percy statement, Norfolk, Virginia, February 12, 1872.

34. 12 Stat. 566. Under the general pension law of July 14, 1862, the amount of pension available to mothers was $8, which was the amount that a soldier would receive for total disability. The general pension law also set agents' and attorney's fees at $5. For changes and information on agents' and attorneys' fees up to 1885, see Frank B. Curtis and Wil- liam H. Webster, *A Digest of the Laws of the United States governing the Granting of Army and Navy Pensions. . . .* (Washington, DC: Government Printing Office, 1885), 222–38.

35. The requirement of dependence would change after the passage of the Dependent Pension Act of June 27, 1890. The Dependent Pension Act can be found in 26 Stat. 182. For an explanation of the changes to parents' requirement of dependence, see Regosin, *Freedom's Promise*, 173–79.

36. Huldah's son Samuel, for example, was approached by a pension attorney who wanted him to apply for his brother's pension without his mother's knowledge. Huldah Gordon pension file, Deposition of Samuel Gordon, March 29, 1883.

37. Donald R. Shaffer, "'I do not suppose that Uncle Sam looks at the skin': African Americans and the Civil War pension system, 1865–1934," *Civil War History* 46, no 2 (June 2000): 147. Shaffer finds that African Americans appear to have been subjected to special examinations more often than whites. See also Donald R. Shaffer, *After the Glory: The Struggles of Black Civil War Veterans* (Lawrence: University Press of Kansas, 2004), 128–31. Larry M. Logue and Peter Blanck explore the ways race shaped the prosecution of African Americans' Civil War pensions in "'Benefit of the Doubt': African-American Civil War Veterans and Pensions," *Journal of Interdisciplinary History* 38, no. 3 (Winter 2008): 377–99.

38. Huldah Gordon pension file, Huldah Gordon deposition, March 29, 1883.

39. Ibid., June 21, 1876.

40. Huldah Gordon pension file, Huldah Gordon affidavit, June 21, 1876.

41. Huldah Gordon pension file, Samuel Gordon deposition, July 5, 1876.

42. Ibid.

43. Huldah Gordon pension file, Edward Gordon deposition, July 3, 1876.

44. Huldah Gordon pension, file, "Mother's Pension," September 26, 1876.

45. By the system's design, it was neither unusual, nor prohibited, for claimants to make multiple bids for a pension. Huldah had a new lawyer, but it is not clear which party found the other and initiated the reopening of the claim.

46. Among the adults recorded in Cohoon's records as living on the plantation in 1863 was listed "Henry," a single man with seven children, purchased with his parents from an owner named Holland. The 1870 census lists Holland as living with several children with the same names as those in the plantation record. See Gutman, *The Black Family,* 130; 1870 U.S. Census, Norfolk County, Virginia, population schedule, Second Ward City of Norfolk, Norfolk, Virginia post office, page 114, dwelling 699, family 1044, Henry Holland household; digital images, Ancestry.com (www.ancestry.com), accessed February 19, 2008.

47. Huldah Gordon pension file, Huldah Gordon deposition, March 30, 1883.

48. Huldah Gordon pension file, "Dependent Parents," April 20, 1883.

49. 22 Stat. 345.

50. Megan J. McClintock, "Civil War Pensions and the Reconstruction of Union Families," *Journal of American History* 83, no. 2 (September 1996): 479.

51. Brandi C. Brimmer, "Black Women's Politics, Narratives of Sexual Immorality, and Pension Bureaucracy in Mary Lee's North Carolina Neighborhood," *The Journal of Southern History* 80, no. 4 (November 2014): 827–58; see also Regosin, *Freedom's Promise,* 96–101. On African Americans' views of women's sexual behavior, see Noralee Frankel, *Freedom's Women: Black Women and Families in Civil War Era Mississippi* (Bloomington and Indianapolis: Indiana University Press, 1999), 97–100.

52. Huldah Gordon pension file, Huldah Gordon, Norfolk, Virginia, to Commissioner of Pensions, Washington, DC, December 31, 1883.

53. Ibid.

54. "Virginia Deaths and Burials Index, 1853–1917" digital images, Ancestry.com (www .ancestry.com), accessed February 11, 2015; citing Index, FamilySearch, FHL film number 2048579.

"By Stealth" or Dispute

Freedwomen and the Contestation of American Citizenship

TAMIKA Y. NUNLEY

On December 16, 1862, Emeline Wedge filed petitions on behalf of herself, her two children, and her sister Alice Thomas, who were all slaves of Alexander McCormick. McCormick refused to take advantage of the compensation provision of the 1862 Emancipation Act when it took effect in Washington, DC. Hoping that the act would be repealed, he appeared before the clerk of court after receipt of a summons. According to court records, McCormick "denied the Constitutionality of the Emancipation Act, and said that he would bide his time until it was declared unconstitutional." McCormick attempted to assess his legal obligations to emancipate his slaves, and the reference to the constitutionality of the Act connected closely to his perceived status as a citizen entitled to the protection of his property rights. Just before his case was decided, McCormick reappeared before the clerk and commissioners of the District and, for the first time, formally contended with the legal claims of what he regarded as his "property" or his slaves. In this case as in so many others, emancipation threatened critical attributes that characterized mid-nineteenth-century representations of American citizenship—property ownership and white supremacy.[1]

Slaveholders in the District of Columbia generally either took advantage of the compensation provision in the Emancipation Act or questioned the constitutionality of the new legal measure altogether. White locals who refused to apply for compensation took a decisive stance against the idea that the government could deny what they understood as a key feature of the rights and entitlements of citizenship. Even as the government offered compensation, for propertied white men like McCormick, who refused to manumit slaves, American citizenship protected a slaveholder's full discretion over the decision to free slaves. White possession of black people, as they understood the practice, was permitted by the law and protected by the Fifth Amendment.[2] Furthermore, for non-slave-holding whites in the District, and the South more broadly, citizenship could be interpreted through a lens beyond property ownership.

In the spring of 1857, Chief Justice Roger B. Taney opined that black people, enslaved or free, were not regarded as citizens.[3] Under the premise that black people were unfit for citizenship and unable to govern their own lives, many slave-holding and non-slave-holding white southerners expressed hostility toward and a purported superiority over free blacks and refugees during the war. Indeed, scholars such as William Novak and Michael Vorenberg posit that formal or legal recognition of citizenship, such as the franchise, alone could not capture the meaning of citizenship during the nineteenth century.[4] Membership in communities and associational privileges of organized groups provided an impetus through which disenfranchised groups assumed responsibilities in civic society. Thus, citizenship conceptually involved various components, political and cultural, economic and social, at the dawn of the Civil War and determined the degree to which one could leverage power.[5] Conflict ensued with the prospect and reality of wartime emancipation, and black and white people alike set out to define the rights and obligations of American citizenship. Although citizenship is never clearly defined at this particular moment of the nineteenth century, it became clear that citizenship could not be acquired without freedom.[6]

Throughout the war, as in much of American history, citizenship was a highly contentious and appropriated concept.[7] Scholars such as Martha Jones and Stephen Kantrowitz have shown that black women and men used the term *citizenship* well before the moment of emancipation, having shaped civic identities in antebellum free black communities and made significant claims to racial equality.[8] Likewise, refugees maximized the opportunities presented by the war to claim rights of their own as an expression of black humanity and desires for freedom and equal citizenship on American soil. While I agree with scholars like Chandra Manning that black men and women seeking refuge with the US government behind Union lines altered the concept of citizenship, access to the privileges of citizenship was not a definitive reality for most black women, men, and children.[9] As Thavolia Glymph points out, many of the interactions between refugees and government officials also reveal experiences of exploitation in exchange for uncertain and inconsistent

protections.[10] The attribution of citizenship often meant the Union government's entitlement to and exploitation of black labor in exchange
for refuge from the Confederacy. Thus, what remained unclear were the
terms upon which refugees would be received within Union lines—were
they citizens or contraband? The unequal conditions of acceptance also
remained a problem of citizenship for refugees. As Michael Vorenberg
has argued, freedom rights had to be realized first.[11] And I would argue
that even with freedom rights, the racial hierarchies implicit in understandings of citizenship too had to undergo revision. Just as US Attorney
General Edward Bates declared that persons of African descent were
citizens, historians can attest to the reality that the reception of black
refugees varied widely across the country.[12]

The variegated responses to wartime emancipation led numerous
black refugees to take steps necessary to secure their freedom while
prompting a social contract between themselves and the government.
This chapter examines the manner in which black women in particular
navigated conflicting ideas about the citizenship status of black refugees.
I argue that formerly enslaved women employed the strategies necessary for realizing their liberty, at times making a series of negotiations
with Federal officials and in other instances taking action of their own
volition that reflected an expression of their legal rights. Furthermore,
black women refugees articulated the rights entitled to a free person,
and therefore initiated the process through which they transitioned
from the status of enslaved to American citizen. This process of self-
actualization and protest proved critical to the process of liberation and
a catalyst to understanding new meanings of citizenship. These incidents
undoubtedly appear at the heart of power right in the nation's capital.

The facts of Emeline Wedge's case reveal the unique position of Washington, DC, and the neighboring Chesapeake counties as a distinctive
regional battleground over freedom and citizenship during the Civil
War. As an enslaved woman, Wedge both challenged the legal validity of
her enslavement and forced McCormick to contend with her testimony
against him. As a feature of the Supplemental Act, passed in the summer
of 1862, enslaved women in the District of Columbia were allowed to
testify against white men and women for the first time. Regarding the
actual case, evidence showed that McCormick's farm was located along
the border dividing the District from Maryland and that, just one day
after the Emancipation Act became law, he instructed the slaves to reside

on the Maryland side of his property. According to the records of the Board of Commissioners, he built a small tenement for the slaves on the Maryland side, while his main living quarters remained in the District, along with the cow pen and other buildings included in the homestead. While McCormick generally prohibited his slaves from traveling to the District side of the property, it was proven that Alice was "required to drive cattle from the pasture to the cow pen," which was located on the District side. Unidentified witnesses also testified that they had seen the women and children in McCormick's Washington home daily and that, for approximately seven or eight weeks, Emeline and her family had resided in the District with an older man also bearing the last name Wedge, who apparently was the father of Emeline's husband.[13]

The Board of Commissioners ultimately acknowledged Emeline's right to claim freedom under the Emancipation Act of 1862. Emeline's case is illuminating because, among other things, Emeline's husband and father-in-law did not file the petition, but she instead took the initiative to claim her rights to freedom. But this was not unusual. Patriarchy did not always feature prominently in black women's quests for emancipation. To the contrary, freedwomen in the moment of local emancipation filed numerous claims and complaints on behalf of themselves and members of their families. Early understandings of citizenship often rested largely on the imperatives of the patriarchal head of the household to uphold the rights and obligations of citizenship.[14] Free black men often made the argument that discrimination denied them the recognition necessary to fulfill their duties as heads of their households. Indeed, white women and free blacks found ways to participate in associational and community-focused forms of citizenship in the absence of more formal privileges of citizenship such as the vote.[15] Regarding the experiences of refugees, patriarchy at times proved inapplicable or unnecessary, and black women making claims to freedom found alternative expressions of their position in society. Their actions transformed the relationship between formerly enslaved women and the Union government.[16]

While prevalent ideas about citizenship tipped the scales in favor of white male property owners, resulting in a legacy of gender and racial inequality, black women litigated, petitioned, and organized as any citizen would. Black women's legal and extralegal actions during the Civil War thus set in motion an array of claims to freedom that challenged the racial and gendered exclusivity of citizenship. White citizens also employed a variety of strategies to prevent black women and men from realizing a life of freedom and equality. Former owners like McCormick attempted to evade new emancipation measures by claiming residence in loyal slave-holding states. Others employed violence or harassment to demonstrate their hostility towards emancipation and the growing presence of free blacks. Slave-holding and non-slave-holding whites in the District and surrounding Chesapeake counties made it clear that they would not simply acquiesce to the terms of emancipation.[17]

The nation's capital had freed slaves residing in the District in 1862, but many of the black women arriving in the city during the Civil War did so at their own risk—confronting a system in which their legal status was deeply ambiguous. Enslaved and free black women took advantage of the geographic and political position of Washington, DC, particularly in instances where they arrived from slave-holding states during or after 1862. Many of them traveled to the District from Virginia, a bastion of the Confederacy, or Maryland, a loyal slave-holding state. According to the laws and customs of the Confederacy, black women coming from Virginia were considered "runaways." Concerned with sustaining the fragile loyalty of Maryland, the Federal government legally protected slaveholder interests of the state by upholding the Fugitive Slave Law of 1850. Depending on whether the laws of the Confederacy or the Union applied, black women traveling from slave-holding states could thus be considered enslaved even as wartime emancipation took its course. Accordingly, black women remained in a state of legal limbo as they navigated wartime policy created in the interests of states loyal to the Union and against the interests of the Confederacy.[18]

The emancipation process in Washington, DC, involved a series of critical policies instituted under martial law, including the First Confiscation Act of 1861, the District of Columbia Emancipation Act of 1862, the elimination of black codes, the Supplemental Act of 1862, the Second Confiscation Act of 1862, the Emancipation Proclamation of 1863, and the repeal of the Fugitive Slave Law in 1864.[19] This complicated sequence of policy changes had varying impacts on the lives of enslaved and free women, particularly those journeying from neighboring slave-holding states. Wartime policy in the District, nestled between Confederate territory in Virginia and the nebulously loyal slave state of Maryland, created uncertain terms of legal freedom.[20]

WARTIME EMANCIPATION IN THE DISTRICT

In the spring of 1862, Congress approved the terms of freeing slaves in the District. On April 16, the Federal government declared the following:

> Be it enacted by the Senate and House of Representatives of the United States of America in Congress assembled, That all persons held to service or labor within the District of Columbia by reason of African descent are hereby discharged and freed of and from all claim to such service or labor; and from and after the passage of this act neither slavery nor involuntary servitude, except for crime, whereof the party shall be duly convicted, shall hereafter exist in said District.[21]

The abolishment of slavery in the District of Columbia legally set in motion the emancipation process, making the violation of this Emancipation Act a felony, and incentivizing compliance with the new order by awarding up to three hundred dollars of compensation for each slave freed. Slaveholders applying for compensation were offered a specific amount of money determined by the assessed value of each slave, which at times exceeded three hundred dollars.

Although some locals denounced the new act as an unconstitutional infringement upon their property rights as citizens, as many as 966 slaveholders filed claims for compensation. The clerk and Board of Commissioners, along with the secretary of the treasury, were responsible for assessing the claims, determining the value of slaves, and transacting compensation. Commissioner records indicate that the majority of the claims involved smaller slaveholdings, ranging from one to eight slaves. For the value of four slaves—which included a slave named Rosanna, and her children William and Alexa Gordon, and Caroline Lucas—the infamous brothel owner Mary Ann Hall requested three thousand dollars. According to Hall, Rosanna alone was valued at twelve hundred dollars. White women appeared as frequently as men in seeking compensation for their property. A woman named Harriet White, for instance, requested a little over $6,800 for the value of twenty-four slaves. White's case was one of many filed by women hoping to profit from the compensation provision in the Act, revealing that both white women and men were invested in the institution of slavery and believed they were entitled to compensation for "lost property" during emancipation. Some locals possessed holdings as large as, if not larger than, White's. District resident George Washington Young, for instance, boasted holdings of sixty-eight slaves, with an attested compensation value set at over seventeen thousand dollars.[22]

Once freed, black residents could remain in the District, or leave the country with the support of government-subsidized emigration initiatives. Former slaves who decided to emigrate outside of the United States could be allotted up to one hundred dollars per person. Thus, while the Emancipation Act represented a significant victory for blacks, as well as white abolitionists, it was clear that Congress encouraged the exodus of black locals. Although such colonization efforts had gained some traction prior to the war, the government could not convince a critical mass to emigrate outside of the country after emancipation, nor could they convince whites to affirm the idea of an American-based black citizenry. Free black people articulated visions of both cultural and legal citizenship long before the outbreak of war, and freedpeople asserted their right to remain in the District when the Emancipation Act took effect. They did not see themselves as citizens of a foreign land. Their labors, struggles, and loyalties had fostered a sense of belonging on American soil.[23]

Realizing freedom and citizenship in America, however, was no easy feat. Local emancipation actually allowed slavery to survive in instances where a black person was convicted of violating the antebellum black codes. Accordingly, legal reform would be necessary in order for the Emancipation Act of Washington, DC, to prove completely effective in releasing black women and men from the tyranny of slavery. Republican senator Henry Wilson, for instance, understood all too well the legislative loopholes that could keep free blacks bound. As former chair of the 1852 Free Soil convention, and a long-standing proponent of abolitionism, Wilson had submitted a proposal, just weeks after the passage of the Emancipation Act of Washington, DC, to eliminate the black codes. By way of background, Senator Wilson, along with Senator James Grimes and the Committee on the District of Columbia, had produced a report on the conditions of "degradation and inhumanity" that blacks faced in the Washington Jail. The concomitant discussions concerning the abhorrent treatment of enslaved and free blacks led to further deliberation over the root of these injustices, which included the black codes and the Fugitive Slave Law of 1850. Wilson then submitted a proposal on May 22, 1862, stating, among other things, that "all persons of color . . . shall be subject and amenable to the same laws and ordinances to which free white persons are."[24] The subsequent repeal of the black codes ended a system of surveillance and control that had circumscribed the lives of enslaved and free blacks since the inception of the nation's capital. The measure proved to be critical in the emancipation process—but white locals would not relent so easily.

Despite the repeal of the black codes, the Emancipation Act itself—passed in order to place pressure on the Confederacy—remained largely deficient in its ability to transition former slaves into free life in Washington.[25] Indeed, it merely exposed the remaining strength of the multilayered regime of slavery and racial hierarchy. Evidence of defiant slaveholders, who resisted their former slaves' claims to a newly freed legal status, shows that white contempt stifled the emancipation process. While Republican legislators and activists spearheaded antislavery and emancipation policies, white locals vehemently opposed the presence of free black locals and incoming refugees. During the Civil War, reports surfaced of white hostility, abuse, manipulation, and disregard of the law.

Despite the compensation provision in the Emancipation Act, many slave owners in the District did not concede to the primary objective of the new law—emancipation. Slaves seeking to solidify their free status thus encountered a number of legal hurdles. The logistical issues presented by this resistance to the Emancipation Act led to the Supplemental Act of July 12, 1862, which set forth the terms under which slaves could claim free status even where a former owner refused to apply for compensation. The Supplemental Act stated, moreover, that "in all judicial proceedings in the District of Columbia there shall be no exclusion of any witness on account of color."[26] This stipulation, which allowed former slaves to testify against whites, was the distinctive feature of the Supplemental Act. Slave testimony would be critical in the efforts of black women and men to counter white arguments that they were not residents of the District, or that they had unlawfully claimed entitlement to the terms of the Act. For the first time in the history of the nation's capital, slaves could exert legal agency in their own self-defense. The testimony of enslaved women offered a critical avenue to freedom that invited them to exercise an important practice of citizenship.

The Fugitive Slave Law of 1850, however, further complicated the emancipation process, particularly for slaves who were "hired out" in the District from Maryland planters or for those who escaped from loyal slave-holding states such as Maryland.[27] The law stipulated that escaped slaves must be returned, and that penalties should be imposed upon officials and locals who refused to return slaves. Therefore, while hundreds of slaves flocked to the District from surrounding slave-holding states to become free, they did so illegally. Even after local emancipation and the abolishment of the black codes, the courts in Washington, DC, enforced fugitive slave laws on behalf of owners residing in states that professed loyalty to the Union. White supremacy was not antithetical to the aims of the Union—rebellion was. Policies that preserved slavery made clear that race- and gender-based discrimination remained acceptable.

Some slaves managed to evade fugitive slave laws with the assistance of military officials acting pursuant to the Second Confiscation Act of 1862. The Second Confiscation Act emancipated Rebel-owned slaves as an "act to suppress insurrection, to punish Treason and Rebellion, to seize and confiscate the Property of Rebels."[28] Essentially, while the First Confiscation Act had only freed those slaves employed in labor that supported the Confederate war effort, the Second Confiscation Act freed the slaves of all disloyal slaveholders.[29] Although the Acts impacted the economic and labor productivity of the Confederacy, particularly as refugees arrived from the states closest to the Peninsula campaign, they did not legalize the freedom of neighboring slave-holding states such as Maryland and Delaware, where a number of slaves came from. This made the emancipation process difficult to manage and complete, leaving black citizenship seemingly out of reach.

CONTENTIOUS FREEDOM

Just as the system of racial slavery was built upon a multifaceted legal framework, emancipation was multilayered. Family networks figured prominently in recorded appeals for freedom in Washington, DC, as black women and men sought to locate and reunite themselves with missing or abducted relatives.[30] When the superintendent of contrabands at Camp Barker gave testimony before the American Freedmen's Inquiry, he stated that, as a general rule, refugees "wish and seek to preserve family ties renewing again their relations as parents, children, husband and wife whenever they are able."[31] These family ties had been complicated and threatened not only by the system of enslavement, but also by the war itself. Many women were left alone with as many as seven children to clothe and feed while their husbands worked for the military or War Department. While most of these women sought employment to support their families, they wrestled with starvation, inclement weather, and disease. Indeed, when their husbands were not paid adequate wages, or died during the war, women and children were subject to the most abject living conditions in the city. Enslaved and free women persistently submitted their grievances, complaining of legal entanglements with manipulative white locals who attempted to evade the terms of Emancipation.[32]

On March 28, 1862, Emeline Brown, a free black woman, submitted a petition for a writ of habeas corpus to the Circuit Court of the District of Columbia, asserting that her daughter, Lucy Brown, was "uniquely and illegally detained and held in custody and keeping by one Benjamin J. Hunt of Georgetown." Twelve-year-old Lucy was "hired out" to Benjamin Hunt prior to the petition, but Emeline discovered that "said child Lucy is maltreated." Emeline thus requested that the court grant her habeas petition "directed to and commanding the said Benjamin J. Hunt, to be and appear" before the court. Her petition, however, was denied—the court did not order Hunt's appearance or Lucy's release. As a result, Lucy continued working for Hunt without the protection of the law to shield her from his abuse. Eight months later, after the passage of the Emancipation Act of April 1862, Lucy's father, John Brown, a newly freed man, submitted a petition, arguing that he was her "natural guardian and protector." This petition was deemed meritorious—Hunt was mandated to release Lucy and she was returned to her parents. Emeline's effort to free her child from the tyranny of Benjamin J. Hunt was one of many cases involving the legally sanctioned reenslavement of free black women and girls, and the mistreatment of female slaves and servants in Washington, DC, during the mid-nineteenth century. Emeline's free status could do little to save her daughter from abuse, but the collective outcome of the Emancipation Act of 1862, and the petition initiated by her father John Brown, worked in favor of Lucy's release. Localized law or customs often prevailed in favor of white interests, but in this instance the persistence of the petitioners and the mounting pressure of wartime emancipation led to Lucy's release.[33]

The blurred boundaries of the District and the complex ties District locals held with the surrounding Chesapeake states resurfaced in another petition. On May 29, 1862, just after the passage of the Emancipation Act of the District of Columbia, an enslaved girl named Maria Diggs submitted a petition for her freedom. Although the slaveholder had applied for compensation for Maria's mother and father who resided with him in the District, he declared that Maria was "not freed by the act." He argued that because Maria had been "hired out" to a man just outside of the District, the new law did not apply to her. While scholars have argued that the "hiring out" system of enslavement undermined

slavery, in this case it preserved the institution by drawing upon its
Chesapeake origins. The commissioners opined that "all who were out
of the District when the bill was approved, do not come within its provisions—are consequently slaves still." Maria thus was not as fortunate
as Emeline Wedge. Because of the "hiring out" system, Maria's owner
not only received compensation for her parents, but also found a way to
invalidate her claims to freedom. The former slaveholder still held the
reins—his citizenship rights were protected accordingly.[34]

While more than nine hundred slaveholders received compensation
for the emancipation of their slaves, this incentive only applied to those
who resided in the District. For those slave owners in the surrounding
counties who were subsequently forced to release their slaves in accordance with the Emancipation Proclamation of 1863, no analogous
provision for compensation existed. The Emancipation Proclamation,
issued on January 1, 1863, simply declared that all slaves within the
Confederacy "are, and henceforward shall be free."[35]

Despite the common misconception that the Emancipation Proclamation freed every slave in the country, the law, like its predecessor
policies, only applied to those states in rebellion. Unwilling to surrender
the men, women, and children who augmented their labor force in a
war-ravaged landscape, slaveholders defiantly resisted these new legal
measures that were designed to entice blacks to join the Union ranks.
Indeed, slaveholders of the seceded states did not see themselves as
subject to these laws; instead, they believed they were only subject to the
laws of the Confederacy, which affirmed their right to slave ownership,
and referred to slaves within Union lines as "runaways." Black women,
however, fought tirelessly to loose themselves and their relatives from
the stranglehold of the old slave system.[36]

Emancipation and new discourses of citizenship could not completely
erase the racial and gendered injustices that prevailed throughout the
Civil War, nor the rampant effects of poverty that kept freedwomen subject to hunger, disease, and inadequate living conditions. Indeed, black
women earned the lowest wages and often found themselves in dire
circumstances as they tried to feed and clothe their children. Josephine
Griffing, an agent of the National Freedman's Relief Association, wrote to
the secretary of war about her encounters with the deplorable condition
in which black women and children lived in the District. After delivering
wood to "over one hundred families," she discovered that many families
composed of women and children were "without food of any descrip-

tion." Griffing was confounded when she saw mothers "confined with infants with four, six, and seven children in their care—their Husbands either in Gov't Service or dead."[37] Facing limited flexibility in terms of childcare, coupled with the low probability of making enough income, freedwomen attempting to survive in the Washington, DC, area faced tremendous odds.

Some freedwomen traveled to "contraband camps" to begin their free life or simply to survive. Freedmen's Village on Robert E. Lee's confiscated estate in Arlington, Virginia housed approximately 1,500 former slaves in 100 family homes. The Village was known for the rather large population of women, children, and elders frequently depicted as "dependents" and not citizens of the government. However, the community cultivated gardens, earned small wages, cared for the homes, sewed clothing, and built a school for the children. Government officials envisioned the camp as a temporary community and hoped to make employment arrangements with white families in need of additional labor in the North. Residents in the Village, by contrast, felt that they had created sustainable living conditions that would allow them to experience the privileges of citizenship within their village in Arlington. Contrastingly, just across the Potomac near 12th and Q Streets in Washington, Camp Barker compared starkly with Freedmen's Village, looking more like a "tent city" with higher mortality rates and unsanitary living conditions. In 1864, when officials decided to move residents of Camp Barker to Freedmen's Village, only 120 agreed to move, while the remaining 685 refused to set foot on the slave-holding territory.[38]

Charged anywhere between five and eight dollars per month for damp and cold shacks exposed to the inclement winters in the District, black women during the war found it difficult to earn a sufficient living and keep themselves and their families healthy. Many black children lost both parents during the war, and were forced to rely upon overcrowded orphanages or their closest relatives as they fought to survive. Their struggle for survival often resulted in casualties. In 1864, as officials began evicting freedpeople from Camp Barker, one grandmother was forced to leave the premises as her grandson was dying beside her. According to reports, "The grandmother who had taken care of it [the grandson] since its mothers death begged leave to stay until the child died, but she was refused."[39] Camp Barker—a "contraband" camp organized by the government to house and employ refugees who escaped from Confederate territory—thus served as an outpost not only of freedom, but also frailty. For instance, Georgiana Willets, a missionary who worked at Camp Barker, observed in 1864 that, "There is now some suffering but it is chiefly amongst the women who have small children—These can barely obtain the necessaries of life."[40]

In the aftermath of wartime emancipation policies, refugees flocked to Union lines searching for asylum and opportunities to reclaim families and find work in sustainable communities built by freedmen and women. Yet life in the contraband camps was often filled with habits and customs that merely reminded freedpeople, and black women in particular, that for the moment, legal emancipation had its limits and that the meaning of citizenship remained uncertain. The story of one black woman named Lucy Ellen Johnson, who lived with her mother at Camp Barker while her husband was employed in the military, is illuminating.

Upon her arrival at Camp Barker, Johnson understood that she was supposed to work in the camp and "earn my food and clothing like other contrabands."[41] In fact, prior to her arrival, she had been a chambermaid on the Steamboat *Zephyr,* so she had a work history and an eagerness to work. Shortly after arriving at Camp Barker, however, Johnson became ill and unable to work. When she asked for rations, a blanket, and clothing, she was interrogated by Mr. Nichols, the white official at Camp Barker who distributed supplies. Nichols could not understand why Johnson's husband had not provided for her, but Johnson pleaded: "I am here to earn my board and the same clothes that others have." She offered to request money from her husband so that she could pay for the needed items, but Nichols responded, "You can't buy them from me—you can't have anything."[42] Johnson argued that if her arrangements at the camp were problematic, then Nichols should have spoken to her husband about the matter so that she could find work elsewhere.

Nichols became angry and ordered Johnson to a room, where she was pinned down and harassed by a corporal, a sergeant, and soldiers. The gang of men took her to a tent, where they kicked her and grabbed her by the throat. She reported: "They fastened a rope round my two thumbs and passing it over the limb of a tree raised me from the ground so that my weight was suspended by the thumbs."[43] They adjusted the rope and hung her by her wrists. "In this position," Johnson recalled, "one kicked me—another choked my throat—another stuffed dirty wool in my mouth." After a half hour of torture, she was finally released.

According to one assessment, more than thirty people filed testimonies regarding the abusive treatment of freedpeople at Camp Barker.[44]

Stories like those of Lucy Ellen Johnson are vivid reminders of the undercurrents of white contempt during the moment of legal emancipation. This contempt for enslaved and free blacks who migrated to Union lines and the District manifested itself in a variety of forms, ranging from abuse in contraband camps, to local mob violence in the city. Wartime emancipation sparked a violent backlash across regional boundaries from those who held the view that freedpeople burdened the nation and should by all means be excluded from citizenship. For instance, Maryland remained a point of contention for wartime emancipation, even after the state adopted a new constitution banning the practice of slavery.

On November 14, 1864, just days prior to the date when Article 24 of Maryland's new constitution, which made slavery illegal, took effect, Harriet Anne Maria Banks wrote a letter stating that her owner, Dr. S. S. Hughes, "treated me badly & this was my principal object in leaving they informed me that Abraham Lincoln could not free me that he had no right to do so."[45] Along with slavery, many of the Maryland black codes were no longer in effect, but the constitution did make leaving an employer a punishable crime for black Marylanders alone. Thus, a constitution intended to inaugurate a free labor system in Maryland actually catalyzed a corrupt system of child abduction, labor exploitation, and rejection of the parental rights of black mothers and fathers.

Within this context, the apprenticeship system in Maryland arose as a convoluted collaboration between former slave owners and local justices committed to the old order of the South. The provost marshal of the District of Maryland, Andrew Stafford, observed that, just four days after the adoption of the new constitution, "a rush was made to the Orphan's Court of this County, for the purpose of having all children under twenty one years of age, bound to their former owners, under the apprentice law of the State."[46] These apprenticeship arrangements were validated by local judges, who typically decided in favor of the former master, regarding black parents as unfit to financially provide for their child, particularly where the father was away at work or war and could not claim the child's labor. Decisions of the court thus reflected a racial and gendered hierarchy that prioritized the interests of whites first, then black men as the head of the household, before those of black mothers. Reminiscent of the plantation, the courts too often reinforced white power and paternalism to decide the fate of black children.

Black mothers who did not have a spouse or whose husbands could not testify in Orphan's Court—often because they had left to support

the Union war effort—were particularly affected by these legal interpretations of apprenticeship arrangements. In particular, black mothers
found themselves burdened with the responsibility of simultaneously
fighting off former slaveholders and providing for their children. Although the labors of all household members were critical to the subsistence of families during the nineteenth century, local justices in the
Orphan's Court often refused to acknowledge a black mother's right
to protect her child's labor. As a result, black women sometimes took
matters into their own hands in order to retrieve their children from
the grips of planter exploitation and create a life where their families
could enjoy the fruits of their own labors. Jane Kamper, a former slave
of William Townsend of Talbot County, Maryland, reportedly told Mr.
Townsend, "of my having become free & desired my master to give
my children and my bedclothes he told me that I was free but that my
Children Should be bound to me [him]." She testified further that, "he
locked my Children up so that I could not find them. I afterwards got my
children by stealth & brought them to Baltimore." Kamper, like many
other freedwomen, thus risked her life to save her children "by stealth"
from unconsented apprenticeship. She concluded her statement saying,
"My Master pursued me to the Boat to get possession of my children
but I hid them on the boat."[47] As characterized by Kamper's story, legal
emancipation made the freedom of black women and children lawful,
but not always tangible. Even upon assuming freedom rights gained
from the war, black women continued the work of resituating their relationship between themselves, the government, and the communities
in which they lived.

CONCLUSION

Black women and men as well as government officials undoubtedly
employed the term *citizen* to describe free blacks and former slaves at
the moment of wartime emancipation. Overstating this fact, however,
wrongly suggests that white Unionists extended to former slaves an
invitation to share equally in the rights of American citizenship. It also
detracts from freedpeople's struggles to define the terms of their inclusion. The perception that emancipation and black equality occurred at
the expense of white entitlements to citizenship brought citizenship into
direct conflict with emancipation for people who refused to free slaves.
For instance, the Union government protected the interests of slave-

holders in Maryland just as emancipation policies took effect in the District of Columbia and the Confederate states. The imperatives of white slaveholder citizenship and black citizenship were at odds in that the economic rights of one violated the human and civil rights of another. Just as government officials in the halls of Congress and within military encampments began to employ the term *citizen,* they also employed terms such as *contraband* and *dependent*—terms rhetorically antithetical to nineteenth-century representations of American citizenship. As I've demonstrated here, black women wielded their political muscles by challenging the notion that American citizenship equated to white control over black life. Using tactics such as litigation, flight, and petitions, black women initiated a wartime challenge to anti-black sentiments expressed by white residents of Washington, DC. The passage of the Supplemental Act, which allowed blacks to testify against white citizens for the first time, charted a critical, albeit limited, path for black women seeking to legally claim their freedom. Accordingly, freedwomen reshaped their relationship with the government and former slave owners.

The actions of freedwomen set in motion a dynamic that positioned formerly enslaved women to confront white resistance and appropriate various channels of recourse recognized by the government.[48] While she initially lost her case, Emeline Brown petitioned the courts—months before the Supplemental Act passed—and ultimately saw her daughter freed. Emeline Wedge, however, took her former owner to court less than six months after the Supplemental Act was passed and won her case. Even in cases ruled in favor of former owners, black women did not allow legal injustices to force them to surrender. Instead, they took matters into their own hands, creating their own system of redress. Jane Kamper, for instance, evaded the law and "by stealth," fled from the grips of slave owners with children in tow. Just as lawmakers enacted important legislation authorizing the emancipation of former slaves, black women and men too decided for themselves their own future in the country where they toiled, fought, and lived. The conditions of the war, and internal conflict more generally, presented opportunities for both former slaves and legislators to conceptualize new ideas about citizenship. This process was multilayered and complex. It would take time for white residents of Washington, DC, to be persuaded to treat black women and men fairly and humanely. The legalization of emancipation did not foreclose antiblack resistance, nor did it offer consistent enforcement of equal access to freedom and citizenship rights. Freedom did not

equate to citizenship, but it marked a critical outcome of long-held beliefs about citizenship that black women and men conceived years prior
to the American Civil War. Emancipation was the culmination of a hope
long deferred, and the beginning of an arduous path towards inclusion
and legal participation as American citizens.

NOTES

1. Records of the Board of Commissioners for the Emancipation of Slaves in the District
of Columbia, 1862–1863, M520, Roll #1; Henry Louis Gates, *The Oxford Handbook of African
American Citizenship, 1865–Present* (New York: Oxford University Press, 2012); Evelyn
Nakano Glenn, *Unequal Freedom: How Race and Gender Shaped American Citizenship and
Labor* (Cambridge, MA: Harvard University Press, 2002).

2. Paul Finkelman, "The Civil War, Emancipation, and the Thirteenth Amendment,"
in *The Promises of Liberty: The History and Contemporary Relevance of the Thirteenth
Amendment,* ed. Alexander Tsesis (New York: Columbia University Press, 2010), 44.

3. David Thomas Konig, Paul Finkelman, and Christopher Alan Bracey, eds., *The Dred
Scott Case: Historical and Contemporary Perspectives on Race and Law* (Athens: Ohio University Press, 2010).

4. William J. Novak, "The Legal Transformation of Citizenship in Nineteenth-Century
America," in *The Democratic Experiment: New Directions in American Political History,* ed.
Meg Jacobs, William J. Novak, and Julian E. Zelizer (Princeton, NJ: Princeton University
Press, 2003), 85–119; Michael Vorenberg, "Citizenship and the Thirteenth Amendment:
Understanding the Deafening Silence," in *The Promises of Liberty: The History and Contemporary Relevance of the Thirteenth Amendment,* ed. Alexander Tsesis (New York: Columbia
University Press, 2010), 62.

5. Ira Berlin, Stephen F. Miller, and Leslie S. Rowland, "Afro-American Families in the
Transition from Slavery to Freedom," *Radical History Review* 42 (1988): 89–121; Laura
Edwards, "Status without Rights: African Americans and the Tangled History of Law and
Governance in the Nineteenth-Century U.S. South," *The American Historical Review* 112,
no. 2 (April 2007): 365–93; Leslie A. Schwalm, *A Hard Fight for We: Women's Transition
from Slavery to Freedom in South Carolina* (Urbana: University of Illinois Press, 1997).

6. Kate Masur, *An Example for All the Land: Emancipation and the Struggle Over Equality in Washington, D.C.* (Chapel Hill: University of North Carolina Press, 2010); Constance
Green, *Washington: Village and Capital, 1800–1878* (Princeton, NJ: Princeton University
Press, 1962); Constance McLaughlin Green, *The Secret City: A History of Race Relations in
the Nation's Capital* (Princeton, NJ: Princeton University Press, 1967).

7. Mary Frances Berry, *Military Necessity and Civil Rights Policy: Black Citizenship and
the Constitution, 1861–1868* (La Jolla, CA: National University Publications, 1977); Judith
Shklar, *American Citizenship: The Quest for Inclusion* (Cambridge, MA: Harvard University
Press, 1991); Rogers Smith, *Civic Ideals: Conflicting Visions of Citizenship in U.S. History*
(New Haven, CT: Yale University Press, 1999); Vorenberg, "Citizenship and the Thirteenth
Amendment"; Joseph Reidy, "The African American Struggle for Citizenship Rights in the
Northern United States during the Civil War," in *Civil War Citizens: Race, Ethnicity, and
Identity in America's Bloodiest Conflict,* ed. Susannah Ural (New York: New York University

Press, 2010), 213–36; Michael Vorenberg, *Final Freedom: The Civil War, the Abolition of Slavery and the Thirteenth Amendment* (New York: Cambridge University Press, 2001).

8. Martha S. Jones, *All Bound Up Together: The Woman Questions in African American Public Culture, 1830–1900* (Chapel Hill: University of North Carolina Press, 2007); Stephen Kantrowitz, *More than Freedom: Fighting for Black Citizenship in a White Republic, 1829–1889* (New York: Penguin Books, 2013).

9. Chandra Manning, "Working for Citizenship in Civil War Contraband Camps," *The Journal of the Civil War Era* 4, no. 2 (June 2014): 172–204; Kate Masur, "'A Rare Phenomenon of Philological Vegetation': The Word 'Contraband' and the Meanings of Emancipation in the United States," *The Journal of American History* 93, no. 4 (March 2007): 1050–84.

10. Thavolia Glymph, "'This Species of Property': Female Slave Contrabands in the Civil War," in *A Woman's War: Southern Women, Civil War, and the Confederate Legacy,* ed. Edward D. C. Campbell Jr. and Kym S. Rice (Richmond: Museum of the Confederacy, 1996), 54–71.

11. Vorenberg, "Citizenship and the Thirteenth Amendment," 64.

12. Edward Bates, "Citizenship," *Opinions of the Attorney General* 10 (November 29, 1862).

13. Records of the Board of Commissioners for the Emancipation of Slaves in the District of Columbia, 1862–1863, M520, Roll #1, Washington, DC, National Archives and Records Administration.

14. Kathleen Brown, *Good Wives, Nasty Wenches, and Anxious Patriarchs: Gender, Race, and Power in Colonial Virginia* (Chapel Hill: University of North Carolina Press, 1996); Amy Dru Stanley, *From Bondage to Contract: Wage Labor, Marriage, and the Market in the Age of Slave Emancipation* (New York: Cambridge University Press, 1998).

15. Nancy Isenberg, *Sex and Citizenship in Antebellum America* (Chapel Hill: University of North Carolina Press, 1998).

16. Ibid.

17. Ernest B. Ferguson, *Freedom Rising: Washington in the Civil War* (New York: Vintage Books, 2005); Kenneth J. Winkle, *Lincoln's Citadel: The Civil War in Washington, D.C.* (New York: W. W. Norton, 2013); James Oakes, *Freedom National: The Destruction of Slavery in the United States, 1861–1865* (New York: W. W. Norton, 2013).

18. Emancipation Proclamation, January 1, 1863, Presidential Proclamations, 1791–1991, RG 11, General Records of the United States Government, NARA.

19. Oakes, *Freedom National.*

20. Board of Commissioners Records for the Emancipation of Slaves, 1862–1863, Records of the Accounting Officers of the Department of the Treasury, RG 217, NARA; Laura F. Edwards, *A Legal History of the Civil War and Reconstruction: A Nation of Rights* (New York: Cambridge University Press, 2015); Oakes, *Freedom National*; Garfield Randall, *Constitutional Problems under Lincoln* (New York: D. Appleton, 1926); Silvana R. Siddali, *From Property to Person: Slavery and the Confiscation Acts, 1861–1862* (Baton Rouge: Louisiana State University Press, 2005).

21. Act of April 16, 1862 [For the Release of Certain Persons Held to Service or Labor in the District of Columbia], National Archives, General Records of the United States Government, Record Group 11.

22. Records of the Board of Commissioners for the Emancipation of Slaves in the District of Columbia, 1862–63, M520, Roll 1, Washington, DC, National Archives and Records Administration; guardians also frequently represented children who had inherited slaves.

23. Green, *Secret City*.

24. Records of the Metropolitan Police Department of the District of Columbia, 1862 (National Archives, Record Group 351); Kenneth Alfers, "Law and Order in the Capital City: A History of the Washington Police, 1800–1886," *George Washington Studies* no. 5, George Washington University, September 1976; *News*, October 12, 26, 1850; John L. Myers, *Senator Henry Wilson and the Civil War* (Lanham, MD: University Press of America, 2008); "An Act Providing for the Education of Colored Children in the Cities of Washington and Georgetown, District of Columbia, and for Other Purposes," *U.S. Statutes at Large*, 12:407; Senate Re. Com. № 60, 37th Congress, 2nd Session, 1–7, 27, 33–37; Congressional Globe, 37th Congress, 2nd Session, 311; Washington National Republican, January 16, February 14, 1862; U.S. Statutes at Large, XII, 37th Congress, 2nd Session, Chap. LXXXIII, 407.

25. Green, *Secret City*, 99; Masur, *An Example for All the Land*, 203–6.

26. Records of the District Court for the District of Columbia Relating to Slaves, 1851–1863, section 1 (National Archives Microfilm Publication M433), Roll 1. Although slaves submitted petitions for manumission certificates in civil suits well before Emancipation, the Supplementary Act of July 12, 1862, allowed slaves to secure their freedom upon the refusal of their owners to do so.

27. The "hire" system of slavery fused the economic and political ties between Virginia, Maryland, and Washington, DC. "Hiring out" constituted an arrangement between a slaveholder and a person in need of additional labor.

28. Second Confiscation Act, 12 U.S. *Statutes at Large* 589 (1863).

29. For debates on Confiscation Acts, see Oakes, *Freedom National*; Randall, *Constitutional Problems under Lincoln*; Siddali, *From Property to Person*,

30. Dylan Penningroth, *The Claims of Kinfolk: African American Property and Community in the Nineteenth-Century South* (Chapel Hill: University of North Carolina Press, 2003); Amy Dru Stanley, "Instead of Waiting for the Thirteenth Amendment: The War Power, Slave Marriage, and Inviolate Human Rights," *American Historical Review* 115, no. 3 (June 2010): 732–65; Laura F. Edwards, *Gendered Strife and Confusion: The Political Culture of Reconstruction* (Urbana: University of Illinois Press, 1997); Julie Saville, *The Work of Reconstruction: From Slave to Wage Laborer in South Carolina, 1860–1870* (New York: Cambridge University Press, 1994).

31. "Liberal Donations for the Contrabands: A Card," from D. B. Nichols, Superintendent of Contrabands at Camp Barker, *Daily National Republican*, July 30, 1862.

32. Testimony from Dr. D. B. Nichols (April ? 1863), Letters Received, ser. 12, Military District of Washington, RG 94 [O-328].

33. Habeas Corpus Case Records, 1820–1863, of the U.S. District Court for the District of Columbia (National Archives Microfilm Publication M434), Roll 2, Record Group 21.

34. "A Case Before the Emancipation Commissioners," *The National Republican*, Washington, DC, May 29, 1862, LOC; scholars such as Barbara Fields, Richard Wade, and Midori Takagi have considered whether slavery was incompatible with city life. Takagi's work focuses on the opportunities that enabled greater resistance from the slaves. David Stroman, *Slavery in Washington, D.C.: Slaves of Washington, D.C.*, Library of Congress, Washington, DC, 2002; Richard Wade, *Slavery in the Cities: The South, 1820–1860* (New York: Oxford University Press, 1964); Barbara Fields, *Slavery and Freedom on the Middle Ground: Maryland During the Nineteenth Century* (New Haven, CT: Yale University Press, 1985); Midori

Takagi, *Rearing Wolves to Our Own Destruction: Slavery in Richmond, Virginia, 1782–1865* (Charlottesville: University Press of Virginia, 1999).

35. Emancipation Proclamation, January 1, 1863, Presidential Proclamations, 1791–1991, RG 11, General Records of the United States Government, NARA.

36. Board of Commissioners Records for the Emancipation of Slaves, 1862–1863, Records of the Accounting Officers of the Department of the Treasury, NARA, Record Group 217.

37. Josephine S. Griffing to Hon. E. M. Staunton, December 1864, Consolidated Correspondence, Central Records, ser. 225, Record Group 92.

38. David Blight, *A Slave No More: Two Men Who Escaped to Freedom, Including Their Own Narratives of Emancipation* (Orlando: First Mariner Books, 2007), 93; Robert Harrison, *Washington during Civil War and Reconstruction: Race and Radicalism* (New York: Cambridge University Press, 2011), 41–43.

39. Testimony of Mrs. Louisa Jane Barker, January 1864, Miscellaneous Records, ser. 5412, Department of Washington, RG 393 Pt. 1 (C-4757).

40. Josephine S. Griffing to Hon. E. M. Staunton, December 1864, Consolidated Correspondence, Central Records, ser. 225, RG 92; Testimony of Georgiana Willets, January 1864, Miscellaneous Records, ser. 5412, Department of Washington, RG 393 Pt. 1 (C-4757).

41. Testimony of Luisa Jane Barker, January 14, 1864, Miscellaneous Records, ser. 5412, Department of Washington, RG 393 Pt. 1 (C-4757).

42. Ibid.

43. Ibid.

44. Ira Berlin, Barbara J. Fields, and Steven F. Miller, *Free at Last: A Documentary History of Slavery, Freedom, and the Civil War* (Publications of the Freedmen and Southern Society Project), (New York: New Press, 1992).

45. Fields, *Slavery and Freedom on the Middle Ground*, 138; Statement of Harriet Ann Maria Banks, November 14, 1864, Letters Received, ser. 12, Record Group 94 [M-1932]; Berlin, Fields, and Miller, *Free at Last*.

46. Captain Andrew Stafford to General H. H. Lockwood, November 4, 1864, Letters Received, ser. 12, Record Group 94 [M-1932]; Mary Farmer-Kaiser, *Freedwomen and the Freedmen's Bureau: Race, Gender, and Public Policy in the Age of Emancipation* (New York: Fordham University Press, 2010); Karin L. Zip, *Labor of Innocents: Forced Apprenticeship in North Carolina 1715–1919* (Baton Rouge: Louisiana State University Press, 2005).

47. Statement of Jane Kamper, November 14, 1864, Letters Received, ser. 12, Record Group 94 [M-1932]; Berlin, Fields, and Miller, *Free at Last*.

48. Gregory P. Downs, *After Appomattox: Military Occupation and the Ends of War* (Cambridge, MA: Harvard University Press, 2015).

Rethinking the Racial Boundaries of Citizenship

Native Americans and People of Chinese Descent

EARL M. MALTZ

Studies of the Federal government's response to racial discrimination during the period immediately following the Civil War tend to concentrate on the treatment of African Americans. This focus is in many respects entirely understandable. After all, the question of how African Americans should be treated was one of the major issues dividing most Republicans from Democrats, as well as one of the central themes of the entire conflict over Reconstruction. Thus, it should not be surprising that the issue of white–African American relations has attracted the attention of most students of the Reconstruction period, as well as those interested in American race relations more generally.

Discussions of the conflict over the issue of citizenship are no different in this regard. In his 1857 opinion in *Dred Scott v. Sandford*,[1] Chief Justice Roger Brooke Taney famously declared that the descendants of slaves could never become citizens of the United States. Initially, the Republican Party was divided over the question of whether free African Americans should be viewed as citizens. However, by the end of the Civil War the party was committed to the principle of birthright citizenship and, over the objections of many Democrats, this principle was embodied in both the Civil Rights Act of 1866 and section one of the Fourteenth Amendment.

But while the struggle over the legal status of African Americans was one of the central issues of the Reconstruction period, both Republicans and Democrats were also well aware that Federal action might affect the status and rights of other racial minorities as well. In particular, the debates also at times focused on issues related to the proper treatment of both Native Americans and immigrants from China.

Often these discussions raised fundamental questions related to the definition and nature of US citizenship. When dealing with the status of Native Americans, Congress was forced to confront a unique problem of separating the individuals and groups who in fact owed allegiance to the US government from those whose primary loyalty was to tribal authorities. By contrast, the debate over measures that would have allowed Chinese immigrants access to the naturalization process turned on the question of whether the government should be willing to confer equal status on members of a group whose worldview differed fundamentally from that of the vast majority of Americans.

THE PROBLEM OF NATIVE AMERICAN CITIZENSHIP

The Union victory in the Civil War was a defeat for many Native Americans, most notably the members of the Five Civilized Tribes that had relocated to Oklahoma after having been expelled from the state of Georgia earlier in the nineteenth century. The institution of African American slavery was well established in these tribes, and tribal members fought against the Union forces during the war itself. Indeed, Stand Watie, a member of the Cherokee tribe, was the last Confederate general to surrender in 1865.[2]

In the wake of their defeat, the tribes that had supported the Confederacy were forced to accept treaties that required them to renounce slavery and recognize their former slaves as full members of the tribes. The treaties that were negotiated also contained a variety of provisions that ultimately contributed to the decimation of not only the Five Civilized Tribes themselves, but also the Native American tribes in the West more generally. But at the same time, during the process of drafting the citizenship clauses of both the Civil Rights Act of 1866 and section one of the Fourteenth Amendment, Congress made every effort to ensure that these provisions would not change the political status of individual Native Americans.[3]

This status was a by-product of the idiosyncratic nature of the relationship of the tribes themselves to the Federal government. While located within the territorial boundaries of the United States, the tribes were not constituent parts of the Federal government. Instead, in the words of Chief Justice John Marshall in an 1831 Supreme Court decision, they were viewed as "domestic dependent nations." In 1856, Attorney

General Caleb Cushing provided a detailed analysis of the implications of this characterization for individual members of the tribes.[4]

The specific question addressed by the opinion was whether a person of mixed ancestry who had been granted eighty acres of land by virtue of an 1854 treaty with the Chippewa Tribe of Lake Superior could also take advantage of an 1841 statute that allowed citizens of the United States to purchase public land at a very low price. After observing that "the word 'citizen' has relative applications, which modify its actual sense in given cases," Cushing declared that "in its highest political sense, [the term 'citizen'] signifies in our public law, the persons who constitute the political society." Citing the case of women and children, Cushing observed that people could be part of this class without having the right to vote. Conversely, referring to the situation of the children of foreign diplomats, Cushing also noted that one could be born within the territorial limits of the United States and yet not be a citizen of this country.[5]

Ultimately, Cushing concluded that Native Americans who remained associated with a tribe were "subjects" of the US government, but were not citizens. In addition, Cushing noted that Native Americans could not take advantage of the Naturalization Act of 1802 because they were not foreigners, and that, in any event, the path to naturalized citizenship that was created by the statute was available only to "free white persons." But at the same time, Cushing also observed that the members of some Native American tribes had been granted American citizenship by treaty.[6]

Against this background, one of the problems that Republicans faced in drafting the citizenship provisions of the Civil Rights Act and the Fourteenth Amendment was to craft language that would definitively establish the citizenship of free African Americans without simultaneously conferring US citizenship on Native Americans who remained members of their tribal communities.[7] Initially, the version of the Civil Rights Bill considered by the Senate simply declared that "all persons of African descent born in the United States" were citizens. Even before any vote was taken on this language, however, Republican senator Lyman Trumbull of Illinois changed the clause to provide that "all persons born in the United States, and not subject to any foreign Power," would have citizenship.

This proposed language created immediate consternation that cut across party lines, as both Democratic senator James Guthrie of Kentucky and radical Republican senator Jacob Howard of Michigan expressed the fear that Trumbull's proposal would naturalize all Native Americans. Trumbull responded that this was not his intention. Noting that the Indian tribes were viewed as separate nations, Trumbull argued that his proposal would only grant citizenship to those Indians "who are domesticated and pay taxes and live in civilized society," and thus had become "incorporated into the United States." Nonetheless, he indicated a willingness to include a provision dealing specifically with Native American citizenship.[8]

At this point, Republican senator Henry Lane of Kansas raised the issue of the status of Native Americans who had taken individual allotments of land as provided by treaty. While Trumbull insisted that these Native Americans were already citizens, Lane disagreed. Seeking to resolve any ambiguities, Lane proposed an amendment that would have specifically conferred citizenship on "Indians holding lands in severalty by allotment." Trumbull objected to this proposal on the ground that some of these allotments remained wholly within the jurisdiction of the tribal governments, and the Lane amendment was rejected.[9]

In an effort to deal with the same problem, Republican senator Samuel C. Pomeroy of Kansas then proposed to amend the bill to exclude "persons . . . subject to . . . tribal authority" from its declaration of citizenship. However, this proposal did not explicitly address the case of people who were born subject to tribal authority and later left their tribes to assimilate into white society. Taking the view that such a person would not become a citizen because he was born subject to tribal authority, Democratic senator Reverdy Johnson of Maryland argued that the Pomeroy language would not solve the problem of Native Americans who took allotments.[10]

Taking the opposing view on the import of the language, Guthrie raised a different objection. Focusing on the potential burdens associated with citizenship, he observed that, while immigrants seeking naturalization were required to affirmatively evince a desire to become American citizens, as written the Civil Rights Act conferred citizenship *by operation of law* on some classes of Native Americans who had not been born citizens. Guthrie declared that "I cannot consent to impose citizenship and its liabilities upon a people without their assent [or the assent of their government]."[11]

Republican senators John Conness of California and Alexander Ramsey of Minnesota then raised a different objection to Pomeroy's formulation. They noted that not all Native Americans were associated with a recognizable tribe. Instead, some lived on so-called "public" reservations, while others traveled in small nomadic groups. Conness and Ramsey pointed out that these nonaligned Native Americans owed no allegiance to any other government, and would thus become citizens under the Pomeroy language.[12]

The existence of this class of Native Americans presented Republicans with a conceptual dilemma. As persons who were born within the territorial limits of the United States owing no allegiance to any other government, they were theoretically entitled to citizenship under the dominant Republican ideology of the early Reconstruction era. As Republican senator John B. Henderson observed, to decide otherwise would be to conclude that "[the government] is made for the white man and the black man, but not the red man."

Nonetheless, most Republicans balked at conferring citizenship on a group that they viewed as "perhaps the lowest class known as Indians." Republican senator George H. Williams of Oregon expressed concern over the extent of the rights that might be granted to these Native Americans if they were made citizens by the proposed Act. He noted that states typically banned sales of firearms and alcoholic beverages to Indians, and observed that, under the terms of the Bill, states would apparently be powerless to enforce such bans against Indians who were granted citizenship.[13]

In the face of the Republican objections to the Pomeroy language, Trumbull finally retreated to the phraseology used in the original Constitution, inserting language that excluded "Indians not taxed" from the definition of citizenship in the Civil Rights Bill. Democratic senator Thomas A. Hendricks of Indiana complained that the right to citizenship should not depend on whether a person pays taxes. Trumbull responded that he was in essence using the phrase as a term of art, connoting "a class of persons who . . . are not regarded as part of our people."[14] Whatever their reservations, mainstream Republicans were willing to acquiesce in this formulation, and it was this language that became law when the Civil Rights Act as a whole eventually was passed over President Johnson's veto.

The same language was incorporated into section two of the proposed Fourteenth Amendment. However, section one made no specific reference to Native Americans, but simply provided that "all persons born in the United States and subject to the jurisdiction thereof" would be citizens of both the United States and "of the States wherein they reside."

The question of the impact of the proposed language on the status of Native Americans once again generated considerable discussion.

Senator James R. Doolittle of Wisconsin—a nominal Republican who was by this point firmly allied with the Democrats—proposed to insert language that, like the Civil Rights Act, would have excluded "Indians not taxed" from the definition of citizenship.[15] But despite using this formulation in section two, having rethought the issue, mainstream Republicans unanimously rejected the idea of incorporating a specific exclusion for Native Americans in the section one definition of citizenship.

Both Lyman Trumbull and Jacob Howard—the floor manager of the Fourteenth Amendment in the Senate—argued that the clause as written required Indians to be subject to the "complete" jurisdiction of the United States in order to claim citizenship, and thus excluded Indians who retained allegiance to their tribal governments. In addition, Trumbull noted that the comments of Senator Hendricks of Indiana during the debate over the Civil Rights Act had convinced him that judges might interpret the "Indians not taxed" language literally, thus discriminating between poor Indians and rich Indians in determining citizenship status. Finally, both Howard and Republican senator Daniel Clark of New Hampshire noted that the "Indians not taxed" language in essence gave states the authority to decide whether to naturalize or not naturalize Indians through their taxation policy—an idea that was fundamentally inconsistent with the Republican view that national citizenship should be paramount. Thus, the Doolittle amendment was rejected on a party line vote, and the definition of citizenship was ultimately adopted without change.[16]

The legal import of the citizenship clause for Native Americans was ultimately determined by the Supreme Court's 1884 decision in *Elk v. Wilkins*.[17] In that case, a person who had been born a member of a Native American tribe alleged that, by virtue of the Fourteenth Amendment, he could become a citizen of the United States simply by renouncing his tribal affiliation and taking up residence among the general populace of the state of Nebraska. However, a majority of the justices rejected this argument, essentially concluding that the citizenship clause had not changed the preexisting rule that determined the conditions under which Native Americans could acquire American citizenship.

The decision in *Elk* left Native Americans in essentially the same constitutional position that they had occupied prior to the Civil War—a goal that was shared by Republicans and Democrats alike in the early

Reconstruction era. By contrast, the debate over the proper treatment
of people of Chinese descent proved to be far more divisive.

RECONSTRUCTION AND PEOPLE OF CHINESE DESCENT[18]

By the end of the Civil War, the question of how best to deal with Chinese immigrants had become a significant issue in American politics.
Substantial numbers of Chinese immigrants had begun to arrive in the
mid-nineteenth century, and by 1870 the population of the United States
included over 60,000 persons of Chinese descent. Further, although they
had not been enslaved in America, people of Chinese descent had been
subjected to a wide variety of racially discriminatory laws in areas in
which they had established a substantial presence.[19]

Not surprisingly, like the defense of African American rights, political
advocacy on behalf of the Chinese carried with it a substantial risk of
alienating important groups of white voters. These risks were greatest
on the Pacific Coast, where the vast majority of people of Chinese descent lived during the Reconstruction era. For example, an aggressive
anti-Chinese posture was the cornerstone of a Democratic campaign that
swept the Republicans from office in the California elections of 1867.[20]

In other ways, however, the political contexts of the respective debates over Chinese and African American rights were fundamentally
different. Unlike the condemnation of discrimination against the Chinese, Republican efforts to protect and empower African Americans
were not based simply on moral condemnation of racial discrimination.
Instead, these efforts also closely intertwined with the battle for political
supremacy between Republicans and southern whites.

During the Reconstruction era, Republicans saw the empowerment of
the newly freed African Americans of the South as a necessary counter-
weight to the perceived threat from an unrepentant white populace.[21]
By contrast, while many Republicans viewed support for Chinese rights
as the natural extension of the basic principles underlying Republican
political philosophy, such support did not directly implicate these overarching issues of national power.[22]

The position of the Chinese community in America also differed from
that of free African Americans in other ways. While white Americans
understood that African Americans had been at least partially accul-
turated to American mores by their long presence in the United States,

white Americans viewed the culture of the Chinese as being fundamentally different from their own. Occasionally, influential Republicans characterized this difference in favorable terms. For example, Republican senator Lyman Trumbull of Illinois described Chinese immigrants as "citizens from that country which in many respects excels any other country on the face of the globe in the arts and science, among whose population are to be found the most learned and eminent scholars in the world."[23] More often, however, the Chinese worldview was described as antithetical to American values.

One of the most potent, recurring attacks focused on Chinese religious beliefs. Thus, Republican senator Henry W. Corbett of Oregon described China as "a pagan nation [whose people] worship their god 'josh,' [*sic*] a god made of wood," and argued that if Chinese people were granted full participation in American society, "you may soon find established pagan institutions in our midst which may eventually supersede those Christian influences which have long been the pride of our country." Republican representative William Higby of California, on the other hand, placed his assault on Chinese religious beliefs within a broader critique of what he characterized as deficiencies in Chinese character, asserting that "the Chinese are nothing but a pagan race. . . . They bring their clay and wooden gods with them. . . . Judging from the daily exhibition in our streets, and the well-established repute among their females, virtue is an exception to the general rule. They buy and sell their women like cattle, and the trade is mostly for purpose of prostitution. That is their character."[24]

But even leaving cultural differences aside, Republicans often emphasized what they viewed as another critical difference between Chinese immigrants and free African Americans—a perception that Chinese people who came to America lacked any desire to create a true permanent connection with this country. By 1866, virtually every black person in the United States was not only a permanent resident but a native of the country. By contrast, almost all of the people of Chinese descent in America had been born in China. They were generally viewed as transients whose loyalties remained with the Chinese government and who intended to return to their homeland. Thus, for example, Higby asserted that "you cannot make good citizens of [Chinese immigrants]; they do not learn the language of the country; and you can communicate with them only with the greatest difficulty, as their language is the most dif-

ficult of all those spoken; they even dig up their dead while decaying in
their graves, strip the putrid flesh from the bones, and transport the
bones back to China."[25]

This difference in national origin had an important impact on the
legal status of most people of Chinese descent in the United States.
Under the Republican political theory that developed during the Civil
War, all free African Americans, as natives of the United States, were
automatically entitled to the status of citizenship and all of the rights
appurtenant to that status. By contrast, the only conceivable route to
citizenship available to immigrants was the process of naturalization,
and the ability to take advantage of this process was denied to Chinese
immigrants by the language of the existing naturalization statute, which
limited access to naturalization to "free white persons."[26]

Nonetheless, the continuing presence of adult immigrants from China
created at least the possibility that they might produce offspring born
in America. This possibility was not lost on those who opposed the efforts of mainstream Republicans to formally enshrine the principle of
birthright citizenship in American law. Thus, for example, in his attack
on the citizenship clause of what was to become the Civil Rights Act of
1866, Senator Edgar Cowan of Pennsylvania—who, like Doolittle, was
a nominal Republican who had chosen to align himself with Andrew
Johnson—complained that "if [the Chinese] are to be made citizens and
enjoy political power in California . . . the day may not be distant when
California, instead of belonging to the Indo-European race . . . may belong to the Chinese." Similarly, criticizing the citizenship clause of the
Fourteenth Amendment itself, Cowan averred that

> I do not know how [Republican senator John Conness] from California
> looks upon Chinese, but I do know how some of his fellow citizens regard
> them. I have no doubt that now they are useful, and I have no doubt that
> within proper restraints, allowing that State and the other Pacific States
> to manage them as they may see fit, they may be useful; but I would not
> tie their hands by the Constitution of the United States so as to prevent
> them hereafter from dealing with them as in their wisdom they see fit.[27]

Mainstream congressional Republicans do not seem to have been
terribly concerned about the political impact of charges such as these in
1866. Thus, rather than disputing Cowan's description of the legal import
of the citizenship clause, both Trumbull and Conness readily conceded

that section one of the Fourteenth Amendment would have the effect of conferring citizenship on people of Chinese descent born on American soil.[28] By contrast, three years later, the debate over the Fifteenth Amendment revealed deeper divisions among mainstream Republicans over the proper treatment of Chinese immigrants and their offspring.

THE FIFTEENTH AMENDMENT[29]

By 1869, the overwhelming majority of mainstream Republicans in Congress had come to the conclusion that the Constitution should be amended to provide that states could not exclude African Americans from voting. However, they disagreed over the precise form that the amendment should take. The question of the impact that a particular formulation might have on the rights of people of Chinese descent played a significant role in the debates.

The reaction to language proposed by Republican senator Charles Sumner of Massachusetts provides one clear example. Rather than focusing solely on racial discrimination among citizens, Sumner's proposal would have prohibited *all* racial discrimination in voting rights. At the very least, this formulation would have enfranchised Chinese immigrants in states such as Michigan and Indiana, which at that time did not limit the right to vote to citizens. Some senators also worried that the proposal would require the enfranchisement of Chinese immigrants even in those states that allowed only citizens to vote.[30]

The latter possibility caused great consternation among Republican senators. For example, Senator Frederick T. Frelinghuysen of New Jersey proclaimed that "I believe that [we] should not introduce into this country hordes of pagans and heathens. I think we are under every obligation to give our own people equal, unrestricted rights. I do not feel that obligation toward the people of Asia." Taking a slightly different tack, Senator Oliver H. P. T. Morton of Indiana noted the mistreatment of the Chinese in California and argued that, if granted the right to vote, "they will sometime come to understand their power and when in the majority they will rise up and seize it. . . . There ought to be some provisions made against a catastrophe of that kind." Stunned by the intensity of the reaction, Sumner chose to withdraw his proposal without a vote.[31]

Similar concerns led some Republicans to press for language that did not confer the right to vote on people of Chinese descent. While only white immigrants were eligible for naturalization at the time that the constitutional amendment was being considered, these senators expressed the fear that this aspect of the naturalization statute might be changed at some later date and wished to guard against the possibility that the states might then be required to enfranchise natives of China who took advantage of the opportunity to become American citizens in the future. Once again, the rhetoric of the Republicans who expressed this fear often focused on perceived religious and cultural differences between the Chinese and other residents of the United States. For example, asserting that the Chinese "bring with them institutions of paganism which they are establishing here" and observing that "in San Francisco they now have their places of worship in which idols are set up," Senator Henry Corbett declared that "the question is whether you desire to allow this class of people to come in and overthrow the Christian institutions established on the Pacific coast by the American people, a Christian people."[32]

While those who shared Corbett's sentiments proposed a number of different formulations that were designed to achieve the objective of leaving Asian immigrants outside the scope of the protection of any constitutional amendment, the most important of the proposals that was specifically aimed at the situation faced by African Americans was engendered by an idiosyncratic concern that was expressed by Senator Jacob Howard. Howard does not seem to have been particularly concerned with the possibility that natives of China might at some point be allowed to vote. Instead, he repeatedly insisted that the formulations initially introduced in both the House and Senate would, by negative implication, vest the Federal and state governments with the authority to impose religious qualifications for voters.

Seeking to eliminate this problem, he proposed an amendment that would have provided that "citizens of the United States of African descent shall have the same right to vote and hold office as other citizens in States and Territories [who are] electors of the most numerous branch of their respective Legislatures." Voicing his support for Howard's proposal, Republican Senator Orris S. Ferry of Connecticut declared that "when we propose to amend the Constitution we should carry our actions just so far as the evil [to be addressed] extends [and] the amendment [that Howard proposes] reaches to the full extent of the evil, the wrong done to a certain class of people, the necessity for which exists."[33]

However, other Republicans decried the effort to limit the protections of the proposed amendment to African Americans. Thus, Republican senator Willard Warner of Alabama asserted that "to single out one race is unworthy of the country and unworthy of the great opportunity now presented to us," and Republican senator George F. Edmunds of Vermont declared that "there is nothing republican in [the Howard proposal]." Despite arguments such as these, at one point Howard seems to have convinced a majority of his mainstream Republican colleagues in the Senate that his proposal was superior to that which had been produced by the judiciary committee. While on February 17 the effort to substitute the Howard language was defeated on a vote of 27–22, the margin of victory was provided by Democrats who, no doubt anxious to keep the issue of the status of the Chinese alive on the West Coast, voted unanimously to leave the general prohibition on racial discrimination intact.[34]

Eventually, after exhaustive debate and intricate parliamentary maneuvering, Congress adopted the current race-blind text of the Fifteenth Amendment. Republicans from the far western states were, however, able to obtain one important concession. The conference committee that produced the final language had before it two different versions of the suffrage amendment. The proposal that had passed the House of Representatives had prohibited discrimination based on nativity as well as race. At the insistence of Republicans such as Senator William M. Stewart of Nevada and Representative Aaron A. Sargent of California, the prohibition on nativity-based discrimination was deleted. Politicians such as Stewart and Sargent contended that this deletion left the states free to bar natives of China from voting, even if Chinese immigrants were later granted the right to become naturalized citizens.[35]

The accuracy of this assertion was debatable. While some of the legislative history of the Fifteenth Amendment seems to support the Stewart/Sargent position, much of the debate over the amendment seems to have proceeded on the assumption that a prohibition on racial discrimination would ban discrimination against people of Chinese descent per se. This uncertainty complicated the process of ratifying the amendment, particularly in the far West. Neither California nor Oregon ultimately approved the ban on racial discrimination, and despite its limitation to citizens, advocacy of the amendment became a major political liability for Republican politicians in those states. Moreover, the Nevada state legislature ratified the amendment only after Stewart himself dispatched a letter assuring legislators that the omission of the language barring discrimination on the basis of nativity left the state free to deny immigrants from China access to the ballot.[36]

But in any event, the dispute over the scope of the Fifteenth Amendment was in reality only a minor skirmish in the Reconstruction-era conflict over the status of immigrants from China. The battle was rejoined the following year, as Congress considered two different measures designed to protect people of Chinese descent from racial discrimination.

THE CIVIL RIGHTS ACT OF 1870

One of these measures, first proposed in the Senate by William Stewart on January 10, 1870, was patterned on the Civil Rights Act of 1866. However, unlike the 1866 statute, which specifically protected only citizens from racial discrimination, the 1870 proposal extended similar protections to all *persons*. As he later explained, Stewart introduced the bill in response to complaints by Chinese immigrants that they were being unfairly treated by the government of California.[37]

Stewart averred that he continued to oppose the admittance of immigrants from China in principle. But at the same time, he observed that the United States was bound by treaty to allow such immigration, and also insisted that so long as Chinese people were allowed to come into the country, they were entitled to equal protection of the laws. After initially failing in efforts to have the full Senate consider his proposal as a separate bill, Stewart succeeded in having the measure attached to the Civil Rights Enforcement Bill of 1870, which became law on May 31, 1870.

While providing Chinese immigrants with significant protections against racial discrimination, the 1870 statute also implicitly reaffirmed the importance of the status of citizenship in some contexts. Unlike the Civil Rights Act of 1866, Stewart's measure contained no language dealing with property rights. This difference was not accidental; the right to obtain and hold real property was associated with citizenship in nineteenth-century legal thought, and Stewart made a conscious decision to omit all references to property rights from his proposal.[38]

Even more significantly, since it was aimed only at the action of state governments, the Civil Rights Act of 1870 made no reference to the explosive issue of naturalization. However, in a different context, the same Congress that passed Stewart's measure would engage in an intense struggle over efforts to repeal the race-based restrictions on the acquisition of American citizenship.

THE NATURALIZATION ACT OF 1870[39]

Reacting to widespread allegations of fraud in the naturalization process, in 1870 Republicans initiated a concerted effort to overhaul the entire system. But while the long-standing provision that allowed only free whites to be naturalized was not the primary target of the reform effort, the bill that was initially reported to the floor of the House of Representatives would have eliminated this limitation.[40]

Not surprisingly, this change was resisted by western Republicans as well as Democrats. Their concerns were embodied in an amendment introduced by Republican representative Thomas Fitch of Nevada that was designed to continue the ban on naturalization of both Chinese and Japanese immigrants. Defending the Fitch proposal, Aaron Sargent noted that the Fourteenth Amendment explicitly distinguished between the rights held by citizens and those belonging to all persons, and also contended that the denial of the privilege of naturalization to people of Asian descent was both constitutional and consistent with basic Republican ideology. Sargent declared that "[while] I believe . . . the Chinaman and anyone else, no matter his color is entitled to the equal protection of our laws in life, liberty, and security . . . we should not go beyond that and make them all citizens."[41]

Both Fitch and Sargent also emphasized the differences between Chinese and American culture and argued that the conditions under which Chinese immigrants entered the country precluded their full, free entrance into American society. They predicted grave consequences for "American laws, American culture and American civilization" if natives of China were allowed to become naturalized citizens.[42]

These and other attacks led to substantial changes in the immigration bill that was originally reported to the House floor. The bill was first tabled and then sent back to committee. The revised proposal that was initially passed by the House would have left the racial limitation on access to naturalization intact.[43]

The struggle took a different course in the Senate. Like the bill that had passed the House, the reform proposal reported from committee would not have allowed nonwhite immigrants to become naturalized citizens. However, shortly before a vote was to be taken on the bill pursuant to a unanimous consent agreement, Republican senator Charles Sumner of Massachusetts introduced an amendment that would have completely removed the racial limitation on naturalization.[44]

In the heated procedural wrangle that followed, both Republican William Stewart and Democratic senator Eugene Casserly of California demanded a full discussion of the Sumner amendment, arguing that it was in effect a new bill, while other senators insisted that a unanimous consent agreement that had been reached in connection with consideration of the bill precluded any such discussion. Initially, the views of the latter group prevailed; a quick vote was taken, and the amendment was adopted by a margin of 27–22. At this point, however, Stewart declared himself absolved from the obligation to respect the unanimous consent agreement, and an extended debate ensued over the course of the next two days.[45]

Some opponents of the Sumner proposal relied in part on the now-standard diatribes about the dangers inherent in naturalizing Chinese immigrants. But in addition, support for the proposal was weakened by other considerations. Republican senator John Sherman of Ohio suggested that the issue needed study and further consideration, while others, including Republican senator Roscoe Conking of New York, expressed the fear that the adoption of the Sumner amendment would endanger the entire immigration reform project.[46]

The supporters of the Sumner amendment, by contrast, took the position that the elimination of the racial limitation on naturalization was a matter of high principle. Sumner himself argued that the Congress was constitutionally required to remove the racial limitation on naturalization. His position emerged clearly in a brief colloquy with Oliver H. P. T. Morton. After Morton asked whether "the Chinaman [has] a natural and moral right to become a citizen of the United States," Sumner responded, "I answer that he has not; but I answer with equal confidence that if the United States undertakes to legislate on naturalization, it is bound by the Constitution of the United States, interpreted by the Declaration of Independence, to make no distinction on color."[47]

Sumner's legal argument thus rested on two basic premises—first was that the Declaration of Independence should be considered to be positive, paramount law, and second, that the Declaration by its terms prohibited government-imposed racial discrimination. While both of these premises had a venerable pedigree in radical Republican thought, neither had ever been fully embraced by a majority of Republican law-makers.⁴⁸ But even some of those who rejected the legal theories of the Radicals in general supported Sumner's proposal in the context of naturalization law. Thus, for example, Lyman Trumbull contended that "the principle upon which the great Republican party is based . . . is to make freemen of all the men of this country. If [the opponents of the Sumner amendment] are right, then refuse [people of Chinese descent] admission to this country; but if you allow them to come, make them a part of the body-politic."⁴⁹

Given the variety of considerations affecting the various Republican positions on the Sumner amendment, it should not be surprising that the voting patterns on the amendment did not break down along normal factional lines. While the core of the support for the amendment on the most critical vote came from the radical wing of the Republican Party, Sumner was also supported by more conservative Republicans such as Trumbull and Senators Matthew H. Carpenter of Wisconsin and Joseph S. Fowler of Tennessee. Conversely, Sumner was opposed not only by Democrats and more conservative Republicans, but also by radicals such as Morton and Senator Zachariah Chandler of Michigan.⁵⁰

The complicated crosscurrents surrounding the issue of racial restrictions on naturalization were clearly reflected in the voting patterns in three roll call votes that were taken in quick succession on July 4, 1870. First, a motion to reconsider the Sumner amendment carried by a vote of 27–14, with two senators who had supported Sumner only two days earlier changing their position and six former Sumner supporters being present but choosing to abstain. On reconsideration, the proposal for race-blind naturalization was defeated by a vote of 30–14. Republican senator Willard Warner of Alabama, who had opposed the Sumner initiative, then moved to extend access to naturalization to "aliens of African nativity and to persons of African descent." This motion carried by a 21–20 margin, with nine senators who had opposed the Sumner amendment supporting the proposal and Republican senator Timothy O. Howe of Wisconsin, who had supported Sumner, opposing the Willard initiative.⁵¹

In 1870, the passage of the Willard amendment was generally understood to be primarily of symbolic importance. As Republican senator George H. Williams of Oregon observed, at that time few if any immigrants were coming to America from Africa. In any event, the final passage of the naturalization bill did not mark the end of the Reconstruction-era conflict over the eligibility of Chinese immigrants for citizenship. Instead, the battle was rejoined two years later in a somewhat different political context.

THE CIVIL RIGHTS BILL OF 1872[52]

The issue of Chinese naturalization was once again raised during the consideration of a bill that was designed to grant amnesty to ex-Confederate officials who were barred from holding office by section three of the Fourteenth Amendment. The indefatigable Sumner offered as an amendment a comprehensive Civil Rights Bill that would not only have banned racial discrimination in a variety of different contexts, but also would have eliminated the word *white* from every state or national law, statute, ordinance, regulation, or custom. Among other things, this proposal would have eliminated the bar on the naturalization of Chinese immigrants that had been retained in 1870.[53]

Predictably, this possibility was once again greeted with alarm by a number of prominent Republicans. Some of the comments on Sumner's proposal reflected the kind of raw prejudice that so often marked debates over measures that conferred rights on people of Chinese descent. For example, noting that Sumner's amendment would allow Chinese immigrants to become naturalized citizens and require states to allow naturalized Chinese to serve on juries, Henry Corbett declared, "I believe that the only thing they recognize as an oath binding upon them is this: that you shall cut off the head of a chicken and the Chinaman swears in the presence of that, or by that, that he will judge of the matter according to that oath. . . . I think we are not prepared to allow our jury boxes to be packed by twelve Chinamen who can be bought and sold."[54] In addition, John Sherman emphasized what he characterized as the incompatibility between Chinese culture and the worldview reflected in American institutions:

> Take a man . . . from any land peopled by the white race, let him come here, and in five years he easily and rapidly assimilates with our institutions; his blood mingles with our blood and on the whole rather improves the stock. But that principle does not extend to [Chinese immigrants]. This [is] partly [because they are] heathen races, who, from the tenor of their minds, could not in five years be made good citizens of the United States, they having a different idea of the sanctity of religion, a different idea of the worship of God; their fundamental ideas are different, and they

cannot make good republican or democratic citizens out of them in five years, and they cannot and will not mix with the body of the population.[55]

Despite these misgivings, Sherman had somewhat mixed feelings about the idea of amending the naturalization statute to provide immigrants from China with the opportunity to become American citizens. Ideally, he would have preferred to return to the pre-1870 regime under which only white people had access to naturalization. But at the same time, he recognized that Congress was unlikely to reinstate the ban on naturalization of immigrants from Africa and declared that "the law ought to be uniform, to exclude [all nonwhites] or exclude none."[56]

By contrast, westerners such as Corbett and Republican senator Cornelius Cole of California had no such ambivalence. Both introduced measures designed to exclude the naturalization statutes from the operation of the Sumner amendment. After these proposals were defeated, the Sumner amendment itself was adopted by the narrowest of margins, as the Senate split equally and Vice President Schuyler Colfax cast the tie-breaking vote.[57]

Ultimately, however, the sweeping ban on racial discrimination did not become law. While the amnesty bill to which it was attached gained a 33–19 majority of the senators voting, the margin fell short of the two-thirds required by section three of the Fourteenth Amendment for the passage of such a bill. Sumner himself opined that, except for the Chinese question, the bill would have obtained the necessary support in the Senate. While this conclusion may have been overstated, the issue of Chinese rights clearly did diminish support for his civil rights initiative.

In any event, the defeat of the Sumner initiative in 1872 marked the end of Reconstruction-era attempts to provide Chinese immigrants with the opportunity to become naturalized citizens. To be sure, natives of China fell within the purview of the prohibitions on racial discrimination embodied in the Civil Rights Acts of 1870 and 1875. However, states remained free to deny Chinese immigrants rights specifically associated with the status of citizenship—most notably, the right to vote, the right to sit on a jury, and the right to hold real property. Perhaps most importantly, natives of China remained subject to deportation at any time, and beginning in 1882 Congress took steps to prevent Chinese immigrants who left the country from returning. It was not until 1952 that natives of China were provided with the means to remove these disabilities by becoming naturalized citizens.

CONCLUSION

The Reconstruction-era discussions of the appropriate treatment of Native Americans and Chinese immigrants raised a variety of issues related to the concept of citizenship. Republican efforts to deal appropriately with the status of Native Americans were concerned primarily with citizenship as a formal, legal concept based on the idea that a citizen is one who pledges permanent allegiance to a government and that government in turn bears the obligation to protect the citizen. Republicans struggled to create a formulation that would recognize the citizenship of Native Americans who in fact owed allegiance to the Federal government, without conferring the same status on Native Americans who owed allegiance to tribal authorities or no government at all.

The terms of the debates over the question of whether naturalization should be made available to natives of China were quite different. By their terms, naturalization statutes posit a situation in which an alien offers to renounce his existing allegiance and establish a new political relationship with the government of the United States. In supporting the change in the statute, Charles Sumner and his allies relied on a principle that transcended the naturalization debate itself, arguing simply that racial discrimination in general was inconsistent with the premises embodied in the Constitution and the Declaration of Independence. By contrast, opponents of the change cast the debate in very different terms. They generally conceded that the Chinese were entitled to enjoy the fundamental rights that belonged to people generally. However, emphasizing culture more than race per se, the opponents contended that the Chinese worldview was inimical to that of the vast majority of white Americans, and that Chinese immigrants should therefore be denied access to naturalization because they lacked the capacity to become "good" citizens. This argument carried the day, and Chinese immigrants remained ineligible for naturalization until the mid-twentieth century.

NOTES

1. 60 U.S. (19 How.) 393 (1857).

2. The role of Native American tribes in the Civil War is discussed in Clarissa W. Confer, *The Cherokee Nation in the Civil War* (Norman: University of Oklahoma Press, 2007); Arrell Morgan Gibson, "Native Americans and the Civil War," *American Indian Quarterly* 9 (1985): 385–410; and Troy Smith, "The Civil War Comes to Indian Territory," *Civil War History* 59 (2013): 279–319.

3. The legal status of Native Americans in the antebellum era is discussed in detail in James H. Kettner, *The Development of American Citizenship, 1608–1870* (Chapel Hill: University of North Carolina Press, 1978), 288–300, and Barbara Krauthamer, *Black Slaves, Indian Masters: Slavery, Emancipation and Citizenship in the Native American South* (Chapel Hill: University of North Carolina Press, 2015).

4. "Relations of Indians to Citizenship," *Official Opinions of the Attorney General of the United States,* vol. 7, 746–55 (1856).

5. Ibid., 748.

6. Ibid.

7. The discussion that follows is taken from Earl M. Maltz, *The Fourteenth Amendment and the Law of the Constitution* (Durham, NC: Carolina Academic Press, 2003), 58–63.

8. *Congressional Globe,* 39th Cong., 1st Sess. 497 (1866).

9. Ibid. at 498–99, 522, 525, 526.

10. Ibid.

11. Ibid.

12. Ibid. at 526–27. The complexities involved in determining the status of this class of Native Americans are discussed in detail in Stephen Kantrowitz, "'Not Quite Constitution-alized': The Meaning of 'Civilization' and the Limits of Native American Citizenship," in *The World the Civil War Made,* ed. Gregory P. Downs and Kate Masur (Chapel Hill: University of North Carolina Press, 2015), 75–105.

13. *Congressional Globe,* 39th Cong., 1st Sess. (1866) at 574, 527 (remarks of Senator Conness), 574 (remarks of Senator Lane), 573.

14. Ibid. at 527, 527, 572.

15. Ibid. at 2892.

16. Ibid. at 2893, 2895, 2894, 2895, 2897.

17. 112 U.S. 94 (1884).

18. Much of what follows is taken from Earl M. Maltz, "The Federal Government and the Problem of Chinese Rights in the Era of the Fourteenth Amendment," *Harvard Journal of Law and Public Policy* 17 (1994): 223–52.

19. For example, the Oregon Constitution of 1857 prohibited any "Chinaman" who might later arrive in the state from owning real property or working mining claims, while the state of California barred people of Chinese descent from testifying in court and sub-jected them to discriminatory taxation. For a detailed discussion of anti-Chinese laws, see Charles J. McClain, *In Search of Equality: The Chinese Struggle Against Discrimination in Nineteenth Century America* (Berkeley: University of California Press, 1996).

20. Elmer C. Sandmeyer, *The Anti-Chinese Movement in California* (Champaign: University of Illinois Press, 1991), 81; Alexander Saxton, *The Indispensable Enemy: Labor and the Anti-Chinese Movement in California* (Berkeley: University of California Press, 1971), 80–91.

21. See, for example, Earl M. Maltz, *Civil Rights, the Constitution and Congress, 1863–1869* (Lawrence: University Press of Kansas, 1991), 36–37.

22. The relationship between Republican ideology and the issue of Chinese rights is discussed in Saxton, *The Indispensable Enemy,* 30–37.

23. *Cong. Globe,* 40th Cong., 2d Sess. 1036 (1869).

24. Ibid. at 939; 39th Cong., 1st Sess. 1056 (1866).

25. *Cong. Globe,* 39th Cong., 1st Sess. 1056 (1866).

26. Act of March 26, 1790, 1 Stat. 103 (1790).

27. *Cong. Globe*, 39th Cong., 1st Sess. 498, 2891 (1866).

28. Ibid. at 498, 2891.

29. The most complete treatment of the history of the Fifteenth Amendment is William Gillette, *The Right to Vote: Politics and the Passage of the Fifteenth Amendment* (Baltimore: Johns Hopkins University Press, 1965). The discussions of the potential impact of various formulations on the rights of people of Chinese descent are reviewed in Najia Aarim-Heriot, *Chinese Immigrants (Champaign: University of Illinois Press, 2003),* 93–101; Xi Wang, *The Trial of Democracy: Black Suffrage and Northern Republicans, 1860–1910* (Athens: University of Georgia Press, 1997); and Maltz, "The Federal Government and Chinese Rights," 231–35.

30. *Cong. Globe,* 40th Cong., 3d Sess. 1036, 1030, 1033 (1870).

31. Ibid. at 130, 1035, 1035.

32. Ibid. at 1035.

33. Ibid. at 1008, 1008.

34. Ibid. at 1009, 1008, 1311.

35. *Cong. Globe*, 41st Cong., 1st Sess. 4275 (1870); Russell R. Elliott, *Servant of Power: A Political Biography of William M. Stewart* (Reno: University of Nevada Press, 1983), 64.

36. The struggle over ratification in the states of the far West is discussed in detail in William Gillette, *The Right to Vote: Politics and the Passage of the Fifteenth Amendment* (Baltimore: Johns Hopkins Press, 1965), 153–58.

37. *Cong. Globe*, 41st Cong., 2d Sess. 3658 (1870).

38. Ibid. at 1536.

39. The conflict in 1870 over the question of whether to allow immigrants from China to become naturalized citizens is discussed in Aarim-Heriot, *Chinese Immigrants,* 140–50, and Maltz, "The Federal Government and Chinese Rights," 236–40.

40. *Cong. Globe*, 41st Cong., 2d Sess. 4267 (1870) (remarks of Representative Davis).

41. Ibid. at 4266, 4275.

42. Ibid. at 4276.

43. Ibid. at 4284, 4318, 4366–68.

44. Ibid. at 4834–36, 5121.

45. Ibid. at 5122, 5122 (remarks of Senator Trumbull), 5124, 5124.

46. Ibid. at 5150–52 (remarks of Senator Stewart); 5156–58 (remarks of Senator Williams); 5152, 5149, 5160.

47. Ibid. at 5156.

48. Eric Foner, *Free Labor, Free Soil, Free Men: The Ideology of the Republican Party Before the Civil War* (New York: Oxford University Press, 1995), 290.

49. *Cong. Globe*, 41st Cong., 2d Sess. 5154 (1870). To the same effect, see *Cong. Globe*, 41st Cong., 2d Sess. 5160–61 (1870) (remarks of Senator Carpenter).

50. Ibid. at 5173.

51. Ibid. at 5173, 5176.

52. The debate over the relationship between the Civil Rights Bill of 1872 and the issue of Chinese naturalization is discussed in Aarim-Heirot, *Chinese Immigrants,* 150–54, and Maltz, "The Federal Government and Chinese Rights," 240–44.

53. *Cong. Globe*, 42nd Cong., 2d Sess. 244 (1871).

54. Ibid. at 898.

55. Ibid. at 845–46.

56. Ibid. at 845.

57. Ibid. at 912, 918, 919. The outcome of these votes reflected the interaction among a variety of different political and ideological calculations. Some radical Republicans, who generally opposed amnesty, viewed the addition of Sumner's civil rights proposal in part as a means to kill the amnesty bill itself. They believed (correctly) that although Democrats and conservative Republicans strongly favored the concept of amnesty in principle, members of these factions would not support an amnesty bill that also contained powerful Federal prohibitions on racial discrimination. Conversely, conservative Republican senator Lyman Trumbull of Illinois argued that supporters of amnesty should oppose efforts to weaken the Sumner amendment in order to make it "just as obnoxious as possible" in the hope of persuading wavering Republicans to vote against the amendment. Ibid., 896. Following Trumbull's lead on this point, Democrats almost unanimously opposed the efforts of Corbett and Cole to weaken the Sumner amendment.

OATHS, OCCUPATIONS, AND THE WARTIME BOUNDARIES OF CITIZENSHIP

Swallowing the Oath

The Battle Over Citizenship in Occupied Winchester

JONATHAN M. BERKEY

By the summer of 1862, Winchester, Virginia native Emma Riely's home-sickness had reached desperate heights. The fourteen-year-old had hurriedly left Winchester with her sister Kate just before Confederate troops under Thomas J. "Stonewall" Jackson evacuated the lower Shenandoah Valley town in March. Emma and her family had hoped that Jackson's retreat up the Valley was a temporary ruse to lure the advancing Union army into a decisive battle.[1] The Riely sisters had packed one small trunk with enough clothing for a week or two, but by August they had been refugees from their home for about six months.[2] As August arrived in Luray, forty-three miles south of Winchester, Emma determined to risk a journey home even though it was occupied by the Yankee army. Kate did not share her sister's boldness (or desperation) and elected to remain a refugee.[3]

Reluctant to travel alone, Riely convinced Fannie Burracker, a Luray resident with relatives in Clarke County, to accompany her. On the day they began their journey, Riely and Burracker stuffed their shoes full of letters from civilians and Confederate soldiers bound for addresses in Winchester and other areas behind Union lines. Although their journey featured several challenges, the party reached the outskirts of Winchester without major incident. They encountered Federal pickets just outside of town, who took them to the provost marshal. There, they learned that all civilians aged eighteen or older had to take the oath of allegiance before entering Winchester. Luckily, Emma Riely was able to provide proof that she was only fourteen; she could cross the Union lines without condition. Fannie Burracker was not so lucky; after she admitted that she was twenty-one, the provost marshal insisted that she take the oath before entering town. Riely recalled that Burracker "broke down and just boo-hooed in the most heart-broken style." She felt sorry for Burracker and urged her to take the oath. Finally, "after a great persuasion she swallowed it, although each word seemed the size of a cannon ball to swallow and you could hear a gulping sound as each one went down." While Burracker was swearing not to provide aid and comfort to the Confederacy, the contraband letters from Confederate soldiers to friends and relatives in the vicinity of Winchester remained in her shoes.[4]

Countless Confederate civilians living in or around Union-occupied areas faced a challenge similar to that of Burracker when they had to make very difficult choices about taking the oath of allegiance to the United States. Many studies of occupied areas suggest that Burracker's response was typical. In occupied Nashville, Memphis, New Orleans, and East Carolina, secessionists swallowed the oath of allegiance to the United States for pragmatic reasons: doing so allowed them to travel and trade freely, and often protected their property from use by occupying military forces.[5]

Despite facing challenges similar to those encountered by their peers in other occupied areas of the Confederacy, relatively few secessionists in Winchester took the oath of allegiance. This essay explores the issues that made Fannie Burracker's decision to swallow the oath, so common-place elsewhere, unique in Winchester. Battles over the oath were battles between different aspects of citizenship. Swallowing the oath marked an explicit rejection of Confederate citizenship. Union authorities attempted to eliminate Confederate allegiance by imposing the oath of allegiance on civilians before they could enjoy the tangible privileges of citizenship like free travel. The Union military's efforts were unsuccessful largely because their campaigns against the formal aspects of citizenship were unable to break the affective bonds of citizenship forged and guarded by Winchester's secessionist community.

Scholars of citizenship have stressed its fluid nature and complexity. More than formal rights and responsibilities, citizenship invokes a sense of belonging to a community. This affective citizenship is particularly strong because it involves an emotional tie to the community—what Stephen Kantrowitz calls "a citizenship of the heart."[6] Fannie Burracker acknowledged the power of affective citizenship when she faced her moment of decision at Winchester. The prospect of taking the oath of allegiance meant breaking her bonds to the Confederate community. When

Emma Riely urged Burracker to take the oath, her first thought was of her community. Burracker lamented, "Oh, Emma, I will be disgraced amongst my friends." When Riely claimed that her friends would never find out that she took the oath, Burracker was unconvinced. "You and Mr. Hart [her driver] will tell on me and they will all say I'm disloyal." Burracker's greatest fear upon swallowing the oath was her community's rejection.[7]

Most Winchester civilians, when forced to choose between the privileges of formal citizenship offered by Union military authorities—such as the ability to trade, travel, and hold property securely—and the affective bonds of the secessionist community, chose the latter. Civilian confidence in the Confederate cause made this choice a little easier. In many occupied areas of the Confederacy, the arrival of Union troops occurred relatively early in the war and, despite occasional threats, Confederate forces did not regain control of these regions. Residents of Winchester were able to hold on to the hope of Confederate deliverance much longer than their counterparts in other occupied areas of the South; indeed, the lower Shenandoah Valley witnessed the return of a major Confederate force as late as autumn 1864.

Examining the struggle over the oath of allegiance in occupied Winchester through the lens of citizenship illuminates the agency that the town's civilians expressed in their struggle to maintain their sense of identity and the social boundaries of their community. Union military authorities could determine who could travel and purchase freely, but only Winchester's secessionist civilians could determine who belonged.

I.

Emma Riely's hometown was the seat of Frederick County and a key market center in the lower Shenandoah Valley.[8] Its 1860 population consisted of 4,392 residents, including 680 free black people and 708 slaves. The town served the region's farmers by providing goods and facilitating the sale and marketing of wheat, the region's main staple crop. Seven main roads fanning out in several directions connected Winchester to its agricultural hinterland. Two macadamized roads dominated this transportation hub: the Martinsburg Pike tied Winchester to neighboring Berkeley County's emerging rail center, while the Valley Pike linked the town to destinations in the upper Valley. Other roadways connected Winchester to eastern Virginia through the passes in the Blue Ridge

Mountains. The Winchester & Potomac Railroad connected to the Baltimore & Ohio system at Harpers Ferry. Baltimore served as the town's primary market for cattle and flour, and many Winchester residents had business and family ties in the city.[9]

When war came, Winchester became an important strategic target for the contending armies. It produced valuable resources coveted by military forces, including wheat, beef, butter, and cloth. Its location heightened its importance. Winchester is north of Washington, DC; a Confederate army occupying the town would threaten not only the northern capital, but Maryland and Pennsylvania as well. A Federal army moving up the Valley would be traveling southwest, away from the Confederate capital of Richmond, but if it could occupy Staunton (about ninety-five miles from Winchester) it would threaten railroad connections to eastern Virginia via the Virginia Central railroad.[10]

Winchester's wartime experience confirms its strategic importance. Frederick County witnessed five significant battles during the war—three of which were fought through Winchester—and numerous skirmishes and raids. The town changed hands thirteen times and was between the lines for about 20 percent of the war. From March 1862 through the end of the war, Barton family scholar Margaretta Barton Colt estimates that Winchester was in Federal hands over 50 percent of the time. Because of the uneven pattern of military activity in and around the town, British observer Arthur J. L. Fremantle dubbed "unfortunate" Winchester the "shuttlecock" of the contending armies in the Valley.[11]

In a town that changed hands so frequently, it is understandable that notions of loyalty among its residents remained fluid. By the summer of 1862, after two Federal occupations of the town, residents had become adept at keeping military officials guessing about their loyalty. The behaviors one Union newspaper correspondent observed in occupied Winchester frustrated him. He noted that he had always been a successful reporter in Washington, DC, despite the fact that many politicians there changed their "political jacket" every four years. In Winchester, "it was done every week without any inconvenience at all!!!!" His report became more heated as he continued:

> These are they who are "loyal" today, but the Lord only knows what they
> may be tomorrow—. These are they who can be "loyal," and yet curse
> the Government to whom that loyalty is due—. These are they who can
> straddle the political fence, and touch the ground on both sides, be ready

to cry "Good Lord or good devil," as the case may require. Periodically, they are "union men," and are very "loyal" just now; but no longer than Jackson's last visit to Winchester they were ready to swing their hats and hurrah for Jeff Davis.[12]

The correspondent's frustration resulted from contested notions of loyalty. What he saw as clear signs of disloyalty were interpreted by Winchester's secessionist community as necessary tactics to ensure survival in an unpredictable environment. Union military officials attempted to use the oath of allegiance as a weapon to solidify the fluid notions of loyalty that Winchester secessionists deemed acceptable. The oath's wording left little room for interpretation. Oath-takers had to swear to support, protect, and defend the Constitution and the government of the United States, and to bear "true faith, allegiance, and loyalty to the same." As Emma Riely observed, "the language of that oath was as strong as it could be made."[13]

Union commanders utilized the oath during the first occupation of Winchester in the spring of 1862. Initially used to ensure that suspicious persons picked up by the army could be released safely, the oath became a tool to limit the privileges of Winchester's secessionists. The first rumblings about the oath in Winchester centered on a pledge to the Restored Government of Virginia.[14] In April, representatives of Restored Governor Francis Pierpont arrived in Winchester to administer an oath of allegiance to county officials. Swearers of this oath pledged allegiance to the United States and the restored state government. County magistrates A. Nulton, J. S. Davis, and R. Bowen took the oath. Nulton later explained to John Peyton Clark that he signed the oath to bring some sense of civil authority to the town, which would allow civil officials to control petty crime and discipline Winchester's black residents.[15]

The furor over the oath to the restored government of Virginia marked the beginning of the lengthy struggle among members of Winchester's secessionist community to resist the Union's assault on Confederate citizenship. Nulton's explanation did not impress most Winchester secessionists. John Peyton Clark noted that there was "much feeling and talk in town upon the subject of the conduct of these men." He joined this chorus, claiming that the magistrates signed the oath because of their "cowardice, ignorance, or inclination." Two days after taking the controversial oath, the magistrates repudiated it, claiming that they had not truly understood the consequences of agreeing to it. As Clark's comments suggest, the most crucial consequence of taking the oath was exclusion from the Confederate community.[16]

Mary Greenhow Lee feared that the magistrates' oath was the first step of a broader assault on the town's Confederate citizens. She had heard rumors that every man, woman, and child in Winchester would be made to take the oath. "Now comes the tug of war, for us who cannot fight for our country," she confided to her diary. "I very much fear there are some who will not stand the test." About a week later, Lee's confidence in her fellow secessionists' fortitude had increased. Reporting another rumor that those who refused to take the oath would not be permitted to practice their professions, she acknowledged that "We are being more & more oppressed every day," but concluded, "the spirit of resistance rises in proportion."[17]

The spirit of resistance that Lee noted rose in response to the Union army's campaign of limiting privileges of Winchester secessionists in order to entice them into taking the oath of allegiance. As Stephen Ash notes, the army could not force civilians to take the oath at gunpoint; it had to be voluntary to be binding. By the middle of April the Federal campaign had begun in earnest. Besides the limitations on Winchester businesses, Union policy forbade clergymen from performing the marriage ceremony unless they pledged their loyalty to the Union government. Civilians who wished to obtain a pass for traveling outside of Winchester also had to take the oath.[18]

Most members of Winchester's secessionist community resisted the temptation to repudiate Confederate citizenship in exchange for the formal privileges of citizenship. After the first battle of Winchester on May 25, 1862, John Peyton Clark jubilantly wrote, "for the first time within two months . . . I went . . . outside the corporate limits of Winchester." When many residents wrote of their freedom that returned with the Confederate forces, the freedom of movement and to practice their livelihoods, which had been tied to the oath of allegiance during the Union occupation, surely were on their minds.[19]

The euphoria of Winchester's secessionists proved to be short-lived. Stonewall Jackson's forces rushed through Winchester at the end of May, heading back up the Valley to avoid being trapped by Union forces under John C. Fremont and James Shields. Federal cavalry dashed into town on June 3. A few days later the Yankees secured their control of Winchester once again.[20]

The Union army's second occupation of Winchester coincided with a turn toward harsher policies concerning Confederate civilians. Gen. John Pope's arrival from the Western Theater marked the end of the Union army's more or less conciliatory policy toward civilians. Jackson's success in the Valley and Gen. George B. McClellan's slow pace on the James River Peninsula convinced President Abraham Lincoln to bring Pope east. His new command, dubbed the Army of Virginia, included the Union forces in the Shenandoah Valley.[21]

Shortly after his appointment as commander of the Army of Virginia, Pope issued a series of orders that electrified public opinion throughout the Union and Confederacy. Issued on July 23, General Order № 11 mandated that army commanders arrest all disloyal citizens within their lines. Those that were willing to take the oath of allegiance to the United States and who could furnish sufficient security for their adherence to it could remain within Federal lines; those who refused were to be sent beyond them with the warning that if they returned they would be considered spies and "subjected to the extreme rigor of military law." The order also forbade any communication between those within Union lines and those beyond them. An editorial in the *New York Times* approvingly noted, "It seems as though we [are] to wage war in downright, deadly earnest."[22]

Even before Pope officially issued his orders, Winchester residents had an inkling of the Federals' new earnestness. One day before General Order № 11 was issued, Mary G. Lee wrote of a decree from Winchester commander Brig. Abraham S. Piatt. "The edict of our 'Pope,'" she learned, "is, that all the male citizens, who will not take the oath of allegiance, are to be sent beyond the lines, & shot, if they venture to return, & that all who write, or carry letters to rebels, will meet the same fate." A few days later, news of Pope's official order reached Winchester. Laura Lee, Mary's housemate and sister-in-law, noted that the Federals had forbidden any supplies to enter the town; a train from Baltimore loaded with goods that had come the evening before was sent back. Lee was incredulous about General Order № 11. "We cannot believe that this last tyrannical order will be carried out," she wrote, "but the Provost Marshal is coming back into town today . . . to apply the test."[23]

If these measures demonstrated that the Federals were conducting the war with a new earnestness, the concerns of the women of Winchester suggested that local secessionists were preparing to meet it. Few women worried that their men would take the oath; rather, they wondered how they would survive when their men refused and consequently were sent south. Mary G. Lee shuddered to think that she and the other women of Winchester would be left "utterly unprotected" in the midst of the occupying Union army. She made a plea in her diary to Stonewall Jackson to come soon and rescue the women of Winchester. Fanny B. Graham had become friends with Jackson's wife Mary Anna when the couple stayed at the Grahams' home during the winter of 1861–1862. Graham told Mrs. Jackson that the town's residents had been "in a state of great anxiety" about the oath. She expressed special concern that she would be left with her four children in occupied Winchester without the protection and support of her husband. John Peyton Clark succinctly summed up the residents' feelings about the oath. He noted that Pope's orders had caused "much uneasiness" in Winchester but expressed confidence that "the major part of the community . . . will refuse to take it under any circumstances." Clark believed that the consequence of this stand would produce "great distress" on Winchester's families, "and will place many to whom it is next to an impossibility to leave their families, some of them large, unprotected, and unprovided for, in a very embarrassing position."[24]

Winchester commander Julius White's enforcement of Pope's order alternated between decisiveness and caution, which kept the town's secessionists on pins and needles. Shortly after taking command, White clamped down on the town's borders. His actions strictly limited those who could enter or leave Winchester, and severely curtailed trade in town. When residents complained that they would be starved out by the measure, White was said to reply that in a few days, "there would be none but loyal citizens left in Winchester & the country would be open for supplies." On July 28 he arrested several citizens and informed them that he would require them to take the oath the following day. However, White's threat would remain unrealized through the beginning of August.[25]

Winchester residents nervously waited for White's next move regarding the oath. Fearful rumors began to frighten them. Already concerned about male secessionists being forced to leave town because of the oath, Mary G. Lee heard a rumor of great consequence to her: after all of the men had taken the oath, women who were the heads of families (like the widowed Lee) would have to take it as well. Lee knew her fate if this rumor came to pass—exile beyond Winchester, for she determined never to take the oath.[26]

As White waited and frightening rumors spread through Winchester, the steadfastness of some local secessionists began to waver. John Peyton Clark noted that the Federal pickets had increased, and only civilians who took the oath of allegiance could obtain passes for travel. Clark admitted that some residents had obliged when confronted with the oath, but he ascribed their behavior to selfish motives—taking the oath allowed them to pass through the lines in and out of Winchester, giving them a monopoly on trade in the town. While Clark passed off their motive as selfishness, he was concerned because some of them had been "good Southern men" recently. Clark had great concern about the subtle way White was reacting to Pope's orders in Winchester:

> The object of the authorities seems to be to exhaust and starve out the town and thus force the citizens into the oath of allegiance. There has been no attempt to enforce the oath according to Pope's order generally, but the policy seems to be stringent, [but] measured[,] by which citizens will be forced into it gradually. Arrest of citizens upon frivolous pretenses are constantly made and the oath offered, which is generally refused but sometimes taken.

On August 20, Mary G. Lee heard another rumor that Union authorities would finally administer the oath in the next few days. She noted that "the men are frightened about it."[27]

The men's fear manifested itself a few days later when many of the "prominent men" in town agreed to take a modified oath from General White. It read:

> I, _____, having been placed under arrest by the military authorities of the United States, with the liberty of the county of Frederick, Virginia, do solemnly swear that, until discharged from arrest, I will not take up arms against the United States, nor perform any act, either overt or covert, prejudicial thereto, nor directly or indirectly furnish aid, comfort or information or allow any member of my family or servant or employee to do so—and will report in person to the Provost Marshal at Winchester whenever required by him.[28]

This modified oath came about through negotiations between White and David W. Barton and Philip Williams. The pledge marked a compromise between the ideals of Union military authorities and Winchester secessionists. The modified oath did not require swearing allegiance to the United States, nor did it repudiate the Confederacy. Therefore, residents who signed it did not foreswear their Confederate citizenship.

Further, it freed those who agreed to it to procure passes from Federal authorities for travel. Barton and Williams insisted on this aspect of the compromise because it allowed them access to their farms on the outskirts of Winchester. While White's modified oath did not force a repudiation of Confederate citizenship, it did guarantee good behavior and prevented its takers from aiding the Confederacy.

The modified oath effectively split the secessionist community in Winchester. When Mary G. Lee first heard that some Winchester men had signed an oath, she flew into a rage. "I had a war of words with Mrs. Barton and Mr. H. M. Brent this evening, about the oath of allegiance," she confided to her diary. Lee claimed that she would cut off her right hand before she would take the oath, and, as she understatedly put it, "expressed my opinion very decidedly." After this outburst she learned that Barton, Williams, and others had modified the oath "as to suit their elastic consciences." The town's secessionists divided into two camps based upon their perception of the modified oath. Barton and Williams led the more moderate group while Robert Y. Conrad led the more radical group. No matter which side they were on, Lee noted that "all of the families are quite violent in their demonstrations."[29]

After she saw a copy of the oath, Lee became concerned that it was a "Yankee trap, which can be closed hereafter on the unwary victim." The key phrase in Lee's view was "until discharged from arrest," which was vague enough to support incompatible interpretations. Many of the men who expressed a willingness to take the oath believed that a return of Confederate forces to Winchester would free them from their pledge, but Lee was convinced that the Yankees would view it quite differently, and an oath-taker who had supported the Confederacy during a return of the rebel army would face grave consequences at the next Union occupation of the town. John Peyton Clark realized that if the oath was binding when a Confederate army returned, the oath-taker "would be obliged under the requirements of the Confederate government to put his oath in his pocket and shoulder his musket, and no man should allow himself to be put in such a position." This conflict in interpretation became evident when Federal officials arrested Robert Y. Conrad, whom Lee dubbed "the champion of our party" for his staunch refusal to take the oath (either original or modified). After his arrest Conrad argued with the provost marshal for nearly two hours regarding the meaning of the modified oath, and especially over how long the pledge would last. The provost claimed that the pledge would last until the war ended, a sentiment at odds with the interpretation of Winchester's moderate secessionists.[30]

On August 25, about twelve of "our most prominent but most *timid* citizens," as Laura Lee put it, took White's modified oath, which led to further tensions among the town's secessionists. Although signers of the modified oath believed that they had not repudiated their Confederate citizenship, and therefore were still viable members of the secessionist community in Winchester, the die-hard elements in town disagreed. Relations between the two groups chilled. "We are amused to find how these *oath-men* try to conciliate us," wrote Mary G. Lee, "& are at the same time so uneasy in our presence." When Lee encountered Philip Williams she observed that he appeared nervous and embarrassed. David Barton's wife Fannie tried to explain her husband's course of action to other women in town, but her justifications fell on deaf ears. "Mrs. Barton will talk to us about it, & try to explain that it is nothing more than a pass," Lee wrote, "but Mrs. B's arguments, second hand, are not at all convincing."[31]

As the secessionists in Winchester sniped at one another, General White began to arrest those who refused to take the modified oath and send them out of town. So many men refused to take the oath, however, that White had second thoughts. He revoked all of the passes given under the modified oath and telegraphed Washington for advice on handling the situation. The affective bond of Winchester's secessionist community proved too strong even for a modified oath of allegiance.[32]

Secessionist concerns about what might happen next were relieved late in the evening of September 2, 1862, when White abandoned Winchester in the face of a large Confederate force moving down the Valley on the way to cross the Potomac and invade Maryland. Although there was some concern that White might try to make some of the arrested men accompany the Union retreat, that fear did not materialize. Late that night when John Peyton Clark heard (and felt) the Federal powder magazine explode, he knew that the Union army had abandoned the town. Clark, who was under arrest at the time, expressed relief that "Gen. White up to that time had not determined what disposition he would make of me, as I determined never to give him, if I could help it, an opportunity to make any disposition whatever of me in the future."[33]

By the winter of 1862–1863 the Federals had returned, and Gen. Robert H. Milroy assumed command in Winchester. His background did not bode well for the town's secessionists. His policies toward civilians in his previous command in western Virginia caused quite a stir. Confederate military leaders reported that Milroy moved to have residents take the oath of allegiance not just to the United States, but also, in Robert E. Lee's words, to "the so-called State of Western Virginia." Confederate general William E. "Grumble" Jones, who notified Lee of Milroy's practices, suggested that Milroy's orders "for harshness and cruel injustice rival the efforts of Pope and Butler."[34]

Milroy brought this harsh attitude toward Confederate civilians with him to Winchester. Shortly after arriving, he boasted to his wife, "I feel a strong disposition to play the tyrent among these traitors." Milroy played this role with gusto; one of his first acts was to proclaim his determination to enforce the Emancipation Proclamation in Winchester.[35]

Milroy tended to be much more heavy-handed with the oath than his predecessors. He tried to use the oath as a tool to reward loyal residents with special privileges and to withhold necessities from secessionists. He established three lines of pickets around town, all within calling distance of each other, to ensure that no one could enter or exit Winchester without a pass. At the same time Milroy announced his intentions to free Winchester's slaves, he also issued a decree forbidding sutlers to sell to anyone who refused to take the oath of allegiance. Nor could anyone bring supplies to town from points north unless he or she took the oath. Laura Lee accused Milroy of trying to starve residents into loyalty.[36]

Travel restrictions remained in effect throughout the Union occupation, and few were willing to submit to the oath in exchange for freedom of movement. Presbyterian minister J. R. Graham continued to comfort his parishioners in Winchester, but he remained cut off from worshippers who lived outside the Union lines, as they refused to take the oath in order to attend services in town. On May 18, 1863, Ann C. R. Jones wrote from her home Vaucluse, several miles south of Winchester, that the day marked the one-month anniversary of the last time she had been in town; she could not venture to guess the next time she would be able to go again. Mary B. Jones, living on the outskirts of Winchester, expressed concern about her extended family who remained in town. "We would be delighted to get all of our dear people out of the Town," she informed her nephew, "but it is impossible to without their taking the oath." On a rare occasion when Margaretta "Gettie" Miller's aunt Kate received a pass to visit Woodstock, Miller reported that her aunt felt "like a bird that was a prisoner and that was left out in the green fields."[37]

As his occupation progressed, Milroy continued to pressure the citizens of Winchester into taking the oath. At the end of January he forbade merchants and sutlers from selling flour or wood to disloyal citizens. Sutlers who disobeyed this order were arrested and their goods confiscated. These tactics imposed great difficulty on residents coping with winter weather. Cornelia McDonald's stepson Edward remembered that trying to feed the family during the winter became a "battle of wits." The McDonald boys stole from the quartermaster tents that occupied their front yard, and the family managed to hide a cow in the basement. Despite these efforts, there were times in the winter when the family subsisted on stolen army crackers and milk. The spring brought little relief. Toward the end of April, Milroy closed every business in town to disloyal citizens. "Not even a place to get a shoe mended," Cornelia McDonald complained. "We have long ceased to expect to buy."[38]

Although a directive like Pope's General Order № 11 did not inform Milroy's policy, he contemplated adopting harsher tactics in Winchester by the middle of May 1863. Most likely, Milroy drew his inspiration from General Orders № 100, more commonly known as the Lieber Code. Article 146 of the code authorized commanders to "expel, transfer, imprison, or fine" citizens who refused "to pledge themselves anew as citizens obedient to the law and loyal to the government." Commanders received their copies of the order around April 24; by the middle of May Milroy, concerned about guerrilla attacks, asked his superior Gen. Robert Schenck, "What do you think of the policy of requiring all persons to take the oath, or move south of our lines immediately? I am very tired of being in the midst of treason." The same day, Schenck wired his approval.[39]

As Richard Duncan has suggested, Milroy's policies seemed to strengthen the determination and resolve of Winchester's secessionist community, especially its women. Toward the end of his occupation one Winchester resident proudly observed, "The Yankees will not allow the people to buy anything without taking the oath, and we would rather starve than do that." After three months of Union occupation, Gettie Miller remained defiant. "I hope that Pa wont take their nasty oath," she wrote, "unless they make him." When Arthur J. L. Fremantle entered Winchester with returning Confederate troops in June, he learned of Milroy's policies. During the six months of Union occupation, residents "could not legally buy an article of provisions without taking the oath of allegiance, which they magnanimously refused to do."[40]

On June 12, 1863, just days before Confederate forces under Richard Ewell swept through Winchester, Milroy wrote an overly optimistic letter

to Robert Schenck. He claimed that his harsh measures were beginning
to bear fruit. Noting that area Unionists had become timid because of
the temporary nature of previous occupations, Milroy asserted that his
longer stay in Winchester had begun to give the Unionists confidence. He
noted that in town and throughout the countryside, "the Union sentiment
has been rapidly improving." He claimed that large numbers of men and
women were coming in daily to take the oath of allegiance, and he reported that Winchester's leading secessionists were only waiting to hear
of the next Confederate battlefield defeat "to come out boldly and take
the stump for reconstruction." This remarkable letter illustrates Milroy's
detachment from reality. Instead of hearing of another battlefield defeat, Winchester's secessionists welcomed Confederate general Richard
Ewell's soldiers with open arms on June 15. Despite Milroy's claims in
his letter to Schenck, Milroy biographer Jonathan A. Noyalas's search
of recorded oaths of allegiance in the records of the Middle Department revealed none taken in Winchester during Milroy's occupation.[41]

Although Winchester's secessionists proved unyielding throughout
Milroy's six-month occupation, his restrictive policies took their toll.
In the weeks following the battle of Gettysburg, Winchester residents
realized that the Confederates could not keep their hold on the town,
and many chose to leave rather than endure another Union occupation.
As she hurriedly began preparations to leave Winchester in the middle
of July 1863, Cornelia McDonald observed that "The whole town seemed
to be trying to get away; every thing that had wheels was in demand,
and even a cart was deemed a prize. Few were willing to risk another
Federal occupation, for the next might be a prolonged one." A visitor
to Winchester in the same month characterized the town as "dead and
rotten," elaborating that there was "no business, nothing to eat. Houses
deserted, population leaving north and south." A month later, Ann C. R.
Jones contrasted Winchester's past glories with its wartime condition.
"You never saw such a place as Winchester has become," she informed a
Florida relative. "So many persons anxious to leave it, selling the houses
& even old inhabitants, & some young, keen for going away, I have become disgusted with the town." Gettie Miller prophesied that "if the war
keeps on [like] this very much longer every person will move away."[42]

Gettie Miller's prediction did not come to pass, but Cornelia McDonald's prognostication of a prolonged Union occupation did. Following
the third battle of Winchester on September 19, 1864, Union forces held
the town until the war's end. The final Union occupation of Winchester,

begun by Gen. Philip Sheridan, was a curious mixture of harsh policy toward civilians combined with some acts of mercy. While Sheridan certainly exhibited callousness toward civilians in Winchester, many residents felt that he was not personally mean like Milroy. Ironically, Sheridan's forces brought a sense of stability to the region that had been absent since the beginning of the war.[43]

Like his predecessors, Sheridan wrestled with the problem of extinguishing the Confederate loyalty of Winchester's secessionists. While Julius White and Robert Milroy threatened reprisals against secessionist civilians, Sheridan was the only occupier to make mass arrests in Winchester. On October 25, 1864, he had all male residents capable of bearing arms arrested, except those who agreed to take the oath of allegiance. Union officials rounded up nearly one hundred men and detained sixty-three. According to Mary G. Lee, nearly every man left in Winchester was arrested. She was unsure why the men were arrested, but she suspected that they would be given the choice of taking the oath or being sent beyond Union lines. Sheridan's explanation for his action showed a change from previous Union commanders in Winchester. He claimed he had no specific charges against the men, but that he wanted, according to Lee, "to show this community that he had the power to compel respect to his soldiers." By late 1864, Sheridan did not need to convince secessionists to swallow the oath; he had the power to compel them without it.[44]

Although Sheridan demonstrated that he had the power to compel Winchester's civilians, his policies proved to be more tolerant than those of his predecessors. In the fall of 1864, Sheridan allowed local farmers to sell their produce in town as long as Winchester's hospitals had the first chance to purchase it. Sutlers remained forbidden to sell to disloyal citizens, but the sale of cornmeal and flour marked an important exception to this rule. Sheridan allowed many residents to travel to Baltimore to purchase goods for their own use. The city also sent relief supplies, including bacon, flour, cornmeal, lard, sugar, and coffee, to be distributed to the destitute throughout Frederick County with Sheridan's approval.[45]

A general sense of war weariness among Winchester's civilians further contributed to fewer conflicts over the oath. Sheridan noted in early October 1864 that "The people here are getting sick of war." The influx of wounded into town after the battles of Third Winchester and Cedar Creek overwhelmed the civilians who remained. Emma Riely remembered that during the winter of 1864–1865 "a kind of Rip Van Winkle sleep had fallen upon the people. All were apparently absorbed with their own cares and poverty, especially the latter."[46] This absorption continued until the war's end a few months later.

II.

Despite repeated attempts by Federal forces to apply the oath of allegiance to Winchester's secessionists, it proved to be an ineffective tool to further Union war aims. Although their tactics severely limited civilians' access to mobility and much-needed supplies, Union commanders found few secessionists in Winchester who were willing to swallow the oath. Several factors bolstered civilians' confidence in their struggle to avoid taking it.

The main reason few secessionists in Winchester would swallow the oath is that they appreciated its significance—because it renounced Confederate citizenship, the oath marked a border that very few were willing to cross.[47] Winchester civilians clearly interpreted the act of taking the oath as abandoning the Confederate cause. Local secessionists interpreted the oath as the limit of membership in the Confederate community. Unlike many residents who expressed trepidation about the possibility of an oath being administered during the summer of 1862, Mary G. Lee looked forward to it. She believed it would clearly show who "was with, & who, against us."[48]

Lee's view suggests that the community values of Winchester's secessionists played a crucial role in steeling individuals against taking the oath. As Stephen V. Ash has demonstrated, civilian morale and resistance in occupied areas drew strength from community ideals. Clearly Winchester's secessionist community thought it was proper to endure any deprivation in order to avoid taking the oath. Toward the end of the first Union occupation of Winchester, residents faced losing the freedom of movement unless they took the oath. Laura Lee declared, "Of course no *decent* person will take such an oath." When Kate Sperry learned that former Confederate soldier Hector Isler took the oath after his capture, she proclaimed, "he's done for—the cowardly fellow." Mary G. Lee had great sympathy for the Breedin sisters who were struggling to pay their rent during Julius White's occupation. They hoped to travel south to pursue an opportunity to serve as governesses, but they could not procure a pass without taking the oath. Lee approvingly noted, "They, very properly, refuse to take the oath."[49]

These examples of determination inspired many in Winchester; other secessionists found fortitude when they thought of their family members who were serving in the Confederate army. During the furor over General White's modified oath, Mary G. Lee recounted a meeting with Dr. R. J. Holliday, whose son Frederick had recently had his right arm amputated after being wounded at the battle of Cedar Mountain. Struggling to hold back tears, Holliday showed Lee a note his son had written with his left hand. He told Lee that he would not sign the oath because doing so would break his son's heart. John Henry Stover Funk realized the influence his status as a Confederate soldier had on his family in Winchester. After cheekily telling his mother, "I am anxious to know how you and Milroy agree upon national affairs," he urged her to prevent his brother from taking the oath, claiming it would be better if he were arrested and taken north—that course would "be an honor to him." Although he pressed hard for his brother to avoid the oath, he held a different view of his father's situation. Funk advised his father to avoid the oath as long as possible, but if it came to the choice of taking the oath or starving, he should take it and "let the sin rest upon the leader of the vandals who imposes it."[50]

The possibility that their reactions to the oath could be reported to others outside their immediate community further steeled Winchester secessionists in their opposition to it. One reason why Mary G. Lee was so opposed to General White's modified oath was that if the men would sign it, the Yankees could claim that many people had taken the oath in Winchester without reporting that it was modified. During Milroy's occupation, Winchester troops in the Stonewall Brigade stationed at Fredericksburg heard rumors that their hometown had been "abolitionized" and that many citizens had taken the oath. In a letter to his family, John Henry Stover Funk responded to the oath-takers in a manner that reinforced local secessionists' communal values: "They [are] unworthy of the title of honest men or worthy women and we spurn [such] false hearted and cowardly specimens."[51]

While Funk heard distressing news from Winchester regarding the oath, local secessionists' strong stand during the first Federal occupation drew admiring comments from the *Richmond Daily Dispatch*. Under the headline "Southern Places Occupied by the Enemy," the paper reported that "The people of Winchester have nothing whatever to do with the enemy. They have shown in a calm and dignified, but most determined manner, that they are no longer *one people* with their enemies." The

Dispatch hoped that the example set by Winchester secessionists in their refusal to take the oath would "continue to be universally followed at the South."[52] The affective citizenship of Winchester's secessionists embraced and drew strength from a broader Confederate community.

Because many Winchester secessionists found ways to get around the oath, it became easier to serve as an example of fortitude. Despite their harsh rhetoric, Union commanders did not consistently enforce the restrictions they hoped to impose upon disloyal civilians. If Winchester secessionists remained patient, they could find times when Federal restrictions were loosened. In July 1862, Unionist Julia Chase noted that the Federals had lifted their usual restrictions on travel, making no distinction between the loyal and disloyal. Many of the travelers smuggled letters into and out of Winchester. Sometimes this inconsistency caused frustration. Cornelia McDonald grew tired of the uneven nature of the enforcement of restrictions, claiming she never knew from one day to the next whether she could buy goods or not.[53]

While many of Winchester's secessionists hoped to take advantage of vacillations in Union occupation policy, other skillful residents were able to play the system no matter the conditions. Mary G. Lee became a remarkable purchasing agent for the Confederate cause as she learned from her experiences under Union occupation. Laura Lee spoke admiringly of her sister-in-law's ability to ferret away supplies during Milroy's occupation. In March 1863, she wrote, "our excitement and amusement consists in buying everything we want without a permit." She noted that even though Milroy had forbidden sutlers to sell to disloyal civilians, Mary was able to purchase one hundred herrings and twenty-five pounds of molasses, eight hams, coffee, and soap. A few weeks later, the Lees had such a successful shopping day that they ended their activities not because of pressure to take the oath, but because they ran out of money.[54]

Few of Winchester's secessionists could match the foraging skills of the Lees, but they often secured support from Union soldiers who did not share the proclivities of their commanders and who desired flour and baked bread that the secessionists could provide. Soldiers stationed near families would often get to know them and become sympathetic to their plight. Cornelia McDonald noted that the soldiers she saw every day were always pleased to help her buy the things she could not because of her desire to avoid the oath. One soldier paid regular visits to her home late at night with a kettle and a bundle. The kettle contained cof-

fee and sugar, and the bundle held a piece of fat bacon. McDonald filled
the soldier's kettle with flour and sent him on his way. Kate McVicar
remembered that George Loy, a Federal soldier in a Wheeling unit, had
been friends with her brother before the war. Loy agreed to act as the
family's purchasing agent, buying goods, including clothes for McVicar's
brother, who was a soldier in the Confederate army.[55]

Winchester residents also received aid from an unlikely source: residents who had taken the oath of allegiance. Some oath-takers believed
that their promise not to aid the Confederate cause did not apply to
Confederate civilians. Frequently the oath-takers cooperated with local
secessionists for economic gain. Kate Sperry, refugeeing in Newtown,
had to cancel her plans for baking one day because she could find no
butter in her neighborhood; everyone had given theirs to a Mrs. Bindle,
whom Sperry described as an old Union woman. Mrs. Bindle had taken
the butter to Winchester to trade for groceries. In his study of wartime
Winchester, Richard Duncan observes that a number of the town's secessionists willingly took the oath in order to travel to Martinsburg to
purchase goods for trade with their secessionist neighbors.[56]

The unsettled nature of military activity in the region further contributed to Winchester secessionists' attitude toward the oath and the
deprivations they endured in order to avoid it. It was one thing to take
the oath in a region that was securely held by Union forces, but those
who took the oath in areas where Union control was tenuous could face
grave consequences when Confederate forces returned. This uncertainty
discouraged some who might otherwise have considered taking the oath.

The inability of the Union army to permanently hold Winchester also
inspired local secessionists to hold out as long as they could, knowing
that Confederate forces could return at any time. While residents of
other occupied areas of the Confederacy initially shared the hope of
deliverance, in most cases their hopes faded as months of Union occupation turned into years. Union control in Winchester remained tenuous
as the war continued. Unionist Julia Chase criticized Pope's General
Order № 11 when she learned of it in July 1862. She noted that many
secessionists in Winchester were willing to risk exile rather than take
the oath, for they believed that Stonewall Jackson would return shortly.
Chase believed it would be "folly" to issue such an order if there was a
chance of the Confederates returning, as a large group of vengeful residents would return with them. During Milroy's occupation Cornelia
McDonald and two of her stepdaughters thought that they had a valid

pass to leave Winchester and head south, but they were returned to town by the Union pickets. They went to visit Milroy, who offered to give them another pass. The women thanked him but refused the pass, one of the stepdaughters explaining, "I think the next pass that carries us up the Valley will be signed by Gen. Jackson."[57]

Mary G. Lee allowed a similar belief to give her comfort as she struggled with the challenges of Union occupation. After one instance of General Milroy's tightening restrictions on disloyal civilians, she learned that several men had been talking about taking the oath. She expressed much less concern than she had during the time of Julius White's modified oath because experience had taught her that "these very stringent measures . . . have always preceded, immediately, our deliverance."[58]

Mary G. Lee's hope of deliverance ended in February 1865, when General Sheridan ordered her to be sent south through the Union lines. The hopes of the secessionists who remained in Winchester that winter had declined as well. In a few months the war would end in Union victory, but most local secessionists could take comfort in the fact that they had never swallowed the oath.

Four years of tenuous wartime struggles could not destroy the affective bonds of Winchester's Confederate civilians. As gatekeepers of the Confederate community, Winchester secessionists defined what it meant to belong to that community. Behavior that Union officials saw as disloyal was often condoned by Winchester secessionists as necessary behavior that loyal Confederates must engage in for survival. The Union military's attempt to weaken the Confederate cause by appealing to the formal privileges of citizenship failed because the Confederacy of the heart proved strong enough to withstand these temptations. While Julius White's modified oath threatened to rupture Winchester's Confederate community, the return of a Confederate army at a critical moment enabled it to survive. Examining the struggle over the oath of allegiance through the prism of citizenship reminds us that rather than being the helpless victims of oppressive Union military policy, Winchester's secessionist civilians were active and able defenders of the social boundaries of their community in the battle over Confederate citizenship. In most cases (Fannie Burracker notwithstanding) affective citizenship proved stronger than appeals to the formal privileges of citizenship and steeled Winchester's secessionists against swallowing the oath. Although military defeat ended any hope for an independent Confederate nation, the Confederacy of the heart that Winchester secessionists so tenaciously defended during the war would play a key role in shaping the way that they faced the postwar challenges of Reconstruction.

NOTES

1. The Shenandoah River drains northward into the Potomac, so travelers heading south in the region are traveling up the Valley, and those heading north are traveling down the Valley.

2. Emma Cassandra Riely Macon and Reuben Conway Macon, *Reminiscences of the Civil War* (Cedar Rapids, IA: The Torch Press, 1911), 12–13, 32.

3. Ibid., 36–37. The best recent account of Jackson's 1862 Valley Campaign is Peter Cozzens, *Shenandoah 1862: Stonewall Jackson's Valley Campaign* (Chapel Hill: University of North Carolina Press, 2008).

4. Macon and Macon, *Reminiscences,* 48, 50–52.

5. Judkin Browning, *Shifting Loyalties: The Union Occupation of Eastern North Carolina* (Chapel Hill: University of North Carolina Press, 2011), 5, 65; Peter Maslowski, *Treason Must Be Made Odious: Military Occupation and Wartime Reconstruction in Nashville, Tennessee, 1862–65* (Millwood, NY: KTO Press, 1978), 62, 69; Joseph H. Parks, "A Confederate Trade Center under Federal Occupation: Memphis, 1862 to 1865," *Journal of Southern History* 7 (August 1941): 310–11; Anne Sarah Rubin, *A Shattered Nation: The Rise & Fall of the Confederacy 1861–1868* (Chapel Hill: University of North Carolina Press, 2005), 86, 97.

6. Stephen Kantrowitz, *More Than Freedom: Fighting for Black Citizenship in a White Republic, 1829–1889* (New York: Penguin Books, 2012), 6. For other works that address affective citizenship, see Kenneth L. Karst, *Belonging to America: Equal Citizenship and the Constitution* (New Haven, CT: Yale University Press, 1989); William A. Link, David Brown, Brian Ward, and Martyn Bone, eds., *Creating Citizenship in the Nineteenth-Century South* (Gainesville: University Press of Florida, 2013); and Michael E. Woods, *Emotional and Sectional Conflict in the Antebellum United States* (New York: Cambridge University Press, 2014). See also the essays of Earl Maltz, Elizabeth Regosin, Caitlin Verboon, David Williard, and Claire Wolnisty in this volume.

7. Macon and Macon, *Reminiscences*, 52.

8. The lower Shenandoah Valley consists of the West Virginia counties of Berkeley and Jefferson and the Virginia counties of Frederick and Clarke. Its natural boundaries are the Potomac River in the north and Cedar Creek in the south. See J. E. Norris, *History of the Lower Shenandoah Valley* (1890; repr., Berryville: Virginia Book Company, 1972), 28–29.

9. Richard R. Duncan, *Beleaguered Winchester: A Virginia Community at War, 1861–1865* (Baton Rouge: Louisiana State University Press, 2007), ix–x; Margaretta Barton Colt, *Defend the Valley: A Shenandoah Family in the Civil War* (New York: Crown, 1994), 6.

10. Colt, *Defend the Valley,* 8–9.

11. Colt, *Defend the Valley,* 9; Arthur James Lyon Fremantle, *Three Months in the Southern States: April–June 1863* (Lincoln: University of Nebraska Press, 1991), 228. Estimates of the number of times Winchester changed hands reach as high as seventy-five. I have used the more conservative estimate of Margaretta Barton Colt, who accurately notes that the higher estimates are "misleading, as the great majority of these engagements were cavalry forays and did not result in a new occupation or even a change of control (9–10).

See also Garland R. Quarels, *Occupied Winchester 1861–1865* (1976; repr., Winchester, VA: Winchester-Frederick County Historical Society, 1991), 131.

12. Unidentified newspaper clipping dated July 28, 1862, placed in the July 17, 1862, entry of the John Peyton Clark journal, Handley Regional Library, Winchester, Virginia (hereafter cited as HL).

13. US War Department, *The War of the Rebellion: A Compilation of the Official Records of the Union and Confederate Armies,* 127 vols., index, and atlas (Washington, DC: Government Printing Office, 1880–1901), series 2, 3:52 (hereafter cited as *OR,* followed by series, number (part): page); Macon and Macon, *Reminiscences,* 45.

14. The Restored Government of Virginia was declared by the Unionist Wheeling Convention in June 1861. It repudiated the Richmond secession convention and declared all state offices held by secessionists to be void.

15. John Peyton Clark journal, April 24, 1862.

16. Ibid., April 26, 1862.

17. Mary G. Lee diary, April 23, May 2, 1862, HL.

18. Stephen V. Ash, *When the Yankees Came: Conflict and Chaos in the Occupied South* (Chapel Hill: University of North Carolina Press, 1995), 60; Mary G. Lee diary, April 3, 1862; John Peyton Clark journal, May 12, 1862; Richmond *Enquirer,* June 9, 1862.

19. John Peyton Clark journal, May 26, 1862.

20. Duncan, *Beleaguered Winchester,* 108.

21. Mark Grimsley, *The Hard Hand of War: Union Military Policy Toward Southern Civilians 1861–1865* (New York: Cambridge University Press, 1995), 85.

22. *New York Times,* July 27, 1862, quoted in ibid., 89.

23. Mary G. Lee diary, July 22, 1862; Michael G. Mahon, ed., *Winchester Divided: The Civil War Diaries of Julia Chase and Laura Lee* (Mechanicsburg, PA.: Stackpole Books, 2002), 49.

24. Mary G. Lee diary, July 27, 1862; Fanny B. Graham to My Dear Friend, August 9, 1862, published in the *Winchester Evening Star,* January 22, 1965. Of course, Winchester Unionists did not share the opinions of their secessionist neighbors regarding Pope's orders. A letter published in the *Baltimore American,* written from Winchester on July 28, 1862, jauntily observed, "since the late . . . orders of Gen. Pope the air seems free, the sky brighter, the step of the loyal man is more elastic, while the physiognomy of [the] Secesh is lengthened indefinitely." See clipping from *Baltimore American* in John Peyton Clark journal, July 31, 1862.

25. Mary G. Lee diary, July 31, 1862; Laura Lee diary, July 28, 31, August 1, 4, 1862, HL.

26. Mary G. Lee diary, July 31, 1862.

27. John Peyton Clark journal, August 18, 1862; Mary G. Lee diary, August 20, 1862.

28. Mahon, *Winchester Divided,* 53; John Peyton Clark journal, September 1, 1862; Robert Y. Conrad characterized the modified oath as a "neutrality oath." See Robert Y. Conrad to Daniel B. Conrad, September 13, 1862, Mss1 C76376287–299, Robert Y. Conrad Papers, Virginia Historical Society, Richmond, Virginia.

29. Mary G. Lee diary, August 22, 30, 1862.

30. Ibid., August 23–24, 27, 1862; John Peyton Clark journal, September 1, 1862.

31. Mahon, *Winchester Divided,* 53; Mary G. Lee diary, August 25–26, 1862.

32. Laura Lee diary, August 27–28, 1862; Mary G. Lee diary, August 27–28, 1862.

33. John Peyton Clark journal, September 8, 1862.

34. *OR* ser. 1, 21:1080–1082.

35. Duncan, *Beleaguered Winchester,* 139–40.

36. Jonathan A. Noyalas, "'My Will is Law': General Robert H. Milroy and Winchester, Virginia" (Master's thesis, Virginia Polytechnic Institute and State University, 2003), 24–25, 27; Richard Parker diary, January 17, 1863; Laura Lee diary, January 17, 1863, in Mahon, *Winchester Divided,* 78.

37. Fanny B. Graham to M. A. Jackson, June 20, 1863, in Winchester *Evening Star,* February 18, 1965; Colt, *Defend the Valley,* 249, 254; Margaretta Miller diary, May 30, 1863, HL.

38. Mahon, *Winchester Divided,* 79; Julia Davis, *Mount Up: A True Story Based on the Reminiscences of Major E. A. H. McDonald of the Confederate Cavalry* (New York: Harcourt, Brace & World, 1967), 110–11; Cornelia McDonald, *A Woman's Civil War: A Diary, with Reminiscences of the War, from March 1862,* ed. Minrose C. Gwin (New York: Gramercy Books, 1992), 123, 142. Milroy closed all businesses, April 26–28, 1863. See Mary G. Lee diary, April 28, 1863. Milroy tended to be more lenient when his policies threatened the health of Winchester residents. When typhoid fever raged through Winchester in May and June 1863, he allowed civilians access to whiskey and medicine. See Colt, *Defend the Valley,* 254.

39. William A. Blair, *With Malice Toward Some: Treason and Loyalty in the Civil War Era* (Chapel Hill: University of North Carolina Press, 2014), 145; *OR* ser. 1, 25(2): 496.

40. Duncan, *Beleaguered Winchester,* 153; letter dated June 4, 1863, in *Richmond Daily Whig,* June 19, 1863; Gettie Miller diary, April 24, 1863; Fremantle, *Three Months,* 229.

41. *OR* ser. 1, 27(2): 178; Noyalas, "'My Will is Law,'" 35.

42. McDonald, *A Woman's Civil War,* 164; Duncan, *Beleaguered Winchester,* 170; Colt, *Defend the Valley,* 269; Gettie Miller diary, July 23, 1863.

43. Duncan, *Beleaguered Winchester,* 207.

44. Ibid., 235–36; Mary G. Lee diary, October 25, 1864; Sheila R. Phipps, *Genteel Rebel: The Life of Mary Greenhow Lee* (Baton Rouge: Louisiana State University Press, 2004), 177.

45. Duncan, *Beleaguered Winchester,* 227, 244–45; Mahon, *Winchester Divided,* 179.

46. Duncan, *Beleaguered Winchester,* 223, 227, 235; Macon and Macon, *Reminiscences,* 117.

47. This outlook is at odds with Stephen V. Ash's view that civilians became lax in their attitudes about the oath as the war continued. Ash asserts that many secessionists took the oath in the later years of the war "with no intention of respecting it and therefore violated it without compunction." See Ash, *When the Yankees Came,* 73.

48. Mary G. Lee diary, August 8, 1862.

49. Ash, *When the Yankees Came,* 45; Laura Lee diary, May 14, 1862; Kate Sperry diary, May 15, 1862, HL; Mary G. Lee diary, August 12, 1862.

50. Mary G. Lee diary, August 26, 1862; Stover to My Dear Mother, March 3, 1863.

51. Stover to Dear Father and Mother, _____ 9, 1863, Fredericksburg and Spotsylvania National Military Park.

52. *Richmond Daily Dispatch,* April 28, 1862; emphasis added.

53. Mahon, *Winchester Divided,* 50; Duncan, *Beleaguered Winchester,* 144.

54. Mahon, *Winchester Divided,* 82, 85.

55. McDonald, *A Woman's Civil War,* 123, 134; *Winchester Evening Star,* December 18, 1912.

56. Kate Sperry diary, February 13, 1863; Duncan, *Beleaguered Winchester,* 147.

57. Walter T. Durham, *Reluctant Partners: Nashville and the Union, 1863–1865* (1987; repr., Knoxville: University of Tennessee Press, 2008), 202; Mahon, *Winchester Divided*, 50; Duncan, *Beleaguered Winchester*, 142.

58. Mary G. Lee diary, April 25, 1863. While continued Federal retreats from Winchester inspired the town's secessionists, Richard Duncan suggests that Federal reverses in the region led to harsher Union policies. See Duncan, *Beleaguered Winchester*, 82, 100.

Citizenship—Compulsory or Convenient

Federal Officials, Confederate Prisoners,
and the Oath of Allegiance

ANGELA M. ZOMBEK

Early summer 1864 dragged on as Albert Vickers remained confined in Johnson's Island Prison. Coercion alone had driven Vickers to Confederate service. The unwilling conscript actively sought an opportunity to desert to Union lines but, ironically, instead earned promotion to lieutenant in Company D, 46th Alabama Regiment. Vickers finally deserted after the November 1863 Battle of Chattanooga, but upon his capture Union authorities confused the purportedly loyal Albert with the disloyal H. L. Vickers, which landed Albert in prison. Vickers repeatedly petitioned the commandant Col. Charles Hill throughout summer 1864, begging recognition of the clerical error. Vickers clamored for the US oath to "atone to my country for the wrong" he had done. He insisted that a hearing would prove his loyalty and closed his petition with a recognition of Federal power, "your prisoner, A. T. Vickers." Vickers's difficult situation reveals how imprisonment could shape the fault lines of citizenship in Civil War America.[1]

Citizenship during wartime, especially in military prisons, was a concept intimately linked with the US oath of allegiance—the latter conferred the former. Union prison officials enticed enemy inmates to affirm their allegiance, reclaim US citizenship, and mitigate the trials of imprisonment. Inmates, however, recognized that they could profess allegiance to fulfill immediate needs, even if their loyalty was actually feigned. Through enticement and profession of allegiance, officials and inmates at Union military prisons shaped the meaning and function of citizenship within the context of imprisonment. When Union officials administered and enemy inmates took the oath, both assumed significant responsibilities—the officials judged oath-takers' sincerity and had to protect reclaimed citizens, while the prisoners were to remain true to their word, at least outwardly, regardless of the risk.

The Civil War's crisis of imprisonment forced Confederate prisoners of all classes to reevaluate allegiance amidst anxiety-ridden circumstances in which they, as captives, lacked rights and remained subject to the decisions of Union officials. Federal officials' administration of the oath of allegiance in military prisons represents an early effort to reconstruct the polity that demonstrated the Union's supremacy and shaped notions about US citizenship. Federal officials had the power to change prisoners' circumstances by offering the oath, and they made enemy inmates sweat psychologically. Some inmates recognized the power of Union officials, at least rhetorically, and advanced anxious pleas for the oath and, by extension, reinstated citizenship. This reclamation, in the context of wartime imprisonment, at best secured release and at least secured protection from angry comrades. Some prisoners truly felt shame for forsaking the southern cause by reclaiming US allegiance, but many prisoners feared that Union officials would punish them if they refused the oath. In either case, Union officials' administration of the oath invited prisoners to make a personal choice regarding allegiance and, consequently, citizenship, and this individual decision harkened back to the individual focus of antebellum years.

The Civil War culminated from almost eighty years of uncertainty surrounding the definition of US citizenship and whether the Union was binding. Southern secessionists—mostly landed, slave-owning aristocrats—believed themselves true heirs of their Revolutionary forefathers. To them, the Federal government, like the British Crown, had become too powerful, necessitating the creation of a new decentralized government that would reflect popular will. Unionists, especially members of the Republican Party, believed the Union was binding and equated secession and its supporters with treason.[2] This ideological conflict spilled onto battlefields, and into military prisons.

By 1861, Americans were long accustomed to focusing on themselves and their localities, preferring individualism unless a national crisis arose. Americans—especially southerners—saw the Union and the Federal government as abstractions subject to modification or even dissolution.[3] For four long, but overall comparatively brief years, Americans in the North and South became actively involved in their national projects through military service, government employment, and personal sacrifice. For many Americans, however, perhaps especially POWs, the tension between local, state, and national loyalties created mental anguish and forced them to weigh self-interest against their oath of service in considering US allegiance and citizenship.

The oath of allegiance demonstrated the Union's supremacy, and individual US prison officials who administered the oath decided who belonged within the polity and when they could be readmitted. Union officials followed in the footsteps of their Revolutionary forefathers as they used the oath to bolster patriotism, however coercive the tactic might have been. The oath, as Lucius Wedge and Jonathan Berkey's essays in this volume show, signified a relationship between civilians, the government, and God. Typically, it was government authorities who controlled this process, conferring privileges on oath-takers and punishing refusal. At the same time, as Anne Rubin has indicated, Confederates who took the oath did not necessarily intend it as a sincere profession of loyalty; it was often used to pacify US authorities while maintaining allegiance to the Confederacy.[4]

Southerners often viewed the oath as fluid, but Federal officials believed it binding. The oath could represent an olive branch welcoming prodigal sons back into the fold, but it was also a political tool, war measure, and practical remedy for alleviating overcrowded prisons.[5] Union authorities, from Secretary of State William Seward, to Commissary General of Prisoners William Hoffman, to prison commandants, knew that simply offering the oath would not persuade hardened Rebels, or even those on the fence, to take it. Federal officials often regained citizens not from democratic impulses, but by coercing inmates to make the "right" choice. Benefits like extra rations, improved living conditions, and the opportunity to work were incentives that Federal officials used to encourage Confederate POWs to swear US allegiance. But reclaiming citizens necessitated that the Federal government protect oath-takers from Confederate inmates who abhorred their comrades' choice. To oath-takers, however, the decision boiled down to calculated self-interest. Many who reclaimed US citizenship believed in the Union, but others took the oath out of recognition that it held the key to returning to their families, the focus of primary allegiance. Ultimately, Federal prison officials who administered the oath and Confederate POWs who subscribed to it were often opportunistic individuals who shaped the motivations for offering and embracing citizenship and molded its consequent obligations within the context of imprisonment.[6]

Early in the war, Federal policy governing the oath fluctuated according to the war's trajectory, creating ambiguity over who could administer the oath and which inmates were eligible for it. This confusion, and Confederate inmates' responses to the oath, indicate not only how inmates' political ideology shifted throughout the war, but also how Federal conceptions of loyalty molded citizenship.[7]

The Federal government, through military prison officials, courted men who rejected US citizenship when they sided with the Confederacy. On October 12, 1861, Assistant Adjutant General E. D. Townsend issued Special Orders № 170, which performed two functions. The first was unwitting: the order, which released the same number of prisoners from Washington and New York Harbor as Confederates released from Richmond, validated Confederates' belief in volitional allegiance and the legitimacy of their political experiment.[8] The second signaled the role that the oath played in reconstructing the nation. Oath-takers swore, "without any mental reservation or evasion," to support, protect, and defend the US Constitution and government, and "bear true faith, allegiance, and loyalty" to its laws.[9] Union officials thus assumed charge over prisoners' political and moral lives as they administered the oath—a sacred pledge that, if broken, constituted both sin and felony.[10]

Some Confederates accepted Federal power and swore fealty to God and Union. Take the case of an unnamed Camp Chase POW, chronicled in a June 1862 *Santa Cruz Sentinel* article. The prisoner petitioned California senator Latham, an acquaintance of the inmate's loyal brother, claiming that he always opposed secession and that its errors became more apparent to him every day. The petitioner desired the "simple boon" of taking the oath and willingly swore "by the God who made me, and by every hope that fills my bosom, and by every sweet memory of the past, ever to remain true to the American Union in all time to come." Religious imagery abounded as he begged the senator to do something so that he "may be *separated from the goats*" and return to Union friends in Tennessee. The penitent closed with a solemn vow to be the senator's and the Union's "humble servant."[11] *Sentinel* journalists were supportive, opining that Federal officials might later employ the prisoner against senseless secessionists. The story's veracity may be questionable since the man remained nameless and his fate unreported, but it taught readers the price for forsaking US citizenship and the penitence required for rectification.

Federal policy surrounding the oath ironically substantiated the idea of volitional allegiance upon which both the Revolutionary-era United States and the Confederacy were founded—both asserted the individual's right to choose allegiance. Even though Federal officials issued overarching directives regarding allegiance, the choice was nonetheless personal. General-in-Chief Henry W. Halleck's General Orders № 107, dated August 15, 1862, appealed to independent-minded Confederate inmates. It mandated that the oath be voluntary, rendering coerced oaths null and void. The order emphasized that "oaths taken and paroles given to avoid arrest, detention, imprisonment or expulsion are voluntary or free acts and cannot be regarded as compulsory."[12] On one level, this directive supported individual decision-making, but languishing in prison was an undesirable alternative. Capt. H. W. Freedley, overseeing prison operations around Springfield, Illinois, acknowledged the difficulty of ensuring volition. He alerted Hoffman on August 16, 1862, that he attempted to make the oath "as voluntary as possible" for POWs. "While no inducement has been offered to encourage them," he commented, "every endeavor has been made to prevent them from being discouraged, threatened, or otherwise prevented from signing." Hoffman blamed prisoners' reluctance on "violent secessionists," speculating that hesitant inmates, if freed from negative influence, would choose *correctly*—an implicit recognition of coercion.[13] Federal authorities thus could and did manipulate POWs to profess allegiance.

The oath, however, did not guarantee absolute loyalty. Trusting Federal officials conferred privileges upon oath-takers as benefits of reclaimed citizenship, but officials who were suspicious of oath-takers' sincerity rescinded privileges. Secretary of War Edwin Stanton and Commissary General Hoffman vacillated from one camp to another since prison commandants often confronted men who professed that they had always been loyal. This forced Stanton to decide how to treat such men, how oath-takers could best serve the Union, and what responsibility the Federal government ultimately had to them. In June 1862, Col. Richard Owen, commandant of Indianapolis's Camp Morton Prison, alerted Stanton that numerous POWs preferred imprisonment over Confederate military service and requested to remain in prison rather than be exchanged. Assistant Secretary of War C. P. Wolcott communicated Stanton's response, directing Owen that POWs who took the oath and whose future loyalty was unquestionable should not be forced within Rebel lines when an exchange was in place.[14] This was a tall order for prison commandants, as Stanton charged prison officials with oath-takers' protection and gave officials the power to separate the sheep from the goats.

This power challenged prison officials and perplexed Hoffman in two scenarios that Camp Douglas commandant Col. Joseph Tucker raised the next month. On July 10, Tucker sent Hoffman a multifaceted inquiry, revealing much about the Federal government's responsibility to those who desired to reclaim citizenship through the oath. First, Tucker asked whether prisoners of war "whose term of life is evidently short" may be released on parole, on the oath, or on any other terms. Tucker essentially requested that Union prison officials, on behalf of the Federal government, have the power to judge life and death, and offer the oath—and consequent freedom—to inmates in critical condition. But regaining faithful citizens was not the sole motivation. Releasing ill inmates was also practical. If sick prisoners were freed, prison officials would not have to care for them, leaving the reclaimed citizens to fend for themselves and relieving Federal authorities from expense.[15]

Tucker's second request proved more problematic. He asked Hoffman if inmates who proved they were forced into the Rebel service and desired to take the oath and give bonds could be released. Here, the burden of proof rested on the inmates, but Tucker's inquiry, pending Hoffman's assent, would have prison officials play judge and jury for a man's intentions.[16] This contentious issue frequently aroused suspicion from prison commandants and exposed Hoffman's anxiety in welcoming repentant men back into the Union fold.

Federal officials were often leery about the intentions of oath-taking prisoners who wanted to join the Union army, but former Confederates saw the oath and voluntary military service as keys to citizenship. As they recognized, military service was a defining feature of citizenship. In July 1862, inmate Joseph Lamb claimed he was forced into Confederate service and petitioned Camp Chase commandant Col. C. W. B. Allison for the oath. Closing his petition, Lamb swore himself willing and anxious to take the oath and "to enlist and fight in the Federal Army till the last gun is fired if I should live or the rebellion is put down." Lamb acknowledged the oath as his ticket back into the polity and offered military service as proof of loyalty.[17] Federal commandants and Colonel Hoffman knew that military service was expected of citizens, but deciding who should receive the potentially deadly privilege was complicated.

During the Civil War, individual Federal officials determined who among the Rebels sought reclamation, judged the worthiness of candidates, and decided what rights and privileges, if any, oath-takers should have. In so doing, Federal officials facilitated the process of national reunification within the context of imprisonment, while simultaneously depriving the Confederacy of manpower and citizens.

The Naturalization Act of 1795 may have guided Federal officials' judgment of foreign prisoners who sought the oath. This act established precedents for admitting foreigners to the United States, allowing any free white alien to claim citizenship if he took an oath of allegiance, renounced prior allegiances, and was never "convicted" of joining the British Army during the Revolution—suggesting that individuals forced into enemy service were eligible for US citizenship.[18] W. F. Lynch, commanding Camp Butler outside of Springfield, Illinois, and its quartermaster George Swain, both sent numerous petitions through the Department of the Ohio to Hoffman proclaiming the loyalty of foreign inmates. Swain, on February 4, 1863, stated that many Confederate conscripts were Irish, German, and Polish. Union forces captured these unwilling draftees after their first engagement at Arkansas Post. Swain thought these immigrants had a strong case for taking the oath since many went south from Illinois solely for employment and still had relatives in loyal states. Swain contended that the men should join the Union army since they, "but for the misfortune of locality," would be in the loyal ranks. Maj. Gen. H. G. Wright responded that POWs generally could not receive discharge on the oath, but acknowledged the "peculiar" nature of this case since the foreigners' compulsory service resulted from a quest for work.[19] Swain and Wright may have also believed that the immigrants belonged in the North, especially given southerners' aversion towards ethnic diversity.[20]

This issue plagued Hoffman and General-in-Chief Henry Halleck as they waffled about whether or not enemy deserters and POWs should don blue uniforms. On February 18, 1863, Hoffman, on behalf of Halleck, ordered Brig. Gen. Jacob Ammen, commanding Camp Douglas, and commanders of "all other important posts" to release Confederate inmates whose sincerity was ascertained upon taking the oath. But there was a caveat—Hoffman directed commanders to explain that the oath made men "liable to be called on for military service as any other loyal man."[21] Here, Halleck and Hoffman supported turning grey-backs into bluecoats and alerted oath-takers that their decision carried responsibility.

Perhaps this dictate affirmed military service as an obligation of US citizenship and, by extension, intended to discourage oath-takers from

deserting Union ranks and rejoining Confederate forces, since violating
the oath meant death if caught. Ultimately, however, Union officials determined that admitting oath-takers into the army was too risky. Almost
immediately after Hoffman affirmed military service as a civic duty,
Secretary Stanton forced him to backtrack. On February 19, Hoffman received a request from Col. Charles Thielman, Sixteenth Illinois Cavalry,
asking that German inmates at Camps Butler and Douglas be permitted
to take the oath and join his regiment since they were Confederate conscripts. It took only a week for Stanton to countermand Halleck's February 18 directive. On February 25, Stanton ordered Hoffman to forbid
enlisting any POW even if he had taken the oath.[22]

Judging from the conflicting dictates of Halleck and Stanton, there
was no consistent Federal policy on deserters taking the oath and joining
US ranks. The Union certainly benefited from more loyalists, but Federal
authorities remained unsure of what to do with prodigal sons. Hoffman,
the conduit for commands from superiors, had his own views, which
he articulated to Stanton on March 24, 1863, regarding Confederate deserters held at Washington, DC's Old Capitol Prison. Hoffman noted that
Washington's provost marshal frequently released oath-taking Confederate deserters into the city, and Hoffman contended that it was not worth
the "trouble and expense" of sending them further north since their
desertion "guarantee[d] that they will not return to the rebel army."[23]
Hoffman's words indicate his belief that deserters would make loyal
citizens by default—execution awaited them if they went south.

Hoffman was naïve about deserters' intentions, and later the same
year he recognized that motives were difficult, if not impossible, to pinpoint. Former Confederate soldiers turned captives could not only feign
loyalty to the United States, but could also pretend that they never intended to be enemy combatants. Hoffman understood that, according to
the laws of war, prisoners could attempt escape, either by scaling walls,
digging tunnels, or putting on a charade.[24] The latter option perhaps
carried the least risk, and Hoffman knew this. On May 11, 1863, he directed Gen. John S. Mason, commanding Columbus, Ohio, to release all
oath-taking Rebel deserters from Camp Chase. But Hoffman cautioned
that many prisoners would "doubtless endeavor to claim to be deserters
with a view of escaping confinement"—a marked shift from his March
letter to Stanton. Hoffman therefore ordered Mason to make "careful
inquiry in each case" to differentiate honest from duplicitous deserters.[25]
In so doing, Hoffman again conferred upon individual Federal agents

the power to judge personal allegiance. These agents, along with the inmates whom they evaluated, knew that this was a grave matter since violation of the oath was grounds for execution.

Brig. Gen. Gilman Marston, commander of Point Lookout, shared Hoffman's mistrust. In October 1863, Marston informed Hoffman that his evaluation of inmates who desired exchange revealed some who wished to remain within Union lines and others who wanted to take the oath and join the US Army or Navy. But Marston had no doubt that many, if allowed the oath, would "find their way into the rebel army."[26] Personal motives drove oath-takers, and no US official could control men once released, but Federals could restrain subversive behavior by keeping reclaimed citizens in prison.

Many southern POWs maintained fidelity to the Confederacy, believed it the correct interpretation of American citizenship, and denounced oath-taking comrades as treasonous. Their threats towards comrades who preferred US allegiance forced Federal officials to be careful about when they administered the oath and necessitated that officials seques-ter reclaimed citizens, illustrating that Rebels wielded considerable power and shaped the obligations that citizenship conferred upon Fed-eral prison officials.

Immediately after the Dix-Hill Cartel became effective in late July 1862, Federal officials knew that they would face the challenge of pro-tecting oath-takers from unreconstructed Rebels who wanted exchange to rejoin the Confederate army. Union officials did not recognize the legitimacy of the Confederate government, but southern politicians cer-tainly did, and Union officials confronted this reality through prisoner exchanges.[27] On July 31, 1862, Adj. Gen. Lorenzo Thomas wrote to Secre-tary Stanton from Fort Delaware, and alerted Stanton that 3,000 Rebels wanted exchange and 301 desired the oath. The lopsided total forced Thomas to separate loyalists from unrepentant Rebels since a number of prospective oath-takers insisted that they "would be shot if exchanged."[28] Threats from comrades and the existence of the Confederate state left these reclaimed southern loyalists in limbo. They clamored for Fed-eral protection since taking the US oath constituted treason against the Confederacy, a fledgling nation that, from inmates' perspective, looked legitimate as it mustered an army, sent men into battle, and negotiated prisoner exchanges.[29]

Similar dynamics plagued Union officials at Camp Chase, Johnson's Island, Camp Douglas, and Old Capitol Prison where they confronted the question of whether exchange or administration of the oath should come first. On August 24, 1862, Hoffman directed Camp Chase commandant Col. C. W. B. Allison that POWs who chose the oath over exchange should be "detained at the camp" and "after the disposition of the others" could pledge allegiance. In his instructions to Johnson's Island and Camp Douglas, Hoffman purposefully ordered exchange before the oath, demonstrating that Union officials controlled the exchange process but nonetheless had to recognize the power of Confederate ideology.[30]

This problem persisted into the summer of 1863, judging from circumstances at Old Capitol Prison. In mid-June, Hoffman complained to Stanton that oath-takers were in a precarious position since they incurred the enmity of loyal Rebel prisoners. The passion of unrepentant Rebels would certainly "jeopardize" loyalists' lives if they were exchanged together. The best remedy, in Hoffman's view, was to send Union proponents to Philadelphia, where they could safely take the oath and go free upon pledging not to go south of Philadelphia during the war unless serving the United States.[31] This allowed the Federal government to indirectly protect reclaimed citizens in Union territory while at the same time precluding duplicitous oath-takers from rejoining Confederate ranks.

After prisoner exchanges collapsed in late July 1863, there was no guarantee that Federal officials would release oath-takers. General Orders № 286 standardized the requirements for administering the oath, but the order also highlighted inconsistencies in Federal policy governing the release of POWs. Thenceforth, the Commissary General of Prisoners, in conjunction with the exchange commissioner, would judge the worthiness of release petitions. Rebel inmates could no longer receive discharge on mere desire to take the oath. Instead, would-be oath-takers had to prove that they were pressed into the Rebel service, or could plead extreme youth followed by "open and declared repentance." The order mandated that candidates take the oath "without qualification" and understand that in no case did it carry "an exemption from any of the duties of a citizen."[32] The order's impact was multifaceted: first, it again entrusted questions of allegiance to a very select few individuals. Petitioners had to advance a compelling case while the Commissary General and exchange commissioner interpreted the plea according to their subjective definitions of repentance and loyalty. The order also intended to clarify policy, but instead created confusion as it reintroduced the possibility that oath-takers could enter the Union army and remained vague about whether oath-takers could be released from prison. Finally, the order highlighted the obligations of citizenship achieved through allegiance: if emancipated, reclaimed citizens had to prove loyalty, but if they were incarcerated, Union officials assumed the burden of protection.

In 1864 and 1865, a paradox surrounded the oath: more Confederate inmates desired it, but loyal inmates became more vehement about threatening oath-takers, an indication of the power of Confederate ideology. Tensions ran high at Johnson's Island in January 1864. Union officials were responsible for maintaining humane prison conditions, but this became especially difficult when solicitations for loyalty divided inmates. Lt. Col. William S. Pierson noted that many inmates vocalized their willingness to reclaim US allegiance and consequently elicited the ire of fellow inmates. "Many of these prisoners are very much afraid of secret assassination," Pierson cried. He nervously contended that the military rank of the imprisoned Confederate officers inspired a deadly tension that required "great moral courage" to combat. The events of January 8 shaped Pierson's views—prison guards stood in line of battle ready to shoot prisoners who pelted, with snowballs and rocks, a French inmate who desired the oath. Consequently, Pierson recognized that "moral courage" was actually prison officials' obligation to protect reclaimed citizens, and he urged construction of separate barracks for oath-takers.[33]

Pierson's request indicates that he thought oath-takers sincere and that US officials had a responsibility to shield their reclaimed sons from harm. I. C. Bassett, colonel of the 82nd Pennsylvania located at the Sandusky Depot of Prisoners of War, notified Hoffman of Pierson's concerns, many of which he shared. Bassett echoed Pierson's call for a separate enclosure, concurring that prospective oath-takers were "roughly used and their lives threatened" by Confederate loyalists.[34] This anecdote reveals how imprisonment shaped the duties of citizenship. All male citizens were required to give their lives for the nation in the ranks, and this obligation spilled over into prisons, creating a situation where repentant US citizens risked their lives not on the battlefield, but by publicly pledging loyalty in prison.

A few weeks later, on February 15, 1864, Hoffman communicated Secretary Stanton's decision, which may be read in two ways. Stanton recognized that oath-takers were threatened, but refused to remove them to another prison where they would face less risk. He instead vowed to protect them on site, leaving Johnson's Island's officers to fulfill the Federal government's responsibility to protect citizens. Stanton welcomed the reclaimed citizens, but clearly wanted oath-takers to sweat their decision, a reprimand for choosing the wrong side initially. He forbade the construction of separate barracks for Union loyalists, but sanctioned moving them to barracks nearest the guard-house "where protection could more readily be extended to them."[35] This decision elicited mixed reviews: oath-takers appreciated it, but nonetheless feared for their lives, braving snowballs, rocks, death threats, and derision as they marched publicly from prison blocks to protected quarters.[36]

Stanton's directive polarized inmates, and his decision to keep repentant men in prison illustrates how war shaped Federal officials' views on class and citizenship. As previously noted, Union authorities, at various points during the war, permitted Confederate deserters and foreign soldiers—conscripts, normally from the lower classes—to take the oath. Similarly, some prison commanders, like Camp Douglas commandant Jacob Ammen—argued for releasing poor inmates based on their strong Union professions.[37] Johnson's Island inmates, however, were different since they were primarily upper-class Confederate officers.

Federal officials' belief in the ability of lower-class Confederates to make good US citizens exceeded their trust of officers who led the rebellion. Government policy regarding the oath sometimes freed lower-class inmates, alerting them that they could be called to serve in the Union army, a responsibility of citizenship. By contrast, officers remained incarcerated, and the government protected them within the prison—a slight improvement from their original situation as enemy POWs. This action stood class bias on its head as Union officials trusted the usually suspect lower classes, but scrutinized the upper class, a stance that guided the release of Confederate POWs in the summer of 1865 and later found its way into the Fourteenth Amendment, which barred Confederate politicians and officers from office-holding.[38]

Federals' trust of repentant Confederates varied throughout the war, as did both the willingness of southern inmates to take the oath and the responses that the decision elicited from the southern press, inmates' family members, and inmates themselves. Union supporters, like P. E. O'Connor, lieutenant and adjutant of the 10th Veteran Reserve Corps, realized that some prisoners—even family members—exercised deceit in clamoring for the oath to gain liberty. In January 1865, O'Connor petitioned Commissary General Hoffman to release his relative, John Brusnan, from Elmira Prison. Brusnan swore that he joined the Rebel ranks "for want of forethought" and repeatedly attempted desertion.

O'Connor was convinced and thought Brusnan a good candidate for the oath until he discovered a subversive letter from Brusnan to his sister. Brusnan thanked his sister for sending desperately needed money for food and reasserted that he "would never take the oath . . . if not starved to do it." Brusnan's reassertion suggests that his sister thought the oath reprehensible, indicating that inmates' relatives supported the Confederate cause despite imprisonment's trials. Unsurprisingly, O'Connor found this turncoat reprehensible and labeled Brusnan an "incorrigible and ungrateful rebel" who, for the remainder of confinement, deserved a bread and water diet used to punish common criminals.[39] Brusnan's loyalty in December 1864, when the Confederate experiment tottered on the brink of defeat, represents the vehemence with which many southerners proclaimed the right of their cause and the importance of preserving personal honor by seeing it through to the end.

Throughout the war, many southern journalists shared this view that the Confederacy was the only correct version of America. Southern journalists influenced civilians' concept of Confederate citizenship through stories in which POWs, despite dire circumstances, emphatically rejected the US oath. These papers imagined a populace loyal to the Confederate experiment even beyond war's end.[40] In January 1862, the *Richmond Dispatch* proudly proclaimed that 161 Confederate officers and men at Camp Chase "indignantly rejected" prison officials' proposition to gain liberty through the oath.[41] Their rejection indicates that loyalty and, by extension, citizenship sometimes necessitated stoic endurance of imprisonment's physical and mental agony. The *Memphis Daily Appeal* similarly noted how Capt. Andrew Mitchell got permission to visit Johnson's Island and rallied inmates against Military Governor Andrew Johnson's efforts to entice Tennessee inmates to take the oath. "Boys, it won't do!" Mitchell bellowed, "I have been an everlasting Democrat—aye, a Johnson Democrat—but we are now Southern men, and if Jefferson Davis falls, we must fall with him!"[42] Press coverage of Mitchell's appeal taught that true southern citizens willingly subordinated individual allegiance to national allegiance, a shift from antebellum days.

Loyalty to the Confederacy also required rejection of the Federal government and defiance of its officials. While this made for good press, it incurred risk for inmates. The New Orleans *Times Picayune* boasted that not a single Texas inmate at Johnson's Island took the oath in March 1865, a time when the Confederate cause desperately needed encouragement. Journalists further contended that suffering imprisonment bolstered inmates' commitment to Confederate citizenship. "The men on the island are better rebels than when they entered the pen," the paper noted, "and are openly defiant of the Yankee Government."[43] At this and other points in the war, southern inmates realized that they could defend their cause by defying Union prison officials. Rebels' family members also understood this. One loyal Unionist refused to send clothing to his brother, an inmate at Old Capitol Prison, since he believed it would "only aid and abet the unholy cause in which you have been engaged." Instead, the Unionist urged his brother to take the oath to atone for sins against God and the United States.[44]

Stories of inmates' devotion to the Confederacy were grounded in the reality that many POWs preferred Confederate citizenship despite incarceration or captors' physical threats. Union prison officials, however, believed that they could treat Confederate prisoners as conquered subjects who, out of degradation, would reclaim US loyalty.[45] Southern journalists suspected that Federal officials manipulated these power dynamics and published stories of Yankee cruelty to highlight the South's moral superiority. After prisoner exchanges began in June 1862, the *Memphis Daily Appeal* reported an exchanged Camp Chase prisoner's claim that prison officials required every man to return a ballot stating whether they desired exchange or the US oath, thenceforth pledging to behave "as good and loyal citizens." The *Appeal* decried this Yankee ploy to "slink the plain requirements of the cartel" as a "specimen of the insidious attempts resorted to defeat the object of the mutual agreement."[46]

Southerners believed in the Confederate government's sovereignty, which enabled negotiations with foreign powers. Conversely, Federal officials believed that the Confederate cause was a rebellion, that the Federal government retained sovereignty over southerners, and that they could hold secessionists accountable for treason.[47] Union officials therefore thought they could press Confederate inmates to take the oath. Federal authorities assumed that imprisonment would reform inmates, making them receptive to the oath, which would spare them from capital punishment. The Special Commission which was convened to judge Johnson's Island inmate Nathan Bernard, who violated parole, uttered treasonable language, and proclaimed he would rather fight for Jeff Davis than for Lincoln, firmly believed in imprisonment's reformatory power. The commission released Bernard, hoping that his two-year term had a salutary effect on him, and that "with the checks of the oath of allegiance upon his conscience, and a penal bond upon his pocket . . . he may be safely discharged."[48]

When inmates did not voluntarily reform, Federal officials either bribed them to take the oath or used a heavy had to convince them to do so, indicating the power Union officers wielded over enemy prisoners. Prison officials used their position to determine the benefits of citizenship and entice POWs to profess loyalty. If inmates remained loyal to the Confederacy, they sat idle, clamoring for physical activity and better nourishment. By contrast, if a POW swore allegiance to the United States, he could join "galvanized" regiments to fight Indians out west, receive better rations, and/or perform prison labor.[49] The first option represented the reclaimed citizen's obligation to the state, while the latter two evinced the reciprocal relationship of citizenship: US officials offered better rations as incentive and as testament to the government's responsibility to protect citizens, while prison labor was the reclaimed citizen's service to the state. Prison officials also protected loyalists from traitors while at work—they closely supervised oath-takers who constructed a fence at Camp Chase and a barracks at Elmira and, at Johnson's Island, strengthened prison walls and dug drainage ditches.

In the former two cases, Federal officials outright privileged oath-takers with work. At Johnson's Island, however, officials let inmates begin work and then made continuance contingent upon taking the oath, leaving Confederate prisoners to decide between southern loyalty, which would leave them idle and ill-fed, and Union citizenship, which would relieve doldrums and ensure full rations. Johnson's Island inmate W. H. Duff proudly noted that all men in his company refused the oath, but some "razorbacks" renounced the Confederacy since it could not immediately improve their quality of life.[50]

If improved conditions did not inspire Confederate inmates to respect Federal power, Union officials, according to POWs, intentionally diminished inmates' living standards. Southerners may have embellished threats, but since imprisonment enabled Union officials to monopolize force, the allegations could have been true to the letter.[51] Joseph Barbiere, an inmate at both Camp Chase and Johnson's Island, recounted that Union authorities at every large prison used systematic cruelty to force the oath upon inmates and, "in the case of their refusal . . . enfeebl[ed] their health to such an extent as to render them unfit for military service on their return to the South."[52] In February 1865, the

Richmond Examiner likewise reported that Camp Chase authorities used "the vilest deception" and "sometimes actual violence to induce or constrain our prisoners to take the oath." Confederate inmates could not opt for exchange in 1865, which, according to the paper, "left them in a lurch" without any way out of prison. One of the three hundred inmates courted refused the oath, and Yankee officials put him in irons for the war's remainder.[53] Federal officials thus demonstrated that refusing citizenship invited negative repercussions, since they held the keys to citizenship in prison.

Despite the dire circumstances in which Confederate inmates found themselves, some ardently rejected the Federals' unrelenting, sometimes cruel, solicitation of the oath. In March 1864, Camp Chase inmate James Hilliard Polk recounted how Yankee requests persisted until inmates' dying moments, but failed to persuade one man on his deathbed to reject Confederate citizenship. When the Federal provost marshal visited the prison hospital and offered a mortally ill POW the oath, the inmate revived at the thought of forswearing allegiance. He cursed the Yankee "from the bottom of his soul" and immediately died yet a Confederate citizen, a small victory for the South.[54] Joseph Barbiere recounted a similar situation at Johnson's Island. He cursed Yankee authorities for denying a dying inmate the privilege of seeing his mother, a courtesy afforded to common criminals. The man could have seen his mother, who traveled a thousand miles, if he had taken the oath. But, Barbiere concluded, Federal officials routinely "out-Herod Herod." The inmate died in good conscience, however, sacrificing the "sweetest feeling of his heart rather than take the oath" and commit treason against the Confederacy.[55]

This was not the only harsh treatment apparent at Johnson's Island. In January 1865, inmate Virgil Murphey condemned the Yankee practice of offering the oath and protecting reclaimed citizens, whom he satirically labeled "galvanized gentry." Confederate inmates understood that their government could not protect its citizens in enemy hands. The US government, however, through prison officials, could, and this enraged Confederates. Murphey's January 21, 1865, diary entry included a copy of Special Orders № 20, which reserved prison Blocks One and Two for oath-takers. Union officers afforded the newfound loyalists better quarters and additional rations, but Murphey proclaimed that he would "rather be a yellow dog and owned by a fine negro than to abandon his country, his honor, stain his character, soil his reputation and craven like crawl up and perjure his soul by taking the amnesty oath." By 1865,

it was unlikely that the Confederate government could punish its soldiers for taking the US oath, but the immorality of perjury and treason
was enough to persuade some Confederate inmates to remain loyal. This
guilt-inspired decision indicates that Confederate ideology yet wielded
enough power to compel some individuals to remain loyal despite political and military weakness. The continued strength of southern ideology
forced Federal officials to sequester oath-takers lest they risk a human-
itarian crisis.[56]

Confederate inmates who rejected the oath had to affront prison officials and, in some cases, concerned family members. Southern POWs
knew that, as citizens, life was the greatest sacrifice they could make
for their country, and some, like Johnson's Island inmate William Starr
Basinger, willingly suffered imprisonment and risked death even after
the cause was lost. Come May 1865, Basinger knew that voluntarily taking
the oath could expedite release, and so did his mother. She accepted the
Confederacy's end and urged Basinger to do whatever necessary, including taking the US oath, to get home quickly. He, however, refused, stating
that he would rather wait than sacrifice honor and duty, since taking the
oath would be "worse than imprisonment or even death."[57]

Some inmates desperately clung to the idea of the Confederacy, but
others begged family members or Union officials to get them the opportunity to take the oath as soon as possible. These men reveal that loyalty
to self and family reigned supreme for many southerners. During the
war, professing loyalty to and serving the Confederacy seemed the best
methods to protect home and family. But once imprisoned, southern
POWs realized that Confederate citizenship meant nothing and they
would have to reclaim US allegiance to return to their dear families. The
conscious ability of some inmates to take the oath depended upon family
members' approval. Old Capitol Prison inmate John Overton Collins
tried to persuade his wife to come north, suggesting that if she did, he
could take the oath and they could be together. The oath, however, was
so controversial that Collins never specifically mentioned it. Rather, he
told his wife to give him some "signal that I may know of your approval,"
urged her to keep the issue private if she disapproved, and instructed
her to tell his father to trust his honor if she consented. Collins closed
hoping that she would not "think hard" of him and urged her to "destroy"
the letter after reading it.[58] Collins was desperate for release through the
oath, though he did not express it in so many words. Johnson's Island
inmate Alfred E. Bell faced a similar predicament. He considered tak-

ing the oath in March 1864 but first sought his wife's approval, asking whether she thought he should wait. Collins's fate is unknown, but exchange spared Bell's honor.[59]

Imprisonment refocused the attention of southern men back on their individual lives and families even though miles lay between home and prison. Southern prisoners' primary loyalty was to home, not to a new nation born of "necessity" to protect slavery, which disrupted their personal lives by requiring military service. Idleness in prison stirred comforting thoughts of home, inspiring in prisoners a willingness, and often desperation, to do anything to get back alive. This led many POWs to voluntarily seek, even vehemently demand, an opportunity to take the US oath. Some men may have viewed the oath as a profession of loyalty to the old, abstract government. But the US government, given prisoners' circumstances, could free them and the dissolving Confederate state could not.

In September 1864 Johnson's Island inmate T. F. Bartlett sent an anxious plea for the oath to Commandant Hill, rejecting exchange since he feared being pressed into Confederate service. Southerners were not the only people Bartlett feared. He wanted to go to California for "fear of being killed" since he worried that his northern friends would scoff at his abandonment of the Rebel army.[60] Bartlett's case indicates that even though oath-takers regained US citizenship, they would not necessarily fit seamlessly back into the polity.

Perceived peer pressure drove Bartlett west, while imprisonment drove Johnson's Island inmate Theodore P. Hamlin to the brink of insanity as he directed his father on how to secure his release. In January 1865, Hamlin begged his father to hurry attempts to get him the oath, instructing him to petition for parole if the former failed. Hamlin understood the gravity of both, but correspondence indicates that his father lacked faith in his son's ability to honor either pledge. Hamlin therefore painstakingly assured his father that such worries were unfounded. "I would rather have my head severed from my body than to be guilty of such an act," Hamlin cried, indicating that he would not violate his oath. Still, neither the oath nor parole came, and Hamlin's directives to his father grew more frantic, urging him to contact the assistant agent of exchange and enlist influential friends to travel to Washington to plead his case.[61] He understood that individual Union officials would have to play judge and jury of his sincerity for him to go free.

Pleas to Union officials poured in after the war as Confederate inmates tired of imprisonment and knew their national experiment was dead. Despite this, postwar pleas indicate that POWs had to demonstrate they would pose no threat to the United States if released, a precursor to the obligations of citizenship that they were about to assume. In June 1865, Johnson's Island inmate W. R. Smith wrote to Andrew Johnson that he joined the Confederate army in a "misguided hour," desired full restoration of forfeited citizenship rights, and pledged thenceforth to behave as a "loyal and peaceable citizen," showing "gratitude to that Government whose magnanimity has been extended to me."[62] The same month, inmate Wyatt M. Elliot enlisted the help of his long-lost friend, Col. E. C. Carrington, US district attorney in Washington, DC, begging the privilege of the oath. Elliot contended that his past record and "General character," to which prominent Whigs like John Minor Botts could attest, indicated that he would "keep it faithfully."[63] Loyalty and US citizenship thus required subservience absent the inherent subordination that Rebel inmates assumed as prisoners.

Elliot used political clout to argue for the oath, but some men, like William H. Young, contended they were powerless and would not threaten the Union. Young's June 27, 1865, application to Attorney General James Speed stated that he was a "young man of no political influence" who was "drawn into the whirlpool of secession by surrounding circumstances."[64] This plea echoes the notion that Confederates of lower sociopolitical standing would make good US citizens since they could not, or purportedly would not, again commit treason or likewise encourage others.

Evacuating prisons at war's end was no easy task. Most Confederate POWs wanted to go home but some remained in denial. The *New York Times* reported on April 15, 1865, that Johnson's Island's authorities announced recent Union victories, eliciting cheers from loyalists in Block One. They raised the Old Flag while "regular secesh hissed it." Secessionists may have wanted freedom, but would not go without an ideological fight. The *Cincinnati Enquirer* reported similar dynamics at Camp Chase on May 27, 1865, noting that 3,400 POWs remained in prison. Of these, fourteen "obstreperous 'cusses'" refused the oath, earning stays at Forts Delaware and Lafayette. Release bled into June and the *New York Times* reported Illinois governor Richard Oglesby's attempt to rally inmates to take the oath. When Oglesby asked if inmates would reclaim US citizenship and "be good boys again," the answer was an emphatic "Yes, sir!" These respondents, unlike stubborn comrades, reclaimed loyalty to the United States.[65]

Before the war ended, 32,000 Confederate prisoners took the oath, leaving 48,400 unreconstructed prisoners in Union hands at the end of May 1865.[66] Judging from the evidence presented, most POWs who took the oath did so because of compulsion that resulted from individual relationships either with themselves, their family, or Union officials. For some inmates, the drive was personal, stemming from a desire to improve their conditions in prison, hopefully get home, or keep from going insane. Others responded, out of necessity or fear, to Federal officials' power, which strengthened as the Confederacy declined. Union officials held the keys to the oath, and through its administration compelled Confederates to change from prisoners into citizens.

NOTES

1. Albert Vickers to Col. Hill, July 13, 1864, Albert T. Vickers, *Compiled Service Records of Confederate Soldiers who Served in Organizations from the State of Alabama*, RG109, M311, National Archives and Records Administration (hereafter NARA), www.fold3.com, accessed July 19, 2013.

2. Drew Faust contends Confederate ideology attempted to make "class interest synonymous with national interest," but that the upper class had to accommodate nonslaveholders' interests. Drew Gilpin Faust, *The Creation of Confederate Nationalism: Ideology and Identity in the Civil War South* (Baton Rouge: Louisiana State University Press, 1988), 16; James H. Kettner, *The Development of American Citizenship* (Chapel Hill: University of North Carolina Press, 1978), 208–9; Alexander D. Brown, *The Galvanized Yankees* (Urbana: University of Illinois Press, 1963), 60; Emory Thomas, *The Confederacy as a Revolutionary Experience* (Columbia: University of South Carolina Press, 1991), 7; Melinda Lawson, *Patriot Fires: Forging a New American Nationalism in the Civil War North* (Lawrence: University Press of Kansas, 2002), 68, 77; William A. Blair, *With Malice Toward Some: Treason and Loyalty in the Civil War Era* (Chapel Hill: University of North Carolina Press, 2014), 67, 88.

3. Paul C. Nagel, *One Nation Indivisible: The Union in American Thought* (New York: Oxford University Press, 1970), 23; Kettner, *American Citizenship*, 334.

4. Harold M. Hyman, *To Try Men's Souls: Loyalty Tests in American History* (Berkeley: University of California Press, 1960), 61; Lucius Wedge, "'I am a citizen of Heaven!': William H. Wharton, Andrew Johnson, and Citizenship in Occupied Nashville," and Jonathan Berkey, "Swallowing the Oath: The Battle over Citizenship in Occupied Winchester," in Paul Quigley, ed., *The Civil War and the Transformation of American Citizenship* (Baton Rouge: Louisiana State University Press, 2018); Anne S. Rubin, *A Shattered Nation: The Rise and Fall of the Confederacy, 1861–1868* (Chapel Hill: University of North Carolina Press, 2005), 86, 95.

5. Hyman, *Loyalty Tests*, 199.

6. Paul Quigley highlights scholars' recent focus on citizenship's fluidity and how ordinary men and women shaped citizenship. Paul Quigley, "Civil War Conscription and the International Boundaries of Citizenship," *Journal of the Civil War Era* 4, no. 3 (September 2014): 375.

7. Glenn Robbins notes that scholars pay little attention to inmates' political affiliation and changing ideology. Glenn M. Robbins, "Race, Repatriation, and Galvanized Rebels: Union Prisoners and the Exchange Question in Deep South Prison Camps," *Civil War History* 73, no. 2 (2007): 118.

8. Nagel, *One Nation Indivisible*, 69; Kettner, *American Citizenship*, 174–75, 208. George Rable contends that southern republicanism involved fear of political power and passion for individual, state, and sectional independence. George C. Rable, *The Confederate Republic: A Revolution Against Politics* (Chapel Hill: University of North Carolina Press, 1994), 15.

9. Special Orders № 170, October 12, 1861, in *The War of the Rebellion: A Compilation of the Official Records of the Union and Confederate Armies* (hereafter *O.R.*), 128 vols. (Washington, DC: Government Printing Office, 1880–1901), ser. 2, 3:51–52; Archibald McFadyen Papers, 1862–1865, Southern Historical Collection, The Wilson Library, University of North Carolina at Chapel Hill (hereafter UNC).

10. John Martin Davis Jr. and George B. Tremmel, *Parole, Pardon, Pass, and Amnesty Documents of the Civil War: An Illustrated History* (Jefferson, NC: McFarland, 2014), 11.

11. *Santa Cruz Weekly Sentinel* (Santa Cruz, CA), June 13, 1862, 1.

12. General Orders № 107, August 15, 1862, *O.R.*, ser. 2, 4:393. Judge Advocate General Joseph Holt declared the oath void if inmates took it under pressure, especially from questionable imprisonment. Joseph Holt to Secretary of War, May 2, 1863, *O.R.*, ser. 2, 5:546.

13. Capt. H. W. Freedley to Hoffman, August 16, 1862, and Hoffman to Freedley, August 18, 1862, *O.R.*, ser. 2, 4:401, 407. Emphasis mine.

14. C. P. Wolcott to Col. Richard Owen, June 21, 1862, *O.R.*, ser. 2, 4:48.

15. Point Lookout commandant James Barnes contended that releasing physically disabled inmates would relieve considerable expense. James Barnes to Hoffman, May 16, 1865, *O.R.*, ser. 2, 8:557.

16. Joseph H. Tucker to Col. W. Hoffman, *O.R.*, ser. 2, 4:166–67.

17. Statement of Joseph Lamb, July 14, 1862, *O.R.*, ser. 2, 4:217–19.

18. United States Congress, "An Act to Establish an Uniform Rule of Naturalization; and to Repeal the Act Heretofore Passed on that Subject," January 29, 1795, www.mountvernon.org/educational-resources/primary-sources/naturalization-acts-of-1790-and-1795/, accessed March 18, 2015. Residency requirements and years' notice required to renounce prior citizenship became significant issues as a result of the Quasi-War with France under the presidential administration of John Adams. The Naturalization Act of June 18, 1798, raised the residency requirement from five to fourteen years, but the residency requirement was again reduced to five years under the Naturalization Act of April 14, 1802. The Act of January 29, 1795, repealed the 1790 Act and required a declaration of intention to seek citizenship at least three years prior to naturalization. The Act of May 26, 1824, reduced the declaration period from three to two years, and this Act would have been on the books at the outbreak of the Civil War. The Naturalization Act of 1795 was the last to comment specifically on whether or how enemy soldiers could become US citizens. US Citizenship and Immigration Services, Legislation from 1790 to 1900, www.nps.gov/elis/learn/education/upload/Legislation-1790-1900.pdf, accessed March 5, 2016.

19. George Swain, Lieutenant and Quartermaster 58th Illinois Regiment, Memorandum February 3, 1863; H. G. Wright to Headquarters Department of the Ohio, February 7, 1863. W. F. Lynch, Col. 58th Illinois, Camp Butler noted he was "satisfied" of the foreigners' truthfulness. W. F. Lynch to Hoffman February 5, 1863, *O.R.* ser. 2, 5:240–41, 243.

20. Merle Curti notes that few immigrants went south, southerners rejected the melting pot idea, and immigrants could prove loyalty through willingness to serve in the Union army. Merle Curti, *The Roots of American Loyalty* (New York: Columbia University Press, 1946), 72, 84.

21. Officers were excluded. W. Hoffman to Brig. Gen. Jacob Ammen, February 18, 1863, *O.R.,* ser. 2, 5:281.

22. Chr. Thieleman to Hoffman, February 19, 1863; Hoffman to Thieleman, February 25, 1863. Assistant Secretary of War P. H. Watson also communicated the ban on Confederate POWs joining the Union army. Watson to Col. W. H. Ludlow, April 7, 1863, *O.R.,* ser. 2, 5:287, 297, 446.

23. Hoffman to Stanton, March 24, 1863, *O.R.,* ser. 2, 5:390–91.

24. *General Orders No. 100*, Art. 77, April 24, 1863, avalon.law.yale.edu/19th_century/lieber.asp#sec3, accessed March 19, 2015.

25. Hoffman to Brig. Gen John S. Mason, May 11, 1863, *O.R.,* ser. 2, 5:593. In April, Hoffman noted that deserters could not be considered POWs and should take the oath, under penalty of death for violation, to prove loyalty. Hoffman to Col. Henry Dent, April 11, 1863, *O.R.,* ser. 2, 5:465.

26. G. Marston to Hoffman, October 7, 1863, *O.R.,* ser. 2, 6:356–57.

27. George Rable notes that the Montgomery delegates created a "powerful and sovereign nation." Rable, *Confederate Republic*, 56.

28. L. Thomas to Hon. Edwin M. Stanton, July 31, 1862, *O.R.,* ser. 2, 4:314.

29. The Confederacy defined treason as "levying war against . . . or adhering to their enemies, giving them aid and comfort." Constitution of the Confederate States, Article III, Sec. 3 (1), avalon.law.yale.edu/19th_century/csa_csa.asp#a3, accessed March 19, 2015.

30. Hoffman to Col. C. W. B. Allison, August 24, 1862; Hoffman to Major W. S. Pierson, August 26, 1862; Hoffman to Col. J. H. Tucker, August 28, 1862, *O.R.,* ser. 2, 4:428–429; 435–436; 458–459.

31. Hoffman to Stanton, June 13, 1863, *O.R.,* ser. 2, 6:14.

32. General Orders № 286, August 17, 1863, *O.R.,* ser. 2, 6:212. Prior to codification, Hoffman communicated this to Ft. Delaware, the Dept. of the Missouri, and Murfreesboro, Tennessee. Hoffman to Brig. Gen. A. Schoepf, August 4, 1863; Hoffman to Maj. Gen. J. M. Schofield, August 5, 1863; Hoffman to Maj. Gen. W. S. Rosecrans, August 7, 1863, *O.R.,* ser. 2, 6:175, 178, 186.

33. Wm. S. Pierson to Col. I. C. Bassett, January 26, 1864, *O.R.,* ser. 2, 6:903; diary, January 8, 1864, Robert Bingham Papers, UNC.

34. First Indorsement, I. C. Bassett, January 28, 1864, *O.R.,* ser. 2, 6:903.

35. Hoffman to Brig. Gen. H. D. Terry, February 15, 1864, *O.R.,* ser. 2, 6:954; Hoffman to Col. C. W. Hill, September 12, 1864, *O.R.,* ser. 2, 7:811. Fort Delaware and Rock Island also had separate quarters for oath-takers. Lonnie R. Speer, *Portals to Hell: Military Prisons of the Civil War* (Mechanicsburg, PA: Stackpole Books, 1997), 176, 220.

36. Diary, January 8, 1864, Bingham Papers, UNC; diary, January 30, 1865, Virgil S. Murphey Diary, UNC.

37. Mark Neely notes that conscription made the Confederate cause a rich man's war and poor man's fight, and that foreigners faced great risk of being conscripted. Mark E. Neely Jr., *Southern Rights: Political Prisoners and the Myth of Confederate Constitutionalism* (Charlottesville: University Press of Virginia, 1999), 75, 148–49. For more on conscription and class bias, see Rable, *Confederate Republic*, 155–56; J. Ammen to Hoffman, January 31, 1863, *O.R.*, ser. 2, 5:230.

38. The War Department ordered all POWs below the rank of colonel released upon taking the oath. War Dept., Adjutant General's Office: General Orders № 85, May 8, 1865, *O.R.*, ser. 2, 8:538. Release of POWs below captain: Executive Order: General Orders № 109, June 6, 1865, www.presidency.ucsb.edu/ws/index.php?pid=72212, accessed March 22, 2015.

39. P. W. O'Connor to Major Blagden, January 10, 1865; John Brusnan to Sister, December 30, 1864, *O.R.*, ser. 2, 8:52–53.

40. Benedict Anderson contends that print capitalism enabled people to think about themselves and relate to others in new ways. Benedict Anderson, *Imagined Communities: Reflections on the Origin and Spread of Nationalism*, rev. ed. (London: Verso, 1983), 36. For information on the southern press's influence, see Harrison A. Trexler, "The Davis Administration and the Richmond Press, 1861–1865," *The Journal of Southern History* 16, no. 2 (May 1950): 177–95; J. Cutler Andrews, "The Confederate Press and Public Morale," *The Journal of Southern History* 32, no. 4 (November 1966): 445–65; Ted Tunnel, "A Patriotic Press: Virginia's Confederate Newspapers, 1861–1865," in *Virginia at War: 1864*, ed. William C. Davis and James I. Robertson (Lexington: University Press of Kentucky, 2009), 35–50.

41. "Confederate Prisoners," *The Daily Dispatch* (Richmond), January 27, 1862.

42. Reprinted from the *Vicksburg Whig*. "From Tennessee," *Memphis Daily Appeal,* September 6, 1862, 1.

43. *Times Picayune* (New Orleans), March 12, 1865, 8.

44. "A Loyal Letter," *National Republican* (Washington, DC), June 4, 1863, 2.

45. *Calvin's Case* (1608) shaped seventeenth- and eighteenth-century treason laws, establishing that the conqueror's power over the conquered demanded allegiance. This describes Federal officials' beliefs about Confederate POWs. Kettner, *American Citizenship*, 50, 192.

46. "The Oath of Allegiance—Bad Faith of the Yankees," *Memphis Daily Appeal,* September 19, 1862, 2.

47. The US government employed a mix of belligerent and sovereign rights in dealing with the Confederacy. According to Stephen C. Neff, "Sovereign rights and powers are applied to citizens of the law-making power . . . whereas belligerent rights and powers are invoked against enemy nationals." Throughout the war, the Federal government reserved the right to prosecute leaders of the rebellion for criminal offenses once hostilities ceased. Stephen C. Neff, *Justice in Blue and Gray: A Legal History of the Civil War* (Cambridge, MA: Harvard University Press, 2010), 4–5, 215.

48. Nathan Bernard, *Papers of and Relating to Military and Civilian Personnel, compiled 1874–1899*, RG 109, M347, NARA, www.fold3.com, accessed August 20, 2013.

49. Galvanized Yankees fought on the frontier between September 1864 and November 1866. Brown, *Galvanized Yankees*, 1–2. Ohio's governor authorized a battalion of Rebel prisoners in late June 1863; see *White Cloud Kansas Chief* (White Cloud, KS), July 2, 1863, 2.

50. Hoffman to Col. W. P. Richardson, August 14, 1864; W. P. Richardson to Hoffman, October 31, 1864; Hoffman to Col. B. F. Tracy, October 3, 1864, *O.R.*, ser. 2, 7:591, 1069,

918–19; W. H. Duff, *Six Months of Prison Life at Camp Chase, Ohio,* 3d printing (Clearwater, SC: Eastern Digital Resources, 2004), 31.

51. Building on Norbert Elias's theory in *The Civilizing Process,* Pieter Spierenburg attributes the rise of the prison in the 1820s to state formation and monopolization of violence. This phenomenon continued with the establishment of Civil War military prisons. Pieter Spierenburg, "From Amsterdam to Auburn: An Explanation for the Rise of the Prison in Seventeenth-Century Holland and Nineteenth-Century America," *Journal of Social History* 20, no. 3 (Spring 1987): 456. Commenting on Elias, Jonathan Fletcher notes that the monopoly on violence is not absolute, but dependent on practical concerns of surveillance and enforcement. This describes the relationship between inmates and guards in Union prisons. Jonathan Fletcher, *Violence and Civilization: An Introduction to the Work of Norbert Elias* (Cambridge, MA: Polity, 1997), 35.

52. Joseph Barbiere, *Scraps from the Prison Table: At Camp Chase & Johnson's Island* (Doylestown, PA: W. W. H. Davis, 1868), 287–88.

53. Reprinted from the *Richmond Examiner,* February 22, 1865, in "Stories from Camp Chase," *Cincinnati Enquirer,* March 1, 1865, 1.

54. Diary, March 18, 1864, in James Hilliard Polk Papers, Folder 2, UNC.

55. Barbiere, *Scraps,* 83.

56. Entries January 30, 1865, January 21, 1865, and February 1, 1865, Murphey Diary, UNC.

57. Wm. S. Basinger to Mother, May 21, 1865, June 11, 1865, and June 16, 1865, William Starr Basinger Papers, UNC.

58. John Overton Collins to Wife, October 27, 1863, John Overton Collins Papers, 1857–1865, Virginia Historical Society, Richmond, Virginia.

59. Diaries March 7 and 9, 1864, Alfred E. Bell Papers, 1861–1865, Western Reserve Historical Society, Cleveland, Ohio.

60. T. F. Bartlett, *Papers of and Relating to Military and Civilian Personnel, compiled 1874–1899,* RG 109, M347, NARA, www.fold3.com, accessed August 24, 2013.

61. Diaries, January 11, January 30, and March 1, 1865, Theodore P. Hamlin Papers, UNC.

62. W. R. Smith, *Amnesty Papers, compiled 1865–1867,* RG 94, M1003, NARA, www.fold3.com, accessed July 20, 2013.

63. Wyatt M. Elliott, *Amnesty Papers, compiled 1865–1867,* RG 94, M1003, NARA, www.fold3.com, accessed July 16, 2013.

64. William H. Young, *Amnesty Papers, compiled 1865–1867,* RG 94, M1003, NARA, www.fold3.com, accessed July 19, 2013.

65. Reprinted from the *Sandusky Register* in *New York Times,* April 15, 1865, 4; "Camp Chase Items," *Cincinnati Enquirer,* May 27, 1865, 1; "News of the Day," *New York Times,* June 9, 1865, 4.

66. Davis and Tremmel, *Parole, Pardon,* 92; Speer, *Portals to Hell,* 289.

"I Am a Citizen of Heaven!"

William H. Wharton, Andrew Johnson, and Citizenship in Occupied Nashville

LUCIUS WEDGE

On June 28, 1862, William Wharton, the serving chaplain at the Tennessee State Penitentiary, awaited an audience with Governor Andrew Johnson. Governor was a new title to Johnson, who had been a senator from Tennessee for the previous five years. When in early 1862 the Union conquered much of central and western Tennessee, Secretary of War Edwin Stanton, presumably with Lincoln's knowledge and consent, tapped Johnson to serve as military governor.[1] While Wharton waited, a group of five ministers met with Johnson and refused to take an oath of loyalty. They offered a range of reasons for this refusal, but in Johnson's eyes their explanations did not excuse the refusal. They were arrested and sent to the state penitentiary.

Wharton began his interview with Johnson as soon as the ministers had been ushered out and handed over to the provost marshal. The interview was direct and to the point. Johnson explained that the US government needed to "know its friends and put down its enemies." He accused Wharton of being hostile to the US government. Wharton responded that he was loyal and obedient first to Tennessee, and as such he was content to live under whichever government might gain authority over Tennessee in the current conflict. Wharton went farther, however, by explaining, "I am a citizen of a higher government than that." Johnson asked which government, and Wharton replied emphatically, "I am a citizen of Heaven!"

While this declaration did not improve the cordiality of the interview, it does offer a unique window into how loyalty and citizenship were

understood and transformed during the Civil War. Both Johnson and
Wharton understood that a relationship existed between Christianity
and the government of the United States, but they arrived at this conclusion from opposing assumptions. Johnson understood democracy as
practiced in the United States to derive from and to realize the promise
of the gospel. As such Johnson viewed secession as heresy, and the loyalty oath as the creed of the patriotic faithful. Any citizen who was not
ideologically aligned with the Confederacy would readily ascribe to the
loyalty oath.[2] Meanwhile, Wharton understood Christianity as a subject
beyond temporal loyalties; regardless of the government in power, as a
chaplain and minister of the gospel, he held a position beyond patriotism and national citizenship. While Wharton maintained that his duty
was loyalty directed toward the "government in power," this meant that
Wharton could not in good conscience ascribe to the loyalty oath.[3] If the
Confederacy regained control of Nashville or of Wharton himself, he
could not hold to his oath and his obligation to the prevailing civil authority simultaneously. Good conscience dictated that Wharton should
remain beyond the political struggle.

The opposing backgrounds from which Wharton and Johnson approached their meeting informed how they attempted to use citizenship
and its associated rights. Fundamentally, neither man approached citizenship from a legal perspective. Both looked at the issue in terms of
social and cultural meaning. This approach was necessary since neither
individual was a legal scholar. They informed their understanding of citizenship from their backgrounds; Johnson, as a politician, understood
citizenship to be a first membership. You were a member of the nation
first and built other identities from that starting place. For Johnson citizenship meant American democracy, and from this foundation Johnson
built his broader identity as a southerner, a plebeian, and a Christian.
This construction was not unique to Johnson, and helped the significant
portions of Americans who participated in the creation of midcentury
civic religion understand the cornerstones of that creed.[4] Midcentury
civic religion asserted that American democracy stood as the realization
of Christian ideals. Wharton, in contrast, approached the creation of
identity from a different view. He asserted Christianity first, and added
identities from that starting point. This again was not a unique approach
to self-definition or citizenship, and during the normal life of the United
States the differences in these approaches would amount to the obvious
differences in occupation, with little perceptible difference in actual at-

titudes or opinions. The Civil War forced both men into an antagonistic confrontation and required them to articulate the implications of their identities. Defining the limits and reach of citizenship was the vocabulary they used for this conversation.

If the dispute between Wharton and Johnson involved only a matter of political philosophy, perhaps greater forbearance could have prevailed. However, Johnson had not randomly selected Wharton for the loyalty oath. While Johnson freely demanded the oath of various residents of Nashville and Tennessee, he tended to use it as a specially targeted means of indicting civilians sympathetic to the rebellion. He had, for example, required the oath of the mayor and city councilors of Nashville. This policy extended, where required, to citizens who seemed particularly rebellious. Johnson's opinion was that any citizen should be willing to freely ascribe the oath at any time, and as such the oath could be used to determine, if not true citizenship, then at least loyalty. A group of twelve men in Rutherford County were required to take the oath and offer bond after a spate of "unlawful acts, said to have been committed, by residents of our town, against officers and soldiers of the Federal army stationed at Murfreesboro."[5] Samuel Baldwin, one of the ministers arrested for refusing the oath just prior to Wharton's disastrous interview, had been asked to swear his allegiance as a consequence of a sermon he had recently preached. Before a congregation dominated by Union soldiers, Baldwin chose to deliver what must have been a rather uncomfortable sermon on the 38th and 39th chapters of Ezekiel. The Union soldiers engaged in conquering and occupying the upper South could not help but notice the relevance of the text to their situation. Ezekiel prophesied, "Thus says the Lord God: I am against you, O Gog, chief prince of Me'shech and Tu'bal! I will turn you up from the remotest parts of the north and lead you against the mountains of Israel. I will strike your bow out of your left hand and will make your arrows drop out of your right hand. You shall fall upon the mountains of Israel, you and all your troops and the peoples that are with you; I will give you to birds of prey of every kind and to the wild animals to be devoured." The two chapters graphically describe the invasion of Israel by the heathen armies and peoples of the north until God, in his ultimate judgment, utterly laid waste to the invaders, disposing of their bodies by burning them on a pyre of their own discarded weapons. Andrew Johnson very quickly required Baldwin to ascribe to the oath.

While Wharton had not attempted to prophesy the divine destruction

of Union invaders, he had issued a report as chaplain of the state penitentiary under the Confederate governor that he would need to answer
for. In the report Wharton observed that he had

> witnessed with much satisfaction the cheerful alacrity and diligence with
> which the prisoners (in the penitentiary) have labored for the state in the
> last few months, in preparing the materials of war, to which they were
> stimulated by a most commendable and patriotic ardor; they have labored
> faithfully for their country, and many of them young men placed in con-
> finement for minor offences, might be judiciously selected as objects of
> Executive clemency, who would endeavor to atone for the misdeeds of the
> past with acts of bravery and heroism on the battle-field.[6]

Johnson, armed with a copy of this report, demanded Wharton explain the proposition that criminals be turned loose from prison in order to bolster the rebellion. The *Nashville Union,* the paper that printed
the transcript of the chaplain's report, thought it more likely that the
release of prisoners had been the idea of Isham Harris, the Confederate governor. But for Johnson the originator of the chaplain's report
mattered much less than the ability to use the loyalty oath as a win-
nowing fork to divine the loyal from the traitor.[7] Wharton replied that
self-defense in response to the invasion of the north had motivated his
report. For Wharton it seems that the report was an example of defending Tennessee rather than acting as a traitor to the United States. The
thin distinction between the two allowed Wharton to imagine his actions
as moral, while still leaving open the option of remaining a loyal citizen
of whatever nation won the conflict. This fundamentally pragmatic approach failed to impress Andrew Johnson.

Johnson already understood the loyalty oath to be a useful means
of determining loyal citizens, but his conviction in applying the oath
seems to go beyond the relatively straightforward necessities of his office. Johnson appears to have accepted the oath as a tool that could
easily uncover the secreted traitors now occupied by the Union. Oddly,
few historians have been interested in the wartime experiences or policies of Johnson. The most notable examination of the northern loyalty
oath, by Harold Hyman, offered a scant two pages on Johnson's use of
the oath despite remarking that the book would be deficient without the
inclusion of Johnson. The inclusion offers no insight into Johnson or
his particular use of the oath. Hyman was, by far, more concerned with
the use of the oath in the North rather than in the occupied South, a

position that seems apt for a McCarthy-era historian. Unfortunately, recent biographers of Johnson have yet to amend the error. Paul Bergeron includes the use of the oath in his narrative of Johnson's wartime experience, but does little to attach the usage to the importance of the practice on a national or cultural stage. William Blair, by contrast, examines the intricacies of Union occupation policy as it developed through the course of the war. Blair's corrective is useful, but limited in its impact. Blair recognizes the importance of several issues inherent to Civil War occupations. The most notable of these was the use of the loyalty oath as a tool to coax an unwilling civilian population into cooperation. Blair effectively links the use of the loyalty oath to the distribution of supplies from the provost marshals in the occupied South. Unfortunately, Blair offers remarkably little consideration of the quasi-military figures, like Johnson, who employed loyalty oaths as coercive patriotism.[8]

Johnson fervently used the oath to advance Union policy, but in doing so he exercised his own unique understanding of American Christianity, namely, that a correct understanding of Christianity required American democracy. Johnson has never been understood as a particularly religious figure.[9] Fortunately, after Johnson's 1844 congressional campaign he felt compelled to address his faith—and left valuable evidence of his religious thinking. Johnson ran against William G. Brownlow, a Methodist minister from East Tennessee. Johnson had made him a political enemy when as a state legislator Johnson blocked a measure to open legislative sessions with a prayer. The action also allowed Brownlow to accuse Johnson of being "an Infidel, and a secret enemy to the Christian religion."[10] After Johnson's victory he published an extended account of the charges against him, and of his defense against them. Johnson began with a constitutional argument citing the clause restricting any religious test from being administered to candidates for office. He also complained that a politician who is overly religious could be charged with politically expedient false devotion as easily as a politician who did not regularly attend church could be charged with atheism. Having made these protestations, Johnson continued on to exclaim:

> THAT THE CHARGE OF INFIDELITY, AS PREFERRED AGAINST ME IN THE LATE CANVASS, IS UTTERLYAND ABSOLUTELY FALSE FROM BEGINNING TO END; AND THAT, SO FAR AS THE DOCTRINES OF THE BIBLE ARE CONCERNED, OR THE GREAT SCHEME OF SALVATION, AS FOUNDED , TAUGHT, AND PRACTISED BY JESUS CHRIST HIMSELF, I NEVER DID ENTERTAIN A SOLITARY DOUBT[.]

This profession of faith could easily answer Johnson's critics and put the matter to rest, but Johnson had more to say on the topic and continued his confession.

> A belief in the pure and unadulterated principles of Democracy, is a belief in the religion of our savior, as laid down while here upon earth himself—rewarding the virtuous and meritorious without any regard to station, to wealth, or distinction of birth. One of the principal tenets laid down in the great scheme of regenerating man, is Democracy in its purity—that is to say, the just and pure in heart are to be rewarded in heaven with crowns of glory, while the unjust and vile sinner is to be punished in a hell "where the worm dieth not and the fire is never quenched," each rewarded according to their merits or demerits, upon their own individual responsibility. My religious creed first, my Democracy next; they are one and inseparably connected. God and my country first—God and my country last.[11]

From this vantage point, Johnson understood his entire career in politics, and the very essence of citizenship in a democratic republic, as tantamount to religious creed. Johnson connected several important ideas in these declarations. Most prominently, he attached citizenship and democracy to Christianity, but equally important he connected the idea of merit and classlessness to the essence of both Christian doctrine and democratic values.

The connection between the state and the Christian faith was not unique to Johnson. A substantial number of citizens throughout the nation arrived at the same conclusion by the beginning of the war. This provided the undergirding of the civic religion that emerged through the prosecution of the conflict. In the South the connection emerged with deep roots in Christian millennialism. This helped white southerners understand and cope with numerical inferiority, increasing privations, and the astronomical human toll of the conflict. The creation of civic religion was not limited to the South, and became an equally important tool in the northern arsenal as the war continued. In both sections, civic religion did not spring forth fully formed as an accident of the war. Rather, civic religion developed as a part of the antebellum understanding of the nature of the United States as part of the world and God's plan for humanity. Johnson's understanding of Christianity and democracy's intrinsic linkages would have been both comprehensible and laudable to his East Tennessee constituency in the 1840s. Moreover, Johnson's understanding of meritocracy being wrapped into both Christianity and the fabric of America would be popular among residents of East Tennessee. The experience of the frontier was familiar enough for meritocracy to be a popular concept, and the soil and climate of East Tennessee did not support a planter class.[12]

These connections proved exceedingly important as Johnson approached the political conflicts of the antebellum period that culminated in the crisis of secession. On topics ranging from the Homestead Act to the Compromise of 1850 and the place of slavery in the American republic, Johnson approached the issues from the perspective that Christianity and democracy rewarded the meritorious regardless of the will or opposition of the wealthy or aristocratic elements of society. The Homestead Act became a proposal invested with the "special Providence" of God and the sweat equity of a republic.[13] Johnson's emphasis on merit through his early political career can partly explain why he broke with the leaders of the South and Tennessee when it came to secession. Johnson viewed secession as a betrayal of the nation and God promulgated by the elite planter class, a group who never quite fit into Johnson's understanding of the divine purpose of America. Where the Homestead Act served to promote the purpose of America in promoting meritocratic labor, the Compromise of 1850 became a chance for the nation to bind itself together through mutual sacrifice.

> We all belong to the same great American family; we all profess to be attached to the Constitution of the country, that Constitution which has been established by our forefathers. Then, in the spirit of the provisions of that instrument, we ought all to come forward and cooperate in erecting an altar to our common country, upon which each of us, whether from the North, the South, the East, or the West, may sacrifice something to preserve the harmony that has heretofore existed between the extremes of this Union.[14]

Johnson understood the supreme significance of these debates for the nation, and to the degree that anyone could, Johnson understood that the peril of the republic hinged on the resolution of the debates over slavery and the common opportunity of citizens in America. Rather than simply wrapping a political point in a vaguely religious image, Johnson recognized, along with some of his contemporaries, that the questions of slavery and the resolution of the Mexican war represented an existential threat to the nation. This is clear by the ongoing protestation in Johnson's speeches over the Wilmot proviso, and the continuing problem of slavery.

In conclusion, I will only say, as relates to this negro question that I trust
and hope in God's name—and I hope there is no irreverence in making
this appeal, which I do with all solemnity, for, if I know myself, and the
deep interest which I as well as others around me have in the welfare of
our country and the harmonious working of our institutions—I trust and
hope that the Whigs and Democrats, the reflecting, the patriotic, the in-
telligent of both parties will look to the extent, to the length, and breadth,
and height of this momentous question. I trust that looking to the amount
of public prosperity and tranquility and happiness, as well as to the great
value of property, which are all involved in the adjustment of our present
difficulty, they will be brought to feel that the preservation of this Union
ought to be the object which is paramount to all other considerations.[15]

By establishing that the issue of slavery, in general, and the Mexican
War Cessations, in particular, represented a threat to the Union, Johnson manages some fairly remarkable assertions. The assertion is rooted
in Johnson's understanding that the political state is a holy creation.
Membership in this union served as the paramount concern, and provided protections to its citizens. Johnson conceived citizenship less as
a legal status than as an earned social privilege through participation
in building American democracy.

The largest crisis Johnson faced was the sundering of the Union.
Considering Johnson's statements in favor of maintaining the nation,
the crisis offered not only a political, but a moral obstacle. Johnson
responded to the impending crisis late in 1860 by chastising those who
threatened and desired secession. On December 18 and 19, 1860, he
spoke to the Senate, arguing that South Carolina and the other states
threatening secession did so from outside the protections of the Constitution, and thus from an untenable and immoral position. More than
simply appealing to those threatening secession, Johnson took pains,
over the course of the two days he spoke, to detail the illegality of secession as proposed by southern states. He argued that for the severance
of a state from the Union to be legal it required the approval of not
only the given state, but also the rest of the Union. He continued this
critique of secession to consider the merits of any state being able to
simply withdraw from the Union. By examining the compact theory of
government on which the nullification crisis and secession had their
intellectual foundation, Johnson concluded that no provision was made
for withdrawal.[16]

Johnson shifted his attack to criticize the South for appearing to prefer rule by a slave-owning oligarchy to the more egalitarian forms of democracy. This attack was not out of place for Johnson because he had long criticized the dominance of slaveholders and their seeming attempts to gain a disproportionate influence in the South.[17] Additionally, the outsized position of slave-holding in the South flew in the face of Johnson's civic religion, which instead of wealth placed value on merit and virtue regardless of class or birth. Johnson ended his prolonged recitation with both a statement of faith and a threat.

> I have an abiding faith, I have an unshakable confidence in man's capability to govern himself. I will not give up this Government that is now called an experiment, which some are prepared to abandon for a constitutional monarchy. No; I intend to stand by it, and entreat every man throughout the nation who is a patriot, and who has seen, and is compelled to admit, the success of this great experiment, to come forward, not in haste, not in precipitancy, but in deliberation, in full view of all that is before us, in the spirit of brotherly love and fraternal affection, and rally around the altar of our common country, and lay the Constitution upon it as our last libation, and swear by our God, and all that is sacred and holy, that the Constitution shall be saved, and the Union preserved.[18]

Johnson's last thought was to the impending conflict if secession persisted. He wanted the government to have the power not to force action from the states, or compel specific behavior; but instead to enforce existing law within the states. Short of this, Johnson saw civil conflict on the horizon and pledged to secessionists, in the words of an Irish patriot addressing the British, "I will dispute every inch of ground; I will burn every blade of grass; and the last intrenchment of freedom shall be my grave."[19] Johnson's rhetoric sounds closer to the pro-secessionist argument than the typical northern efforts at conciliation. Rather than accepting the grounds that the South acts to protect their rights, Johnson points out and argues in this speech that the best means of protecting the rights of the South is to maintain the constitution as a document that inherently accepts southern opinion on slavery.[20] The use of freedom as a trope provided Johnson the opportunity to intellectually and rhetorically claim patriotism, the favor of God, and the high ground. This trope would not be lost on the burgeoning Confederate nationalists; they used the same language to assert the validity and correctness of their actions.

Johnson had made his decision regarding secession, and he would not have to wait long to discover the attitudes of southerners toward his decision.

It was against this background that Johnson interrogated Wharton on June 28, 1862. Wharton had a very different understanding of his citizenship and how he came to be seated before the military governor, as his responses to Johnson's questions demonstrated. In response to Johnson's interrogatory concerning Wharton's chaplain's report, he ascribed his motivations in presenting the recommendation to the necessities of self-defense. Johnson retorted by reminding Wharton that South Carolina fired on Fort Sumter, and that the Confederacy first violated Kentucky's neutrality. Wharton responded, "I don't wish to argue the case with you, Governor. My mission is to preach Christ. I am no politician and submit to whatever government may get the power." Johnson continued to attack Wharton, but in Johnson's retort the attack moved quickly from sectional and political matters to theological issues. "Do you pretend that your gospel is confined to the limits of your Southern Confederacy? I always thought its precepts of love and charity were co-extensive with the world."[21] Johnson very carefully managed two actions with this statement. First, he deprived Wharton of US citizenship; Wharton, at best, was a citizen of the foreign Southern Confederacy. In supporting the regime of Isham Harris, Wharton had surrendered his social status of citizen of the United States. Further, in so far as Wharton declared himself to be a "citizen of heaven," Johnson moved the terms of the crime committed to a moral rather than criminal action. In reality, it is difficult to define Wharton's action as being fundamentally criminal. Having expressed an opinion in a state report, Wharton had no further power to enact policy. A case could be made that floating the idea represented a form of aid to an enemy of the United States, and as a result the action was treasonous. However, as substantial portions of the nation were simultaneously under arms to militarily divide the nation, this instance of treason seems like the least of the problems confronting Johnson and the nation at large.[22]

Johnson and Wharton approached this confrontation from fundamentally different perspectives. Many of Johnson's contemporaries would recognize his conjunction of the political state and the religious world. In his speeches and public statements the references to God blend seamlessly with political positions in a form recognizable to most of his contemporaries. The consequences of building civic religion with the American State as the centerpiece are made clear in this encounter. Johnson approached the conversation from a perspective that required political allegiance prior to any other consideration. Wharton understood his Christian faith to be his primary consideration, with adjustments for political realities a decided afterthought. Approaching this encounter from differing starting points, Johnson could easily employ his civic religion to justify and require the arrest of Wharton. In claiming religious rather than political citizenship, Wharton lost hold of the arguments Johnson might have responded to.

William Henry Wharton had never been particularly invested in political discourse. He descended from a family of means. His ancestors had been English gentry, and moved to Culpepper County, Virginia prior to the Revolution. They established their roots there, and went on to spawn several generations of professionals. Much of the family, including William Wharton, practiced medicine. He attended the University of Pennsylvania at Philadelphia, and on graduating he moved to the recently founded village of Tuscumbia, Alabama. Here he met and married one of the original inhabitants of the settlement, Priscilla Jane Dickson, in 1823. The young couple would go on to produce seven children, with the oldest eventually going to Philadelphia to study medicine. Wharton spent the next several years running his medical practice as well as a pharmacy in Tuscumbia and Huntsville.[23]

Until 1841, Wharton seems to have concentrated on his medical practice and his family, with very little activity in political or religious life. But at that point he became pastor of "the Christian Church" in Nashville. After the move to Nashville and the death of several family members, Wharton established a normal, uneventful life as the part-time pastor of the "Christian Church" and simultaneously a full-time pharmacist and physician. The church that Wharton led belonged to the still-forming Disciples of Christ. The denomination emerged from the revivalism of the Second Great Awakening as a mixture of several revivalist branches with some substantial Baptist influences. As late as 1849 the various groups were still attempting to develop a national structure to unify the denomination. [24]

Wharton played a role in this unification in the state of Tennessee. He seems to have done so from a position of ecumenicalism rather than an ardent doctrinal stance. Wharton's moderate stance on doctrine also helped him to advise his family members who had moved away, or lived at a distance or in locations that his young national church might not

be able to reach.[25] The limited reach of the Disciples of Christ helped
Wharton to avoid any particular concern with denominational rivalries.
He wrote to one of his daughters at some point after his wife's death to
advise her, "You do as your cousin Susie wants about joining the Episcopal Church—if you can become as good a Christian as she is I know
you will both meet your dear mother again in the 'shinning above.'"[26]
Despite Johnson's charges against Wharton, he seems to have practiced
a genuinely inclusive understanding of the Christian Gospel, and moreover he seems to have had absolutely no interest in playing a role in the
political maneuvers that led to the outbreak of war.[27]

In 1858, Wharton wrote a long letter to his son on a Sunday after-
noon. Wharton had been inspired to compose this missive while preach-
ing at the prison in the morning on the thirteenth chapter of Acts. Much
of the letter, as a result, outlined Wharton's understanding of Christianity. It was within this chapter of Acts that Wharton found the core
of the evangelism of Paul, and by extension the means of continued
evangelism. Wharton sought a more primitive interpretation of the bible. "A person taught only the scripture cannot understand many modern phrases which greatly perplex persons and misleads them when
seeking to be religious—'the new birth' 'change of heart.'"[28] He chastised
those who heard the gospel to accept the veracity of Christ, and confess
their belief without implementing these truths by their own good works
in visiting the poor, sick, and widows to minister to their needs. He
criticized the use of "hope" as something that one could receive in the
present. He stated that instead, hope resided in the future, that it could
not reside in the past or present, and that it required action in the present to achieve hope in the future. Wharton's critique of the antebellum
practice of Christianity emerged from fear over the fate of his son, who
had seemingly begun to doubt the veracity of the gospels. Despite this,
Wharton urged faith on him, and to commit himself to action in that
faith. Wharton argued that the truly telling examples of the spirit in
action did not come from the parables of Jesus, or the words of comfort
in the Psalms, but instead from the genuine examples of the actions of
the spirit recorded in the bible. These records provided the template for
Christian living and evangelism. His letter advocated the forgiveness of
all sins by the merit of Christ's life and sacrifice.[29]

Whereas Johnson heard the Christian message and understood it as
a political message requiring meritocracy and democratic citizenship,
Wharton took the gospel as a guide to social behavior. Neither perspec-

tive was unique. Many ministers throughout the South would welcome Johnson's understanding of political theology, though they would likely disapprove of the ardent belief in Unionism that sprang from that theology in Johnson. Likewise, many politicians would approve of the moral evangelicalism of Wharton, though many would deride the recommendation of arming prisoners. The uniqueness of the exchange between Johnson and Wharton stemmed from the intersection of religious sentiment and political power in this singular moment of decision regarding the rights of a citizen of the United States. Wharton would not have imagined his actions as a minister, even as the minister of the state penitentiary, to be fundamentally political acts. Wharton understood these actions as matters of faith, separate from his political existence as a citizen. His status as a citizen seems to have never entered his mind until the moment when Johnson began his discourse. Johnson, in contrast, understood fully that the political and the religious were linked in the American experience. Thus, a religious action or position that threatened the community was treason equivalent to taking up arms against the government. Citizenship in this moment seems to have been as much a protection of the government as a guarantee of the rights of the individual.

This type of treason happened throughout the war and was regularly punished by Union authorities where they were able to prosecute individuals. Much of the prosecution of traitors could easily be described as a suppression of dissent. In the case of Johnson and Wharton the prosecution of this treason or dissent is a genuinely unique incident. Johnson held authority in Tennessee as the military governor of the state. He, however, commanded no troops and in most ways was not able to express the military authority that backed his position. The military generally understood Johnson as a political figure, yet as a political figure Johnson lacked the authority of an electoral victory. This ambiguity of authority likely is what made Johnson so sensitive to civilian acts of dissent and treason. This ambiguity has also made Johnson a difficult figure to deal with in his historical context. Johnson's wartime experience was quickly overshadowed by his disastrous presidency. Importantly, Johnson approached the problem of occupation differently than his more directly military counterparts. When military leaders occupied territory they could more easily accept lip service oaths from civilians that might be made with practicality rather than patriotism in mind. Johnson, however, needed to establish a longer-term loyal civilian population for the political purpose of restoring Tennessee to a correct relationship with the United States. Anything short of the full-throated support of the civilian population represented a very real threat to that project, especially if it originated from the moral leaders of southern communities.[30]

After Wharton's heated conversation with Johnson, he was arrested and sent into the prison camp system that was developing in the North. He eventually ended up at Camp Chase, Ohio. By October of 1862, US policy encouraged the emptying of POW camps. Despite Johnson's resistance, the political prisoners he had sent north were quickly being paroled, and Lincoln's government was placing pressure on Johnson to expedite the process.[31] Johnson offered Wharton a parole, the terms of which mirrored the loyalty oath Johnson had asked of local clergy in Nashville. The parole required of Wharton that he

> solemnly pledges his honor without any mental reservation or evasion that he will not take up arms against the United States or give aid or comfort or furnish information directly or indirectly to any person or persons belonging to any of the so–styled Confederate States who are now or may be in rebellion against the government of the united states that he will not write or speak against said government and holds himself subject to all the pains and penalties consequent upon a violation of this his solemn parole of honor and that he will report himself to this office within twenty days after his acceptance of this parole when and where terms of his release are to be arranged.[32]

These terms were far from generous, especially for a prisoner who had neither been tried for treason nor ever raised arms against the government of the United States. Wharton's civil liberties would remain dramatically restricted throughout the remainder of the conflict. He continued to make a living as a doctor and preacher, and in 1864 he asked Andrew Johnson for an extension of his parole so he could travel through the lines to deliver the funeral sermon of a close friend elsewhere in Tennessee. Johnson was willing to offer the extension with certain provisions attached. Wharton, however, was unwilling to accept the added restrictions and chose to remain in the city. Wharton explained to the governor that he was unsure how he could "in a funeral sermon 'pledge my honor to protect and defend the constitution and government of the U[nited] States against all enemies whether domestic or foreign."[33] The fundamental misunderstanding that motivated the first disastrous meeting had clearly not faded. Military requirements necessitated the demands placed on Wharton, despite the fact that he had no expectation of exercising anything beyond a religious role. Wharton's rights as a citizen were subsidiary to the necessities of maintaining the war that would restore proper citizenship to the entire Union. Johnson's position on the issue had not fundamentally changed, despite Wharton's passive-aggressive reply. Johnson understood the declaration of loyalty to be a fundamentally innocuous issue. If a man was a loyal citizen, he should have no issue taking the oath of loyalty, which caused no limitations on the individual's rights. Johnson would assume that rather than having to actively preach on the glories of the Constitution at a funeral, Wharton's oath in this instance would simply remind him of his relationship with the government. Wharton, however, seems to have had no room for the state in issues of theology, and rejected out of hand Johnson's fusion of the two.

Wharton remained in Nashville after the war's end, and was able to secure the position of state librarian from the General Assembly of Tennessee in 1870. Wharton remained in this post until his death from a lingering illness the following year.[34] For his part, Johnson ascended to the vice presidency and the presidency in turn as the war drew to a close. As president, Johnson seems to have shed his previous identity as the staunch Unionist in favor of conciliation. This naturally caused continuing convulsions as the nation attempted to resolve the lingering issues of the Civil War. In most estimations Johnson failed to live up to the lofty expectations, and even loftier tasks set before him through the course of Reconstruction. Rather than making treason odious, as he claimed was required early in the war, Johnson pardoned large numbers of traitors and rejected aid to the freedmen and women of the South. Johnson had every reason to look for a quick political solution to the war. While political dissent was treasonous during the war, once hostilities ended the same speech was simply political discourse. Once there was only one government claiming citizens' loyalty, a much greater range of opinions could be permissible. After the war's conclusion, Johnson needed to secure a political resolution to match the military victory. During the war the military could accept thinly veneered loyalty oaths from occupied Confederate civilians; now Johnson could accept the same devotion and call it loyalty instead of treason.

Johnson maintained a consistent intellectual compass for his actions. The war had been treason and apostasy, but not an actual legal division of the nation. Since the nation had not actually divided, its restoration could be effected quickly, and Johnson seems to have found room in his political theology to support forgiveness rather than punishment. In his New York address during the "Swing around the Circle," Johnson rather explicitly explained his position:

> I am not for destroying all men, or condemning to total destruction all men who have erred once in their lives. I believe in the memorable example of Him who came with peace and healing on his wings; and when he descended and found man condemned unto the law, instead of executing it, instead of shedding the blood of the world, he placed himself upon the cross, and died that man might be saved. If I have pardoned many, I trust in God that I have erred on the right side. If I have pardoned many, I believe it is all for the best interests of the country; and so believing and convinced that our southern brethren were giving evidence by their practice and profession that they were repentant, in the imitation of Him of old who died for the preservation of men. I exercised that mercy which I believed to be my duty.[35]

Johnson's missteps on the Swing around the Circle were many, but he provided a good explanation of his actions. If loyal citizens are the only kind who would subscribe in good conscience to the loyalty oath then clearly the South had repented, en masse, their misdeeds during the rebellion. With repentance came forgiveness. Likewise, after Wharton accepted the penitent terms of parole he was free to return to Nashville, and would have had greater freedom had he continued to affirm the loyalty oath in all future wartime encounters. With a return of professed loyalty Johnson accepted the return of citizenship with all its rights and privileges.

Johnson was a politician with many deficiencies, but his fundamental beliefs regarding the loyalty oath remained constant during and after the Civil War. Despite the harsh and potentially extralegal uses to which Johnson put the oath, he nonetheless relied on it as a divination rod in guiding punishment against the traitor while sparing the innocent. William Wharton's experience demonstrates the deficiencies of this policy. While Wharton was not innocent, he was clearly not actively engaged in rebellion. Wharton might easily have passed the war in ignominy had Johnson moderated his attacks, or had Johnson simply fired Wharton as the chaplain of the penitentiary instead of arresting and imprisoning him. Johnson's understanding of politics, however, meant that the immorality of disloyalty necessitated imprisonment. The fusion of

Christian theology with American democracy for Johnson ultimately meant that where punishment once was necessitated, forgiveness could eventually be extended.

Wharton largely resumed his life after the war. He recovered his medical practice and continued tending to his small congregation. Wharton stepped away from his moment as a foil for the political philosophies of Andrew Johnson. Ultimately, he proved no more disloyal than most white southerners, and revealed very little in terms of continued political consciousness. For a singular moment during the war Wharton provided a provocative third path for southern civilians: an attempt to define citizenship not as a political status but instead as a lived cultural expression. Wharton's motivation may have been self-serving—a third path would have saved him considerable turmoil—but it also represented a dangerous problem for the political stability of the United States. During the war any expression of alternative citizenship offered an unacceptable act of treason.

NOTES

1. Andrew Johnson, *The Papers of Andrew Johnson: Volume 5, 1861–1862* (Knoxville: University of Tennessee Press, 1979), 177.

2. This opinion was commonly held among northern officials to the point that they often would intentionally ignore the impact of the oath in communities that might be reoccupied by the Confederacy. If the Confederacy regained control of a community, any residents who had ascribed to the Union oath would face retribution. Harold Melvin Hyman, *Era of the Oath: Northern Loyalty Tests during the Civil War and Reconstruction* (Philadelphia: University of Pennsylvania Press, 1954); William Alan Blair, *With Malice toward Some: Treason and Loyalty in the Civil War Era*, The Littlefield History of the Civil War Era (Chapel Hill: University of North Carolina Press, 2014), 139–42.

3. If the officials governing over occupied territory understood the oath to be a blunt instrument of division into loyal and disloyal, then the occupied citizens understood their positions to be much more tenuous. For many, especially civic leaders, occupation meant finding a way to maneuver between impossibly competing demands. Thus, civic leaders like Wharton attempted to find alternatives to declaring loyalty to one of the rival governments. Mitchell Snay, *Gospel of Disunion: Religion and Separatism in the Antebellum South* (New York: Cambridge University Press, 1993), 186–88; Blair, *With Malice toward Some*, 140; Stephen V. Ash, *When the Yankees Came: Conflict and Chaos in the Occupied South, 1861–1865*, Civil War America (Chapel Hill: University of North Carolina Press, 1995), 89.

4. While civic religion is a useful tool and requires more critical examination to comprehensively explain, this essay only uses it as a tool to contextualize Johnson's approach to religion. For a more in-depth examination of civic religion, see Harry S. Stout's excellent book on the subject, *Upon the Altar of the Nation: A Moral History of the American Civil War* (New York: Viking, 2006).

5. Johnson, *The Papers of Andrew Johnson: Volume 5, 1861–1862*, 410.

6. Ibid., 518.

7. "A Ramble through the Penitentiary—How King Isham Managed His Workshops," *The Nashville Daily Union*, June 28, 1862, chroniclingamerica.loc.gov/lccn/sn83025718/ 1862-06-28/ed-1/seq-2/.

8. Hyman, *Era of the Oath: Northern Loyalty Tests during the Civil War and Reconstruction*; Paul H Bergeron, *Andrew Johnson's Civil War and Reconstruction*, 1st ed. (Knoxville: University of Tennessee Press, 2011); Blair, *With Malice toward Some*.

9. Roughly two pages, out of 377, in the biographical companion to Andrew Johnson, from ABC-CLIO Biographical Companions, comprise the entire historiography related to Johnson's religious belief. Those two pages attribute to Johnson a general belief in god, but offer little further examination. Glenna R. Schroeder-Lein and ABC-CLIO Information Services, *Andrew Johnson: A Biographical Companion*, ABC-CLIO Biographical Companions (Santa Barbara, CA: ABC-CLIO, 2001), 242–44.

10. Brownlow and Johnson had a long and contradictory political relationship. Johnson was a higher-ranking politician than Brownlow, and advanced farther and faster. Brownlow took over the governorship of Tennessee after Johnson ascended to the vice presidency. While both men were struggling for influence in Tennessee, they fought regularly on political and religious issues. One of the more visceral confrontations emerged from the Landmarkist controversy initiated by James R. Graves. Graves brutally assailed Methodism, and Brownlow took up the mantle of defender of the faith. Johnson, either out of doctrinal sympathy or a sense of political advantage, began speaking favorably of a Landmarkist fellow traveler who was heavily cited by Graves. The encounter deepened the animosity between Brownlow and Johnson. For more on these issues, see James Patterson's biography of James R. Graves or Eugene Genovese's article on religious discourse in East Tennessee. Andrew Johnson, *The Papers of Andrew Johnson: Volume 1, 1822–1851*, ed. LeRoy P. Graf and Ralph W. Haskins, vol. 1 (Knoxville: University of Tennessee Press, 1967), 222–23; James A. Patterson, *James Robinson Graves: Staking the Boundaries of Baptist Identity* (Nashville, TN: B&H Publishing Group, 2012); Eugene D. Genovese, "The Dulcet Tones of Christian Disputation in the Democratic Up-Country," *Southern Cultures* 8, no. 4 (November 1, 2002): 56–68.

11. Johnson, *The Papers of Andrew Johnson: Volume 1, 1822–1851*, 240.

12. Stout, *Upon the Altar of the Nation*; Snay, *Gospel of Disunion*; Richard Carwardine, *Evangelicals and Politics in Antebellum America* (New Haven, CT: Yale University Press, 1993); Stephen V. Ash, *Middle Tennessee Society Transformed, 1860–1870: War and Peace in the Upper South* (Baton Rouge: Louisiana State University Press, 1988).

13. Johnson, *The Papers of Andrew Johnson: Volume 1, 1822–1851*, 559.

14. Ibid., 540.

15. Ibid., 551–52.

16. Andrew Johnson, *The Papers of Andrew Johnson: Volume 4, 1860–1861*, ed. LeRoy P. Graf and Ralph W. Haskins, vol. 4 (Knoxville: University of Tennessee Press, 1976), 5, 6–7, 24–25.

17. This critique had come largely in criticizing attempts to reapportion the representation of the state of Tennessee to include the 3/5 clause in determining population. Johnson, coming from the low-slave-holding mountains of East Tennessee, strongly condemned the

idea as a means of diminishing the voice of the common man. The measure would have weighted Tennessee's representation much more toward Central and West Tennessee, areas that produced more cotton, held more slaves, and generally supported measures that had less benefit for the agriculturally and culturally distinct regions of Appalachia. The opposition of Johnson to this reapportionment led his political rivals, particularly William Brownlow, to attack Johnson as an abolitionist. Their attacks were overstated. Johnson, *The Papers of Andrew Johnson: Volume 1, 1822–1851*, 101–4.

18. Johnson, *The Papers of Andrew Johnson: Volume 4, 1860–1861*, 44.

19. Ibid., 45–46.

20. Johnson regularly argued through the 1850s that continuation of the Union was the best option for preserving slavery. In this respect he accepts a mainstream southern argument of the period. After Lincoln's election, maintenance of the existing government falls out of favor with most of those groups replaced by secession. Johnson remains ideologically and intellectually dedicated to the continuation of the government. This makes particular sense given his willingness to attach the consistency of the government to his religious sentiments. Johnson, *The Papers of Andrew Johnson: Volume 1, 1822–1851*; Johnson, *The Papers of Andrew Johnson: Volume 4, 1860–1861*.

21. Johnson, *The Papers of Andrew Johnson: Volume 5, 1861–1862*, 518.

22. Historians have only recently recovered the cultural understanding that the Civil War was fundamentally a religious contest. For many of the participants, the Civil War offered the opportunity to connect the nation (either the Confederacy or the Union) to a deeper divinely ordained cosmic plan. Mitchell Snay and Richard Carwardine provide able demonstrations of the cultural context that informed these connections through the antebellum period. The manifestations of these connections emerge in the willingness of soldiers to brutalize civilian populations and fellow soldiers, as Harry Stout describes in *Upon the Altar of the Nation*, and Mark Noll in *The Civil War as a Theological Crisis*. Moreover the implications of fusing the religious understanding of the nation with the political and legal reality of the United States continued to be a pressing cultural issue throughout Reconstruction, as demonstrated by the work of Charles Regan Wilson and Daniel Stowell. The difficulty with this burgeoning historiography is that while it has begun to draw the clear connections between the practical concerns of the military, the pressing demands of the individual's understanding of prevailing culture, and the haphazard progress of legal fact, as of yet no work has drawn all three topics into a coherent narrative. Stout, *Upon the Altar of the Nation*; George C Rable, *God's Almost Chosen Peoples: A Religious History of the American Civil War* (Chapel Hill: University of North Carolina Press, 2010); Snay, *Gospel of Disunion*; Carwardine, *Evangelicals and Politics in Antebellum America*; Daniel W. Stowell, *Rebuilding Zion: The Religious Reconstruction of the South, 1863–1877* (New York: Oxford University Press, 1998); Charles Reagan Wilson, *Baptized in Blood: The Religion of the Lost Cause, 1865–1920* (Athens: University of Georgia Press, 1980); Mark A. Noll, *The Civil War as a Theological Crisis* (Chapel Hill: University of North Carolina Press, 2006).

23. Frederick Jonas Dreyfus, "The Life and Works of George Michael Wharton, MD (Psuedonym 'Stahl'), 1825–1853," *Tennessee Historical Quaterly* (1947): 316–19; "Death of William H. Wharton," *Republican Banner*, May 9, 1871; T. G. Wharton, "Letter of Judge T. G. Wharton of Miss. to Mrs. Mary W. Bass, Nashville Tenn.," June 27, 1895, Yeatman-Polk Collection, Tennessee State Library and Archives.

24. Frederick Jonas Dreyfus, "The Life and Works of George Michael Wharton," 320–21; "Died," *Republican Banner*, August 10, 1853; "Death of William H. Wharton"; T. G. Wharton, "Letter of Judge T. G. Wharton of Miss. to Mrs. Mary W. Bass, Nashville Tenn."

25. Herman Albert Norton, *Tennessee Christians: A History of the Christian Church (Disciples of Christ) in Tennessee* (Nashville: Reed and Co., 1971), 55, 61, 64–65; Donald G. Mathews, *Religion in the Old South* (Chicago: University of Chicago Press, 1977).

26. William Wharton, "Dear Mary," n.d., Yeatman-Polk Collection, Tennessee State Library and Archives.

27. Norton, *Tennessee Christians*, 74–78.

28. William Wharton, "My Dear Son," April 18, 1858, Yeatman-Polk Collection, Tennessee State Library and Archives.

29. Ibid.

30. Blair's recent work on treason, in particular, would benefit from an examination of the few figures who, like Johnson, were involved with the political occupation of the South. Blair offers a remarkable account of the military prosecution of treason in the Confederate States, but does not provide an examination of the prosecution of treason by the figures who attempted wartime political restoration with rebellious states. Blair, *With Malice toward Some*; Paul H. Bergeron, *Andrew Johnson's Civil War and Reconstruction*, 48–51; Peter Maslowski, *Treason Must Be Made Odious: Military Occupation and Wartime Reconstruction in Nashville, Tennessee, 1862–65*, KTO Studies in American History (Millwood, NY: KTO Press, 1978), 121.

31. Johnson, *The Papers of Andrew Johnson: Volume 5, 1861–1862*, 446.

32. Andrew Johnson, *The Papers of Andrew Johnson: Volume 6, 1862–1863* (Knoxville: University of Tennessee Press, 1983), 21–22.

33. William Wharton, "Wharton to Johnson" (Nashville, TN, July 27, 1864), Johnson Papers, Library of Congress.

34. T. G. Wharton, "Letter of Judge T. G. Wharton of Miss. to Mrs. Mary W. Bass, Nashville Tenn.," 2; "Death of William H. Wharton"; Will Wharton, "My Darling Sister," May 8, 1871, Yeatman-Polk Collection, Tennessee State Library and Archives; "Classified Ads 2—No Title," *Republican Banner*, January 26, 1867; Norton, *Tennessee Christians*, 75–77.

35. Andrew Johnson, *The Papers of Andrew Johnson: Volume 11, August 1866–January 1867*, ed. Paul H Bergeron, vol. 11 (Knoxville: University of Tennessee Press, 1994), 163–64.

FORGING NEW FORMS
OF CITIZENSHIP
AFTER 1865

The "Fire Fiend," Black Firemen, and Citizenship in the Postwar Urban South

CAITLIN VERBOON

At 4 o'clock in the morning on December 12, 1872, a fire alarm shattered the quiet predawn peace of downtown Columbia, South Carolina. Though residents likely found this disruption annoying, unpleasant, and even frightening, they did not find it unusual. Seven years earlier, a huge conflagration coinciding with the departure of Confederate troops and the arrival of Union soldiers had left much of the downtown district in ashes. In the years since the infamous burning, buildings continued to catch fire, and fire remained a real threat to Reconstruction-era Columbia. This alarm actually signaled the third time in only fourteen hours that fire had threatened the lives and property of Columbia residents. This particular early morning fire had broken out in the ruins of St. Peter Catholic Church's vestry room, and upon hearing the signal, the Vigilant Fire Company sped to the church and successfully extinguished the flames.[1]

Columbia in the 1870s was not divided into neat fire districts, nor did it have a comprehensive telegraphic alarm system to alert specific companies to nearby fires. Instead, the city relied on fire alarm bells and the response of as many fire companies as heard the signal. These companies' engine houses tended to cluster in the downtown, densely populated areas, so depending on where the fire broke out, firemen might have a long way to go.[2] Sometimes, even upon hearing the signal, companies could not determine what was on fire, which could lead to a "floundering about in the mud for a time" until they either located the fire or gave up and went home.[3] No matter how experienced and efficient the firemen were, protecting the urban South from fire was an exercise in controlled chaos. The sight of a volunteer company charging down the street at the sound of a bell, often hand-pulling a two-ton engine, was familiar to Columbia's residents.

In fact, most antebellum cities and towns in the United States relied on volunteer fire companies to protect their citizens and property from fire, and these companies were integral to the growth of cities before the Civil War.[4] While large urban centers in the North began professionalizing their forces in the 1850s, medium-sized and growing southern cities like Columbia continued to rely on volunteers well beyond the end of Reconstruction.[5] The amount of municipal oversight varied from city to city, but most cities required the captains of all companies to fill some sort of leadership position in a larger umbrella volunteer department. In Columbia, this was the Board of Fire Masters. While city governments sometimes also provided assistance in purchasing larger, more expensive equipment, volunteers' own dues supported the day-to-day operations and repairs of their engines and engine houses. Because these volunteers were not paid for their fire-extinguishing services, most firemen had day jobs as well. For example, in the mid-1870s, the leadership of Columbia's volunteer forces included bookkeepers, a driver, a cooper, a farmer, a tailor, a carpenter, a state senator, and South Carolina's secretary of state.[6] These men might spend their days in a workshop, in a field, or drafting state legislation, train as firefighters in the evenings, and then be woken at midnight to race to extinguish a dangerous blaze. Volunteering to be a fireman was not something to be taken lightly.

Despite the prevalence and the importance of antebellum volunteer fire companies, in the post-Emancipation South, activities like the Vigilants' routine fire-extinguishing in 1872 took on new significance. The Vigilant volunteer firemen were all black. From the captain, John Dennison, to the ordinary axemen, the Vigilant Fire Company was a black organization by 1872. This in and of itself was not necessarily remarkable; many southern cities had utilized slave and free black labor in antebellum fire companies. The Vigilants themselves may have been black in the 1850s.[7] However, war and emancipation fundamentally changed the context in which these black firemen operated. Without slavery as a legal fact and behavioral guide, independent black service organizations could be parlayed into larger systemic changes. Just as Federal legislation and constitutional amendments affected relationships at the local level, a widening of public engagement at the local level could translate into changes at the state and Federal levels. This jurisdictional migration meant that what might have been seen as a local phenomenon began to be viewed, particularly by white southerners, with a wary eye as to how it might effect systemic change.

Across the South, the number of black firemen increased significantly during Reconstruction. The local Democratic paper in Columbia, the *Daily Phoenix,* attempted to downplay the importance of these black companies by derogatorily referring to their formation as part of an "epidemic" of fire company organization. By using the word *epidemic* to describe the growth of black fire companies, the *Phoenix* characterized them as part of a passing and unwelcome, if not downright dangerous, phenomenon caused by largely uncontrollable external factors. White leaders in Charleston revealed similar yet more openly hostile attitudes towards black fire company organization. In justifying their rejection of a black company's petition to join the volunteer department, the acting fire chief claimed that the department was "already overgrown." "It is deemed inexpedient and detrimental to admit any more companies," he continued.[8] Absolute numbers aside, the 1870s did witness a marked increase in the visibility of black fire companies, as companies such as the Vigilant, the Richmond Fire Company, and the Enterprise Fire Engine Company in Columbia; the Comet in Orangeburg, South Carolina; and the Pioneer Axe Company in Savannah, Georgia, took to the streets and made it impossible for municipal leaders to ignore the role of African Americans in southern cities.

When a Freedmen's Bureau official learned of Charleston's refusal to recognize the black fire company, he urged reconsideration, emphasizing "the importance of interesting colored citizens in measures for the common protection."[9] Despite the official's paternalistic tone, he hit upon a fundamental way that southerners understood citizenship, as a relationship between individuals and a larger collective. He was mistaken, though, in assuming that African Americans needed encouragement to become interested in the common good; their very petition to join the department illustrated they already had a deep interest.

Despite white attempts to downplay their significance, these black firefighting organizations played key roles in the renegotiation of daily life and in the conflicts over freedom, citizenship, and equality in southern cities. Black firemen built on experiences they had gained in antebellum fire companies—after all, associational service and citizenship had long been intertwined—but they realigned the stakes of black firefighting in the South. A newspaper editor in Charleston called firemen an "unsung band of heroes," and characterized them as "the benefactors of their race, in a far truer and more practical sense than your agitators for universal suffrage."[10]

The role of black firemen was indeed profound, as this white observer noted. Black firemen staked a claim to what one might call cultural citizenship. However, the line between their activities and electoral politics was not so sharply defined. Rather, those were two sides of the same coin of meaningful black citizenship. Narrowly defined rights—voting, testifying, sitting on juries, holding elected office—mattered enormously, but so did the unofficial and unprotected practices and customs that shaped southerners' everyday lives. Black firemen helped to mold what postwar society would look like just as surely as jurists or legislators did. Their presence and performance in urban public space defined broad rights they felt they should have, regardless of whether they were guaranteed by law or the Constitution.[11] Paramount among these broad rights were equality and full participation within their urban communities. US citizenship might have been debated and defined at the Federal level, but people experienced it at the level of their overlapping communities, and firemen acted out what citizenship meant on that local, everyday level.

Many white people—southerners and visiting northerners alike—complained that freedpeople only understood the rights side of citizenship. They lamented the sight of people "unemployed and lounging around the streets and corners."[12] But black firemen clearly proved that African Americans not only understood the obligations of citizenship, they actively sought out ways to fulfill them. In congregating and in defending their cities from conflagration, black firemen performed those obligations, and in doing so, both accessed and redefined politicized public spaces in the urban South. White southerners responded to black firemen's presence in urban public space by celebrating the service aspect of their jobs and delegitimizing the more revolutionary implications, especially those that threatened established definitions of citizenship.

CITIZENSHIP AS A CIVIL-SOCIAL CONTRACT

Black firemen recognized their responsibilities as citizens and public servants. These responsibilities went beyond fighting fires. Firemen, both black and white, performed other services when called upon by the city. One such incident took place in the early fall of 1874 in Columbia. For years, the city seasonally suffered from poor water quality and unreliable distribution. Residents' complaints filled local papers. The editor of the *Daily Union Herald,* for example, compared the water to tar in 1871, describing it as "so black and muddy."[13] Two years later, the complaints remained largely the same: "At Mr. Seeger's Grocery," it was reported, "a lot of hair was pulled from the pipes . . . other things taken from several of the pipes are not calculated to make one sing 'the pure sweeter water.'"[14] This dirty water clearly posed a public health risk in terms of sanitation and disease. However, in 1874, Columbian officials realized that the city's water system posed an even greater immediate danger: the water supply and shoddy pipe system might not be adequate to put out a large-scale conflagration. This was no idle fear: their own city had suffered massive fire destruction less than a decade earlier, and Chicago had just been razed by the Great Fire of 1871. "Extensive conflagrations," as one newspaper editor termed them, were more than a remote possibility.[15]

The mayor, therefore, ordered a practical test and public demonstration. In the fall of 1874, the four largest fire companies in Columbia, including two of the black companies, reported to their test locations, attached hoses to their hydrants, and prepared to test the water pressure and supply. When the alarm bells sounded, the Palmetto Company, the Vigilant Company, the Enterprise Company, and the Independent Company all began to pump as much water as possible for the duration of the fifteen-minute exercise. At its termination, the acting chief of the Fire Department concluded that "in the event of a large conflagration," the water "would be exhausted in a day."[16] As the Chicago fire had raged for two full days and was only extinguished by a rainstorm, this water supply was clearly inadequate. Black firemen played an important role in discovering the extent of the water supply problem, and they did so in an official, recognized capacity and on an equal footing with their white counterparts. In a society where the relationship of the state to the people and of white and black people to each other remained in flux, such official service helped to lay the groundwork for blacks' claims as equal members of that society.

It was their work more directly related to combatting fires that made the greatest practical impact on Columbia, however. Black firemen's appearance on the city streets gave meaning to urban freedom. In responding to fire alarms day and night with expensive and complicated machinery, they dramatically challenged assumptions about the nature and appearance of black freedom and right to space. They protected

black and white property. Southerners across the South struggled to rebuild shattered economies during Reconstruction, and urban residents
envisioned their cities as booming modern destinations for businessmen
and tourists alike.[17] In order to fulfill their dreams of urban (re)develop-
ment, residents needed efficient and reliable methods of preventing fire
from destroying their growing cities, and the physical space the firemen
occupied in the city was important.[18] Black firefighters in Wilmington,
North Carolina explicitly tied the city's future to the conditions of the
firehouses, claiming that in their present state they stood "out boldly
as a shame on any city like Wilmington, that pretends to boast of its
might and power and progressive spirit."[19] A city's prospects for future
prosperity could be read in the facades of its firehouses.

   At the same time, black firemen's actions made it clear that they understood citizenship to be part of a reciprocal relationship with the government, in terms of both resources and respect. Slaves had been unable
to demand anything of the government, so the very act of laying claim to
municipal resources became an act of claiming citizenship. They served
their fellow citizens rather than white masters; protection from fire
came at an ideological and a financial price, especially for those white
southerners who resisted accepting their former slaves as fellow citizens.

   For example, in 1870, after acquiring a new engine, the Vigilants
asked the municipal government to provide them with a new engine
house closer to the crowded downtown area. "The present house now
occupied by them is totally unfit for an engine house," Captain Dennison
wrote in what was a common refrain across southern cities during Reconstruction. "Besides, its location is in an isolated part of your city. He
also wrote that "on account of not being in the central part of the city,
we cannot do as we would like."[20] This was a sophisticated petition. On
the one hand, Dennison underscored their independence and financial
responsibility by alluding to the fact that they had recently raised the
money necessary to repair their engine, thereby discouraging criticism
that they were asking for free handouts from an already overburdened
and bankrupt city government. On the other hand, they made a specific
demand of the government in exchange for a service they rendered for
the good of all Columbians. They underscored this by implying that they
wanted to serve the citizens even more comprehensively. Even so, in
demanding resources, black firemen forcibly cast themselves as citizens
and legitimate members of Columbia's civic community.

   In Wilmington, North Carolina, black firemen made the reciprocal nature of citizenship even more explicit. They wrote, "it is a wonder that they even consent to act as firemen, when they have been treated so shamefully." They complained that black companies' engine houses were barely more than "shanties," and asked the city alderman to appropriate funds to repair and enlarge their facilities. "If this is done," they argued, "the citizens will find the colored firemen take a wider and deeper interest in protecting them from fire."[21] In other words, the government owed black firemen respect and better resources in exchange for their continued service in fighting fires. Black firemen thus used their role as official protectors to demand a more equal share of municipal resources.

Black firefighters further underscored their claims to equal status and equal access by acting in cooperation with white fire companies in pressing the city for more resources. In the late 1860s, for example, frequent fires ravaged Columbia, which resulted in overuse of fire companies' equipment.[22] The hoses bore the brunt of the wear and tear, and by 1870, they were "very much injured," the chiefs of three major companies reported, "so much so as to greatly impair the successful operation of our engines."[23] The three captains who signed this petition represented white and black fire companies. Fires did not respect racial lines; thus, firemen had to embrace a degree of interracial cooperation whether they wanted to or not.

As they sped to fires at all hours of the day and night, by putting their own lives at risk, black firemen demonstrated that they understood citizenship as a relationship with the government that not only conferred rights and access to resources, but also obligated them to protect each other and their neighborhoods. Unlike many urban residents who only responded to the fire bell if the "fire-king" appeared to threaten their own property, the black fireman, upon hearing the bell, "springs from his bed instinctively, dons his fire-scarred hat and coat, and, in large and rapid strides, hies him to the engine house."[24] Their very vigilance allowed the majority of urban residents to remain comfortably at home. Thus, performance of civic duties in the form of fire companies underscored black claims to civil rights and citizenship and demonstrated a commitment to a civil-social contract.

PUBLIC PERFORMANCE, CITIZENSHIP, AND MANHOOD

Black firemen helped define black people—particularly men—as citizens even when they were not actively performing a municipal service; that is, they had a symbolic as well as a practical role in the city. They regularly reminded officials and residents alike of their importance through public parades and exhibitions, which functioned as both practice and spectacle. Wanting proof that their city had adequate protection, for example, members of the Raleigh, North Carolina city council passed an ordinance in 1869 that *required* these events quarterly as a form of "exercise and inspection."[25]

On the morning of these exhibitions, firefighters lined up at their engine houses in full dress. These uniforms followed a general design and were likely chosen to elicit citizens' respect and awe. For example, Columbia's Enterprise Fire Engine Company members wore black pants and a red flannel jacket with mother of pearl buttons and black velvet trim. A wide black belt and large black hat completed the look.[26] The Victor Fire Company of Raleigh uniforms were equally elaborate with their blue-trimmed red shirts, black belts, and blue caps trimmed with red and black. Black firemen reserved these distinguished uniforms for organized public occasions. They gave the lie to white opinions that black people were vagrant and lazy, and their patriotic color schemes reinforced their Americanness and discipline in a dramatic and unmistakable way.

Parades for both black and white companies followed a standard script. Firemen marched a specific parade route that usually led them through the main thoroughfares and past the most important government buildings. Though fire companies organized at the local level and were largely governed by municipal or state statutes and legal decisions, they nonetheless made themselves visible to all potential sources of power—local, state, and Federal. Black and white companies usually exhibited and paraded separately, but they followed the same general routes. As they marched, they periodically broke into a run to demonstrate their speed and efficiency. At predetermined intersections, the companies stopped and "played off." Playing off consisted of connecting a hose to the nearest hydrant and pumping water by hand as fast and as far as possible in the time allotted. Both black and white spectators found these performances impressive and reassuring. Businessmen and casual spectators alike turned out to watch two black fire companies in Columbia in 1873. Local newspapers characterized these throngs of spectators in such terms as "joyous crowd[s]" who loudly vocalized their appreciation of the firemen's performances.[27]

These parades not only showcased black firefighters' skill and manliness, but also provided symbolic reassurance to a city rightfully frightened of being ravaged by another destructive fire. Columbians, like other urban dwellers around the South and the nation, needed to believe they could be saved. As city leaders hoped when they encouraged and required fire company demonstrations, the Vigilant, the Enterprise, and the Congaree provided this reassurance. The published account of a joint Enterprise-Vigilant parade reported that "many made remarks on their fine appearance, and often congratulated themselves and our fair city that we have such willing and valiant protectors from the fire fiend."[28] An observer in Charleston was even more explicit. "The colored fire men . . . deserve credit," he wrote, "for their valuable services in the many conflagrations which have visited this city."[29] Urban southerners recognized that black men were protectors of their cities.

As these sentiments suggest, firefighting thus proved particularly suited to African Americans' citizenship struggles. Not only could they use the service they rendered as a way to assert their value in a society that refused to recognize them, but it also provided black men an opportunity to prove their manliness.[30] Fighting fires in the nineteenth century was a physically taxing activity. Though steam engines had been invented by the 1870s, Columbia's black fire companies could not afford such a pricey piece of machinery, so they continued to battle flames with their hand-pump engines. Firemen thus required physical strength to operate the hand pump as well as courage to get close enough to the fire that their water would reach the flames. Their engines were also hand-drawn, meaning that in these public performances, urban residents witnessed black firemen pulling two-ton engines without any equestrian help. Black firemen, a white spectator wrote, were "strong, muscular men, capable of doing gallant and effective service in an emergency."[31]

In using manly service to show fitness for citizenship, they tapped into a long tradition that connected manhood and freedom. Serving in the military as an enlisted soldier was an idea rich with images of manly defense of civilization and a just society.[32] Frederick Douglass himself argued that black men secured "manhood and freedom" by fighting in just and civilized warfare.[33] The Federal government evidently agreed; during the Civil War, enlistment in the Union army had effectively freed more enslaved men (and their wives and children) than the more famous Emancipation Proclamation. Thus while military service was not the only way to prove eligibility for manliness, it was the most obvious.

In fact, any organization that publicly showcased manly service served a similar function. Public performance of manliness was important because manhood was not an inherent status deriving from one's sex.[34] Manhood was an achievable construction of self, but only through the performance and public acknowledgment of manly traits. Scholars have shown that African Americans in particular had to resuscitate their manhood in order to prove their fitness for citizenship. In doing so, they had to balance what historian Stephen Kantrowitz terms "gentlemanly restraint" with "manly defiance."[35] This was most obviously achieved through military service, but other organizations that allowed African Americans to demonstrate that they were people other citizens could call on for defense, rather than people who threatened their person and property, also allowed black men to prove their manliness. In many ways, fire companies allowed black men to walk this fine line more easily than militias.

Black fire companies also played integral roles in urban commemorative celebrations, particularly in patriotic parades. They often led processions on the Fourth of July, Washington's birthday, and Emancipation Day. These public gatherings on streets and sidewalks were orchestrated performances of citizenship because they manifested participants' status in the nation and in their local communities. Because of their distinctive uniforms, firemen were among the most easily recognizable group at large events. Just as colonists and early Americans celebrated the nation into existence after the American Revolution, black southerners celebrated and performed into existence their freedom and citizenship.[36] Black leaders made speeches and worked with white Republicans to develop plans for parades and barbecues and conventions; hundreds, and sometimes thousands, of African Americans attended these gatherings throughout the South as enthusiastic spectators. Organizations such as fire companies allowed for a larger percentage of black southerners to stake a place in the official agenda and in the commemorative community. These physical bodies in the streets and sidewalks of southern cities underscored the arguments that well-known figures made in written or spoken conversations. While membership in black fire companies certainly overlapped with local political leadership, many black firemen were ordinary southerners whose names remain lost to history. Participating in important commemorative celebrations allowed nonelite black men to take an active part in shaping a new American nation in which they were free rather than enslaved. They consciously cast themselves into contentious public interactions that characterized the American public sphere in order to claim inclusion in civil society.

Black fire companies asserted their claim to public space even more vehemently when they staged tournaments in which they invited companies from other cities to compete against them. Though often categorized flippantly as "frolics" by their white neighbors, these intercity competitions allowed African Americans to cultivate ties to black communities throughout the South. They did this through tests of technical skill and physical strength, and through social events that included firemen, their families, and supporters.

The case of Columbia is once again instructive. In May of 1873, the Vigilants invited the Union Star Fire Company of Charleston and the Yellow Jacket Fire Company of Charlotte for a two-day tournament. The Vigilants, accompanied by the Chicora Brass Band, met the companies at the train station and marched with them back to their engine house. The next morning, the tournament commenced with an inspection of the companies by the Columbia mayor and the city aldermen. After a favorable judgment, all three companies began their parade. They were not relegated to the outskirts of the city, but marched through the "principal streets" of downtown Columbia. They played off in front of the statehouse and in the central business district. The firemen concluded the tournament with a ball and a picnic.[37]

Tournaments served both as social space and as political incubators. The leaders of Columbia's black fire companies were also the city's leading black Republicans, and likely the same held true for Charlotte's and Charleston's companies. While they maintained no official ties to, nor were they sponsored by, the Republican Party, they nonetheless served as informal political organizing space, providing meeting venues and sponsoring diverse fundraisers designed to aid local black communities.[38] A Wilmington funeral in 1870 underscored the informal connections between the Republican Party, local politics, and black fire companies. When Henry N. Jones, an important black Republican official, died, all the black firemen in the city escorted the body to the cemetery in solemn and public procession.[39]

In addition, this tournament, unlike intracity parades, obviously transcended simple municipal service and utility. Charleston's firemen had no obligation to protect Columbia from any fires, nor would they have the opportunity to do so even were they so inclined. Thus, white property owners could not pretend that these public events served their own interests. Black firemen, their friends, and their families practiced and socialized with their counterparts from another city, building ties across communities, and in the process, they helped give citizenship rights tangible form outside the ballot box or legislative hall.

WHITE RESPONSES

Interestingly, in the 1860s and 1870s, white spectators seemed to accept black firemen with aplomb. The often rabidly conservative *Columbia Daily Phoenix* more than once judged them "fine-looking men."[40] On the other side of the political spectrum, the Republican *Daily Union Herald* also reported themselves impressed with the black firemen who, they said, "looked fine and well."[41] In fact, local newspapers described black firefighter performance in the same complimentary terms they used for white firefighters.

Given the ways firefighting and public performance were connected to manhood and citizenship claims in the post-Emancipation South, this white acceptance at first seems remarkable. Firemen played a symbolic role similar to that of black soldiers and militias, to whom white southerners consistently voiced opposition. In fact, they frequently petitioned military officials to have black troops removed. "These troops, many of them but recently slaves, look upon all the people of the South as their enemies," the *Columbia Daily Phoenix* asserted, "and in their new position are disposed to lord it over them as much as possible, which, of course, is extremely distasteful and annoying."[42] Armed African Americans threatened to alter society irrevocably, because their presence, said the *Phoenix,* changed "the whole character and conduct of the [black] laborer, making him neglectful, insubordinate, insolent, and beguiling him off from the plantations."[43]

Black militias supported and armed by the government were beyond the pale. They gave civic participation an armed and potentially dangerous component. At a special conference in Columbia in 1871 called by the South Carolina governor, Robert K. Scott, in response to escalating Ku Klux Klan violence, prominent citizens from around the state "urged—and not without some reason—that the arming of the colored militia was regarded by the whites as dangerous to peace and good order; and, whereas, before such arming was done, men could go to bed in peace and security, without fear of molestation, now they were compelled to go armed themselves as a measure of self-protection." The delegates blamed white Klan violence on the mere existence of armed African Americans. "The debate upon this subject was long and exhaustive, but the conclusion reached by all was, that the arming of the colored militia was at least an unwise measure," concluded Lewis Carpenter, the editor of the Columbian Republican newspaper, the *Daily Union*.[44] Even some Republicans held black men responsible for the actions of their white neighbors and were reluctant to include armed organizing as a right black men could access.

White objections to black military service provide clues as to why white southerners were more inclined to tolerate black fire companies during Reconstruction. While participation in fire companies offered black urban residents a way to prove manliness and thus include the right to organize such civic groups in postbellum understandings of male citizenship, it stopped sort of including a martial or armed component within that right. Protecting cities from the "fire fiend" did not require the use of guns or other weapons. Fire companies provided the community, discipline, and purpose usually found in militia organizations, and while their uniforms invoked a martial spirit, they did not arm their members. They inverted society in a way that seemed less threatening to whites because the sight of unarmed black men in service of white interests and property was decidedly unrevolutionary. It also did not remove a single black worker from the southern labor force.

Yet even amidst this white acceptance, hints of latent unease surfaced, centered around how the spaces black firemen created could be used for more revolutionary ends. The history and lineage of the Vigilants in Columbia is suggestive. The Vigilant Fire Company had existed in antebellum Columbia; according to anecdotal evidence, even then it was a black fire company, though the officers appear to have been white.[45] It was inactive between 1865 and 1870. White Democrats controlled the city and state governments in Columbia until 1868, when the Federal government stepped in, and the 1867–1868 city directory failed to include the Vigilant Company in the city's fire department.[46] Given the fact that it had to be rechartered in 1870, it seems likely that it had ceased to exist sometime during or immediately after the Civil War. One can only speculate that were it a largely black company as one observer claimed, race played a factor in its lapse.

Columbia's fire department was not the only one affected by changing circumstances of black freedom. What had been accepted before Emancipation seemed threatening afterward. In Savannah, for example, local whites tried to eject black firefighters and replace them with white Confederate veterans.[47] With Emancipation, racial inequality was not naturalized, nor yet legislated. If black people had the same privileges and responsibilities as white people—as firemen, for example—there was no mechanism stopping them from seizing equality elsewhere. It was a slippery slope. Historian Howard Rabinowitz has argued that the number of black police and firemen correlated with the strength of local Republican rule.[48] It is probable, then, that it was only as Republicans entrenched themselves in Columbia's municipal government that they could dispense these significant, if unpaid, patronage positions such as firefighter to the black Vigilants.

Nevertheless, given the service black firefighters provided for urban residents, most white people, even conservatives who opposed Republican rule, chose to accept black firemen and to celebrate that service while conveniently ignoring its larger implications. They could take some comfort in the fact that volunteer fire departments remained segregated throughout Reconstruction. Indeed, this segregation from their white counterparts can obscure black fire companies' importance in helping establish meaningful freedom in Columbia and other southern cities. Freedom and equality did not necessarily mean integration. Nor did integration mean freedom. In fact, having all-black units allowed for a more equal share of leadership within volunteer fire departments than integrated companies would have. The Vigilant, Enterprise, and Richmond had black officers, whereas integrated companies would most likely have had white officers.[49] The Board of Fire Masters, a group composed of the captains of all the companies, controlled Columbia's volunteer fire department. Self-segregation ensured that black firemen literally had a seat at the table. It allowed them to jointly sign the petition asking for new hoses in 1870. It also meant that they were able to petition the government on their own behalf without having whites purport to speak for them or to represent them.

CONCLUSION

The antebellum definition of citizenship was predicated on black enslavement, and it did not necessarily make sense in the postwar South. Citizenship denoted inclusion in a community, and white men did not want to make room for their black neighbors. They wanted to reinforce connections between citizenship and whiteness, while black southerners wanted to divorce citizenship from race. Black and white people used a process of civic reinvention to achieve a sense of social order in the chaos after Emancipation. Social order looked different to different people; southerners had to grapple not only with who was a citizen, but also with what citizenship even was. Black firemen played a crucial role in the public performances that began to work through these problems.[50] Their presence on streets and sidewalks legitimized their right to access these spaces, and they took to these spaces on their own terms. These terms allowed black men to claim inclusion in American civil society and in their local urban communities in both implicit and explicit ways.

Mobility and access to space and resources was not an abstract citizenship right, but a fundamental, practical one. Physical spaces in the city offered black citizens a way to make their citizenship and freedom meaningful, and they used this to their advantage by maintaining voluntary organizations such as colored firemen's companies. But that same space also provided a way that white southerners could limit black freedom without amending the Constitution. Citizenship, whites insisted, did not necessarily mean equality, nor did it mean freedom. They redrew the boundaries so that African Americans, while remaining citizens in the most narrow, legal sense, were confined outside the sphere of cultural or community citizenship in their own cities and states.

Twenty years after the *Columbia Daily Phoenix* recorded an "epidemic" of fire company organizing, Columbia's black fire companies voluntarily disbanded because of a situation concerning a black fire master and the space he occupied. The integrated Board of Fire Masters' duties included the investigation of suspicious fires, and in 1892, a black fire master, John Simons, captain of the Vigilants, entered a building to determine the cause of a fire. A white police officer ordered him to leave, and when Simons refused, the policeman arrested him and the Mayor's Court subsequently fined Simons ten dollars for doing his job. Neither the policeman nor the Mayor's Court overtly challenged Simons's right to be a firefighter, nor even his right to act as fire master. Instead, they focused on his right to enter the damaged building. The result was the same—without access to the burned building, Simons could not perform his duties as a fire master. In protest, Columbia's nearly two hundred black firemen quit. When the department was professionalized in 1903, therefore, it did not include any black firemen. In fact, the department would not include black firefighters at all until 1953, and even then, units remained segregated through 1969.[51] For two of the most turbulent decades of its history, the 1870s and 1880s, Columbia included black men in its ranks of city protectors. They remained active and visibly laid claim to their citizenship until the day they withdrew their services in protest. Even in their act of disbandment, black firemen used their service as a way to give citizenship a tangible, physical definition in the southern city after the Civil War.

NOTES

1. Untitled, *Columbia Daily Phoenix (CDP)*, December 13, 1872, 3.

2. Untitled, *Daily Union Herald* [Columbia] *(DUH)*, February 3, 1873.

3. "False Alarm," *DUH*, January 21, 1873, 3.

4. Amy Greenberg, *Cause for Alarm: The Volunteer Fire Department in the Nineteenth-Century City* (Princeton, NJ: Princeton University Press, 1998), 4.

5. Even in the South, some larger cities had professionalized their fire departments by the time the Civil War broke out. Richmond, for example, had a professional, paid city fire department. Greenberg details myriad reasons for this shift, including changes in public perception of volunteer firemen, the rise of fire insurance, and financial considerations. Columbia did not make its fire department a paid municipal service until 1903. On national trends, see Greenberg, *Cause for Alarm*, 31.

6. Beasley and Emerson, eds., *Columbia South Carolina City Directory, 1875–1876* (Columbia, SC: Phoenix Job Office, 1876); Manuscript Census Records, 1880.

7. J. F. Williams, *Old and New Columbia, 1786–1929* (Columbia, SC: Epworth Orphanage Press, 1929), 61.

8. Endorsement by R. M. Alexander, August 27, 1867, on letter of William Geo Rout et al., June 20, 1867, L-62 1867, Letters Received, ser. 4111, 2nd Military Dist., RG 393 Pt. 1 [SS-70A].

9. Endorsement by A. J. Willard, September 1867, on letter of William Geo Rout et al., June 20, 1867, L-62 1867, Letters Received, ser. 4111, 2nd Military Dist., RG 393 Pt. 1 [SS-70A].

10. "Firemen's Tournament," *Charleston Daily News*, May 18, 1871, 3.

11. Kate Masur calls this tactic making "upstart claims"—that is, demanding protection of rights that had not previously been guaranteed to any American, regardless of race; Laura Edwards, on the other hand, frames it as a conflict between conceptions of individual rights versus "what was right." See Masur, *An Example for All the Land: Emancipation and the Struggle for Equality in Washington, DC* (Chapel Hill: University of North Carolina Press, 2010); Laura Edwards, "Law Outside the Nation: Overlapping Jurisdictions and Conflicting Conceptions of Citizenship" (paper presented at "Citizenship in the Era of the Civil War," Blacksburg, Virginia, April 23–25, 2015).

12. "Local Miscellany," *DUH*, September 8, 1871, 3.

13. "Local Miscellany," *DUH*, August 16, 1871, 3.

14. "The Water We Drink," *DUH*, May 28, 1873, 2.

15. "The Water Supply—Trial of Fire Engines," *CDP*, September 9, 1874.

16. T. Purse, "Report from the Office of the Fire Department, September 10, 1874, printed in *CDP*, September 19, 1874, 2.

17. Newspapers were full of articles and editorials extolling the virtues of cities. In the case of Columbia, see, for example, "The 'Coming' City—Columbia," *DUH*, December 22, 1870, 2; "Columbia Growing," *CDP*, March 28, 1871. See also Columbia Board of Trade, *Columbia, S.C., the future manufacturing and commercial centre of the South* (Columbia, SC:

Phoenix Printing Presses, 1871). Personal letters likewise reported the growth of cities. See Charles Duke Stanley, letter to Sallie Rivers, April 26, 1872, Charles Duke Stanley Papers, South Caroliniana Library (Columbia, SC), 3. Columbia was not unique, however: see "Improvements," *Raleigh Semi-Weekly Record,* July 16, 1867, 3; "Trade and City Improvements," *Raleigh Semi-Weekly Record,* November 29, 1867, 3; Charles McKimmon, Letter to Kate McKimmon, July 7, 1869, Kate McKimmon Papers, PC 1244.2, North Carolina State Archives (Raleigh, NC), 2.

18. Greenberg, *Cause for Alarm,* 31.

19. Neptune, "Untitled," *Wilmington Post,* January 31, 1869, 3.

20. John Dennison, Petition to the Mayor and Alderman of the City of Columbia, September 1870, Columbia City Council Material, "Petitions to the City Council Fire Committee," Series L1006002, South Carolina Department of Archives and History (SCDAH) (Columbia, SC); Dennison, Petition, September 5, 1870, Series L1006002, SCDAH.

21. Neptune, "Untitled," *Wilmington Post,* January 13, 1869, 3.

22. Cities across the South found their equipment after the Civil War to be sadly worn out or in disrepair. Companies in Augusta, Georgia, made complaints similar to those heard in Columbia. See Augusta City Council Minutes, July 10, August 4, October 6, November 21 and 28, 1865, January 2 and 3, 1866, Augusta Municipal Building (Augusta, GA).

23. John Dennison, George A. Shields, J. S. Sutphen, Petition to the Mayor of and Alderman of the City of Columbia, September 6, 1870, Series L1006002, SCDAH.

24. "Firemen's Tournament," *Charleston Daily News,* May 18, 1871, 3.

25. "Concerning Fire Companies," *Raleigh City Ordinances* (1869), 52.

26. Untitled, *DUH,* July 22, 1873; "Fireman's Parade," *DUH,* October 4, 1873, 4.

27. "The Colored Firemen," *CDP,* May 19, 1873, 2.

28. "Fireman's Parade," *DUH,* October 4, 1873, 4.

29. "The City Fire Companies," *Charleston Daily News,* October 30, 1868, 3.

30. Sean Wilentz and Amy Greenberg note similar uses of volunteer firefighting in northern cities before the Civil War. Wilentz, *Chants Democratic: New York City and the Rise of the American Working Class, 1788–1850* (New York: Oxford University Press, 1984), 259–62; Greenberg, *Cause for Alarm,* 6.

31. "Firemen's Parade," *DUH,* October 4, 1873, 4.

32. Much valuable historical scholarship focuses on the confluence of manhood, military service/valor, physical struggle, and citizenship. Much of the scholarship around manhood and black citizenship focuses on an idea that African American men had to resuscitate their manhood in order to prove their fitness for citizenship. This was most obviously achieved through military service, as historians of antebellum northern free blacks and Civil War African American troops have noted. See Jim Cullen, "'I's a Man Now': Gender and African American Men," in Darlene Clark Hine and Earnestine Jenkins, eds., *A Question of Manhood: A Reader in U.S. Black Men's History and Masculinity,* 2 vols. (Bloomington: Indiana University Press, 1999–2001), 1:489–501; Christopher Bonner, "Blood of Our Fathers: The Military, Manhood, and Citizenship in Black Protest, 1831–1865," unpublished work cited with permission of the author; Amy Dru Stanley, "Instead of Waiting for the Thirteenth Amendment: The War Power, Slave Marriage, and Inviolate Human Rights," *American Historical Review* 115 (June 2010): 732–34; Brian M. Taylor, "'To Make the Union What It Ought to Be': African Americans, Military Service, and the Drive to Make Civil War Service Count" (PhD diss., Georgetown University, 2015), 1–78.

33. Frederick Douglass, quoted in Cullen, "'I's a Man Now,'" 493.

34. Gail Bederman rightly argues that manhood (and gender more broadly) is an ideological and historical process, legible only in its specific historic and cultural context. Bederman, *Manliness and Civilization: A Cultural History of Gender and Race in the United States, 1880–1917* (Chicago: University of Chicago Press, 1995), 7.

35. African Americans were careful to imagine themselves as "people the polity could call on for defense rather than as people it should fear." Stephen Kantrowitz, *More than Freedom: Fighting for Black Citizenship in a White Republic, 1829–1889* (New York: Penguin Press, 2012), 175–222, quotations from 198 and 219.

36. David Walstreicher, *In the Midst of Perpetual Fetes: The Making of American Nationalism, 1776–1920* (Chapel Hill: University of North Carolina Press, 1997). For the antebellum context of how parades wielded political influence, see also Susan Davis, *Parades and Power: Street Theatre in Nineteenth-Century Philadelphia* (Philadelphia: Temple University Press, 1986), 1–22; Simon Newman, *Parades and the Politics of the Street: Festive Culture in the Early American Republic* (Philadelpha: University of Pennsylvania Press, 1997). Kathleen Clark makes a similar argument in her book about urban black commemorations during Reconstruction. My concern is less with the content of these black commemorations and more with the fact that they occurred in public settings and that their very existence impacted race relations in southern cities. I build on her argument about black written and spoken conversations about citizenship to argue that the physical bodies on the streets and sidewalks of southern cities underscored any arguments they made in their commemorative program. *Defining Moments: African American Commemoration and Political Culture in the South, 1863–1913* (Chapel Hill: University of North Carolina Press, 2005), 17–31.

37. "The Colored Firemen," *CDP*, May 19, 1873.

38. "Festival Tonight," *Knoxville Daily Chronicle*, May 25, 1871, 4.

39. "Funeral of a Colored Alderman," *Daily Journal* [Wilmington], January 7, 1870. Scholars have found that fire companies played similar organizational roles in the North. See Greenberg, *Cause for Alarm*; Amy Bridges, *City in the Republic: New York and the Origins of Machine Politics* (New York: Cambridge University Press, 1984); Wilentz, *Chants Democratic*.

40. "The Colored Firemen," *CDP*, May 19, 1873, 3.

41. Untitled, *DUH*, July 8, 1871, 3.

42. "Colored Troops," *CDP*, August 1, 1865, 2.

43. Untitled, *CDP*, September 5, 1865, 2.

44. "That Conference," *Daily Union*, 15 March 1871, 2.

45. J. F. Williams, *Old and New Columbia, 1786–1929* (Columbia, SC: Epworth Orphanage Press, 1929), 61; J. T. Hershman, *The Columbia City Directory* (Columbia, SC: The Steam Power Press of R. W. Gibbes, 1859), 69.

46. *Columbia South Carolina City Directory* (Columbia, SC: W. W. Deane, 1868), 21.

47. Edmund L. Drago, *Black Politicians and Reconstruction in Georgia: A Splendid Failure* (Baton Rouge: Louisiana State University Press, 1982), 108–9.

48. Howard Rabinowtiz, *Race, Ethnicity, and Urbanization: Selected Essays* (Columbia: University of Missouri Press, 1994), 121.

49. This was the complaint of many black Republicans throughout the South for the duration of Reconstruction—that the Republican Party relied on black mass support but failed to distribute meaningful patronage jobs, and thus power, to those black supporters.

See, for example, Eric Foner, *Reconstruction: America's Unfinished Revolution, 1863–1877,* 2nd ed. (New York: Perennial Classics, 2002), 351–53.

50. My interpretation of the performative nature of reinvention is influenced by cultural historians Joseph Roach and Grace Elizabeth Hale. Roach, *Cities of the Dead: Circum-Atlantic Performance* (New York: Columbia University Press, 1996), 1–10, and Grace Elizabeth Hale, *Making Whiteness: The Culture of Segregation in the South, 1890–1940* (New York: Vintage Books, 1999), 6–7.

51. My account of the breakup of the black fire companies and subsequent exclusion and segregation of the city department is based on the Harden Street Substation National Register of Historic Places application, www.nationalregister.sc.gov/richland/S108177440135.pdf, accessed March 30, 2015, 7–8; Darrick Lamont Hart, "Overcoming the Flames of Prejudice: The Integration of the Columbia Fire Department, Columbia, South Carolina, 1948–1969" (Master's thesis, University of South Carolina, 2000).

An Ideology beyond Defeat

*Confederate Visions of Work and Citizenship
in the Reconstruction South*

DAVID C. WILLIARD

When he finally brought himself to acknowledge the collapse of the
Confederacy, Lt. Charles E. Dabney thought it would destroy his world.
Dabney forestalled that acceptance for as long as he could. Along with
most of his comrades in the Sixth Virginia Cavalry, he cut through Federal lines in April 1865 rather than surrender with the remnants of Lee's
army at Appomattox. "After much dodging & roundabout travelling"
(he reckoned that he traveled nearly five hundred miles) in search of a
Confederate army still in the field, he and a companion discovered that
"everybody had abjectly submitted & that all organized resistance, even
west of the Mississippi, had ceased." Dabney's personal Confederacy
had outlived any of the would-be southern nation's larger military or
governmental manifestations; when that realization sunk in, the young
officer submitted to "the bitterest humiliation which providence has yet
inflicted on me" and gave his parole to the Yankees.[1]

Like thousands of other young men who had given their whole selves
to the Confederate project, Dabney's moment of reckoning threatened to
unravel all that his adult life to that point had meant. To sustain themselves as the costs of war threatened to become ever more unbearable,
ardent Confederate nationalists had created a powerful collective culture
in which soldiers' personal virtues and the fate of the Confederacy grew
increasingly intermingled. This culture carried an inherent bipolarity.
If the Confederacy prevailed, its adherents believed that it would do so
because of the superior military commitment, religious piety, racial and
ethnic purity, and degree of sacrifice that its soldiers exhibited. Yet in
binding their selfhood so completely to the fate of the Confederacy, sol-

diers left themselves with little to fall back upon in the event that their cause failed. Confederates had mortgaged the survival of their nation against their own self-image, and at their moment of final defeat, the soldiers in grey found themselves paying the cost of that transaction in full.[2]

Yet those who went on living had to find a first step into the world after the Confederacy. To do so, they required an ideology that could transcend defeat and function in the world that the Confederacy's failure had produced. They sought a replacement for what they had lost in the war: a coherent vision of their place in the world that linked the household to the courtroom and the ballot box, and would thus provide traction for defeated Confederates as they made simultaneous claims to belonging in both the changed terrain of postwar southern society and in the restitution of their legal relationship to the US government that they had fought so hard to be rid of. Charles Dabney's first tentative foray into describing his postwar aims contained a potential answer— one that would gain power, substance, and dimension as what Gaines Foster has termed "the trauma of defeat" abated and white southern men began to consider how they would define citizenship and civic virtue in the Civil War's wake.[3] Dabney declared that he would "return to Virginia; certainly by the last of August," where he would "go to work if the Yankees will allow me & swallow up, if possible, in unremitting labors, the haunting sense of individual and state degredation."[4]

For former Confederates finding their footing in the post–Civil War world, any claim for a new basis for citizenship had to come to terms with how the war had severed the bonds between the formal world of the state and the realm of social custom and expectation. The Confederacy had been built on a conception of citizenship in which both the legal regime and cultural sanction located both power and governance of all levels of society in the hands of white men. That vision was the most radical product of an antebellum southern order that cast white men as what Laura Edwards has called "paradigmatic legal individuals"—people capable of ruling households and, by extension, possessed of the fitness and independence necessary to wield political authority.[5] Wartime had added a new dimension to that relationship as the men in the armies grew ever more synonymous with the Confederacy itself, both as cultural symbols and as enforcers of practical governing authority when home front disaffection and occupation by the United States Army widened the void between the Confederate nation and the reach of the Confederate state. Defeat destroyed this nexus of coherence by eradicating both the legal relationship between the Confederate state and its citizens and the cultural standing that soldiers gained from defending their dependents at a single stroke—the "individual and state degradation" that Dabney referenced. With their legal status in peril, the roots of their personal identities threatened, and their role within southern society in disarray, Confederate veterans needed to remake themselves as well as to find structure in their relations to others.

Rebuilding their worlds around an ideology grounded in work, or "unremitting labors" as Charles Dabney put it, seemed to allow former Confederates to address all of those unresolved consequences of the Civil War. When they wrote about the virtues of dignified work, former Confederate soldiers articulated a common theme with many subtle yet distinct variations in order to locate themselves in a series of increasingly broad relationships. As a gendered concept that not only transcended the domestic and public worlds of returning veterans but also provided a barometer of manhood that crossed race and region, the ideology of productive labor promised to allow Confederate men to reclaim authority over their own actions, their households, and ultimately, over their region's political future. If they could continue to serve the people whom they had protected in war by providing for them in peacetime, Confederate soldiers could both restore their own self-image and lay claim to the status and reciprocal obligations of domestic dependency.

Beyond the individual and the household, Confederate veterans hoped that an ideology of dignified work could provide the foundations for claims to political citizenship as they faced state and national governments controlled largely by their wartime enemies. At least in the short term, Confederate soldiers wishing to secure their membership in the national body politic had to demonstrate to the victorious North (and, to a lesser extent, to southern Unionists) that their wartime experience had reformed their civic beliefs. Work and productivity as the basis of manhood and, ultimately, of male citizenship cohered with antebellum northern critiques of southern indolence and lassitude as well as Republican ambitions for a productive, free-labor southern economy in the postwar years. As a signifier of fitness for citizenship, moreover, an inclination to value work produced no obvious conflict with either of the war's central verdicts: that secession was treason, and that slavery was dead. Because work provided a competitive terrain for men to demonstrate their fitness regardless of race or wartime loyalty, Confederates reasoned that if the North truly sought to restore national unity, the

Federal government would protect the civic rights and political power of those southerners who best exemplified this most Republican of virtues.[6]

Confederate veterans would find their pursuit of reconstructed citizenship curtailed, however, by their encounters with the consequences of emancipation and military defeat—the very reckoning that a focus on work was designed to forestall. Even as former Confederate soldiers attempted to substantiate their claims to citizenship by men's productivity in the postwar years rather than loyalty during the war years, they participated in a parallel debate about the relationship between race, masculinity, and status. While Federal and state officials assessed the penalties they would levy against Confederate soldiers for their participation in a failed insurrection, a simultaneous deliberation about freedom's meaning in the aftermath of emancipation engaged governing institutions as well as individuals at every level of postwar southern society. During and after the war, white southerners juxtaposed their own potential to rebuild their lives, their individual economic destinies, and their region against their perceptions of the laziness of free African Americans. Confederate veterans would levy many of the same claims to dominance in the aftermath of their defeat as they had in the era of slavery by attempting to replace racial entitlements fixed in the law with racialized assessments of societal worth as defined by men's disposition toward work.

Understanding how Confederate soldiers used the concept of work to envision a path from defeat and exclusion to legitimacy and then to dominance demonstrates that Americans crafted citizenship claims in the Civil War era to appeal to multiple audiences: national and local, governing authorities and household dependents, people to whom they needed to demonstrate humility, and others from whom they needed to command respect. When white southern men appear in narratives of the Civil War and Reconstruction, their presence is usually characterized as intransigent resistance to the changes sought by others. Of course, many did oppose the cumulative changes brought about by the war, which disaggregated white manhood from power in the realms of law, politics, and society and seemed to confirm Confederates' fears about the reach of the national government. Yet lumping their actions and ideas together under the labels of resistance mistakes the way former Confederates interpreted their world. Interpreting Reconstruction as a binary of progressive change and stubborn resistance obscures the process by which ordinary Americans—Confederate veterans and others—simultaneously

engaged with multiple audiences to make their lived experiences cohere
with their aspirations. In affecting a new ideology of citizenship, ex-
Confederates assumed many different postures: subservience to secure
the restoration of their political and civil rights, dominance to quell the
ambitions of black manhood, and reliable dependability to reconstruct
the gendered domestic order of the family and the household. Former
Confederates hoped that relying on work as a basis for their claims to
citizenship would prove flexible enough to justify their place in a set of
dissimilar but linked relationships. Their ultimate return to political
and social power in southern life a decade after Appomattox came not
because of their unwavering resistance to change but because they understood how successful pursuit of citizenship meant reconciling diverse
audiences in a changed world.

The resonance of work as a postwar marker of masculinity originated
at the grass roots of white southern society, in the moments when white
southern men laid down their arms and assessed their bleak surroundings. Upon returning to their communities, former soldiers tried to cope
with the totality of their defeat by immersing themselves in the routines
of domestic life. They were driven in part by the necessity of economic
productivity and in part by a desire to establish an identity as valued
providers. Most of all, however, they sought a common, comprehensible
terrain of experience to link the worlds of soldiers and civilians in order
that postwar reunions might not succumb to a host of mutual misun-
derstandings, each of them rooted in different understandings of what
war had done to the men who fought it. Work allowed former soldiers to
leverage their productivity in order to return home as valued community
members without having to discuss the war and its attendant strains.
By rewarding effort with measurable and tangible progress, work provided a venue for productivity and contribution for men whose efforts
on the battlefield, no matter how courageous or skillful, had proven
insufficient. A Confederate captain from North Carolina lamented that
"all our efforts hardships and privations have been for nothing indeed
this is the worst feature of the whole." The pain of two wounds and an
amputated leg paled by comparison; "I have cried more and felt worse
because we were unsuccessful than I ever did before this," he wrote,
and would "rather be dead this day than alive was it not for my mother
Julia and George but I feel it my duty now to do all I can to assist them."[7]

The prospect of productive labor amidst family and community enabled Confederate soldiers, at least momentarily, to channel their energies away from bitterness at past failures or trepidation at the concerns that loomed on the horizon. Veterans used work to distance themselves from dead comrades, emancipated slaves, and the prospect of land confiscation and redistribution to freedmen—in short, the products of the war that threatened to envelop them in despair—and instead espoused a sense of optimism and determination when speaking of their labors.

George Washington Finley Harper returned to his Caldwell County, North Carolina home and determined to do the best he could to restore tranquility and prosperity to his family life. In diary entries, he indicated that he spent May 1865 "[at] Lenoir and Fairfield working on farm and garden occasionally hunting squirrels." Renewed public engagement was too painful for Harper to consider in the immediate aftermath of the war. "*No mail and no public business* or trading," Harper emphasized. Unwilling to interact with his neighbors, Harper derived satisfaction from reasserting his role as provider. On June 8, 1865, his entry read: "Trying to thrive by holding the plough!"[8] William L. Amonett of the Twelfth Louisiana Infantry agreed. "I have now gone to work," Amonett wrote to a minister in his hometown, "given up all ideas of law for fear that it would lead me into public life."[9] For veterans like Amonett and Harper, labor offered a private, temporary sanctuary from both the unpleasant past and the uncertain future. By focusing on productivity, former soldiers could concentrate on their capabilities rather than their failures and forestall the prospect of public engagement in a changed society.

Former Confederates did not reserve such sentiments for their private reflections. Instead, they constructed a domestic identity around their work. In the wake of defeat, former soldiers needed reassurance from their society that their masculine identities had not been lost with the Confederacy. Emphasizing the manly virtues of honest labor allowed southerners, especially women, to remind Confederate soldiers that they still could win the esteem of friends and family even after failing to achieve victory. A Georgia woman wrote to Isabella C. Hamilton praising the "young men belonging to the old aristocracy" whom she found engaged in various odd jobs to scrape together a living. "If I admired them as heros," Hamilton's correspondent wrote, "I admire them still more as *woodcutters* and *fishermen.* How nobly do they bear adversity! What an exhibition of real strength and independence of character!"[10]

Veterans encouraged family and friends to subordinate questions about their wartime experience to immediate concerns. Floride Clemson took solace from her brother's determination upon returning from service with the First South Carolina Light Artillery. "Calhoun," as she called John C. Clemson, "is very anxious to get to work, & is much more sober than he used to be."[11] Eliza Carolina Middleton Huger Smith delighted in her two sons who returned from the war "active & capable in every way, working well & cheerfully in the details of our refugee life. As soon as they are allowed to work," Smith optimistically believed that she "[could] count on a future."[12] Veterans and their families shared a stake in the pleasant delusion of a singular focus on labor. Eva B. Jones noted with approval that her husband Charles had "been hard *at work*" ever since his return from his wartime role as chief of artillery for the military district of Georgia, and that his genteel features had given way to "hands hard and burnt like a common laborer's."[13] For former soldiers, work partially occluded both memories (and, in many cases, traumas) of wartime service and anxieties about the future. Family members, meanwhile, hoped to assuage their own fears about how military service might have negatively changed their loved ones. In the turbulent and uncertain moments in which soldiers became civilians and began to rebuild their domestic worlds, a focus on work offered a crucial point of departure. It allowed the men of the Confederate armies to give priority to what could be done in peace rather than what had been done during, and as a result of, the war.

That shift in focus toward peacetime productivity met with encouragement from the southern press, which urged defeated Confederates to focus their efforts on rebuilding their region rather than lamenting their losses. The Columbia *Phoenix* encouraged veterans in particular to work in order to reconstruct themselves as well as their society, seeing in productive labor a tonic for both personal and social discord. "The whole body of our people now labor under a painful mental *unrest*," the paper declared, and "those who were in the war are especially the victims of this sort of unrest. But let not these despair or despond," the paper continued, "or hesitate or delay too long in grappling with the simple tasks of industry . . . through whatever medium the necessity needs to be pursued. Let each grapple with the task that is most ready to his hand, without pause or questioning, and do the thing that promises the best return, quite satisfied if the result shall be no more than the simple maintenance of existence, through the daily sweat of the brow."[14] Such exhortations sought not only to spur a disheartened populace to imagine a brighter future, but also to galvanize white men to prove their own worth in the aftermath of emancipation. "If young and old, instead of repining and grieving about their recent losses, would go to work and exert a little healthful energy," proclaimed the editors of the North Carolina–based *Western Democrat* in the summer of 1865, "they might recover and again live in prosperity; but idleness will not only destroy their own prospects, but greatly injure those who are industrious." The *Democrat* saw productivity as a prerequisite for postwar claims to political leadership and power, and embedded in its calls for diligent work a clear racial dialectic that implored white men to work as a way to draw distinct contrasts between themselves and formerly enslaved men. "*Working* men will rule this country, and those who do not work will be counted as trash," the paper declared. "The prospect is that very little work will be got out of the Negro, and that he will go into general decay and die out. The white man must not depend upon the Negro, but he must go to work himself."[15]

Most former Confederates quickly discovered that hard hands and burnt skin carried more symbolic value than the material fruits of their labors. The destruction of the southern economy meant that the link between the individual's act of work and the relational status of provider which it conveyed had eroded. Eva Jones, who had praised her husband Charles for his commitment to work, noted with concern its lack of effect on either his personal outlook or the family's economic fortunes when that labor failed to bring tangible rewards. Charles Jones seemed wearied by the circumstances that his immersion in labor, which had offered a brief reprieve, now compelled him to face. He knew, Eva lamented, that there was "no way for him, or anybody else scarcely, to make money now. His wheat crop has utterly failed, and we are all as poor as church mice."[16] Soldiers blamed members of their own society as well as wartime devastation and emancipation for their economic setbacks. Charles F. Barnes of the Eleventh Virginia Infantry railed against southerners who sought profit by employing business-conscious northerners over former Confederates. "Shameful to say, that most of the old merchants here have employed fancy Yankee Clerks & salesmen while numerous poor Confed's walk the streets in utter idleness, searching for work but finding none," Barnes fumed.[17] For Confederate veterans, initial feelings of solace drawn from productive activity gave way to crushing doubts when that activity proved fruitless. The very institutions they had relied upon for support seemed to offer little but a bleak future.

The inability of work to erase the consequences of the war or to provide former soldiers with positions of domestic authority was compounded by Confederates' precarious legal position, as both civil governments and military powers sought to hold the officers and men of the Confederate armies responsible for their participation in the rebellion. The personal vulnerability this imposed on Confederate veterans was exacerbated by the clear, unambiguous demonstration that power in postwar southern institutions of governance lay outside the hands of former Confederate soldiers. Men inclined to view Confederates as repressors of the rights of US citizens, not as potentially virtuous postwar members of that class, would control the process of reconstruction. The first attempts to bring southern communities under control came from the United States Army. In many cases, army officers initiated prosecutions against former Confederate soldiers based on wartime episodes. Indicted soldiers ranged from privates to major generals and appeared before military tribunals. The army initiated proceedings against the Confederate officers George Pickett and John H. Gee during the summer of 1865 for mistreatment of Union prisoners during the war. Military tribunals indicted Pickett, who fled to Canada to escape prosecution, and convicted Gee.[18] Less prominent offenders also found themselves called to account before military courts. Capt. Reuben Wilson of North Carolina languished in Libby Prison during the summer of 1865 as the army's adjutant general's office gathered evidence to prosecute him for the murder of Unionist civilians in the closing months of the war.[19] John Willis McCue, a member of Col. John Singleton Mosby's partisan rangers, stood trial for killing a Union soldier during a raid into Maryland. McCue was found guilty and sentenced to life imprisonment, while the army turned Wilson over to civilian authorities.

With its zealous prosecutions of former Confederate soldiers, the United States Army declared that accounting for wartime violence constituted a prerequisite to resuming normal relations. Confederate soldiers and their families saw the military's actions as evidence that their fears about a vindictive and tyrannical occupation had become reality. "These military commissions before which he will be probably tried are organized to *convict*," the relative of one accused Confederate declared, and they "rarely disappoint their masters."[20] John McCue's father, himself a major in the Fifty-First Virginia Infantry and a former prisoner of war, believed that only the northern desire to punish ex-Confederates explained his son's conviction. His son's actions were "in obedience to orders and [in] legitimate accordance with Mosby's mode of warfare."[21] Although it hardly surprised many southerners who ended the war convinced of Yankee perfidy, the presumption that the victorious Union would treat Confederates as criminals on the slightest pretext left former soldiers believing that they would pay the price of peace and Reconstruction with their own liberty and security.

Beyond the men prosecuted by the army or in state courts, a much larger cohort of former Confederates who never faced a trial nevertheless feared that they would meet with similar treatment. "I may soon be an exile and forbidden to return to the land of my birth," wrote Ezekiel John Ellis to his father at the end of the Civil War. "Will I can submit to this though the thought is almost death."[22] Samuel Barron, a Confederate naval captain from Virginia, returned home from Europe only when he received assurances that "the day of arrests has passed & a quiet & unobtrusive gentleman like yourself will become an object of respect" rather than a hunted outlaw.[23] Like the overwhelming majority of Confederate veterans, neither man ever faced judicial scrutiny for his wartime conduct or suffered any recriminations from political authorities. Yet the specter of arrest or exile at the hands of the national and state governments kept many Confederate soldiers from believing that they could return to civil life as protected citizens. Instead, they contemplated futures in which they faced a stark choice: submit to rule by a hated enemy who nursed wartime grievances, or convince state and national governing authorities to evaluate civic capacity based on postwar dispositions rather than wartime allegiance.

Try as they might to forge a future unhampered by the war's legacies and devoid of public engagement, Confederate veterans therefore found themselves drawn inexorably into considering the world beyond their hands, brows, and arms. This meant confronting novel limitations on the political and social power they had grown accustomed to wielding as white men in a society built on racial slavery. Sustaining their focus on work required suspending the bonds of society, because as defeated soldiers' horizons expanded, their power, confidence, and faith in the future diminished—hence their renunciations of "public business," "public life," and other forms of engagement beyond the domestic realm. Yet in their economic capacities and in their political identities, the social consequences of the war came to Confederate veterans, no matter how unwilling they proved to face them. Former Confederates met those challenges with a campaign of words and actions that featured two

stark alternatives. In their rhetoric, they emphasized personal reform
and a capacity for citizenship rooted in a disposition to work; in their
actions, a large proportion of veterans seemed unwilling to surrender
the prerogatives of mastery and racial dominance that such a reformed
character would require.

As the political contours of Reconstruction began to take shape, Confederate soldiers deployed the same rhetoric of work on which they built
their claims to a place at the top of their domestic social worlds to claim
the right to inclusion and trust within the body politic of the restored
nation. Theirs was an uphill struggle, since the Republican Party had
built its sectional appeal by contrasting visions of northern productivity
and inclination to work against the laziness and dissipation that slavery
engendered among southern whites and blacks alike. Such rhetoric was
key to Republicans' stances on issues ranging from tariff policy to the
fate of western territory, as it allowed that party to equate the outcome
of such questions with the fate of the American republic itself. Because
free labor ideology was at once a claim of the value of work and a jus-
tification of the social and economic outcomes that emanated from it,
it allowed the Republican Party to link questions of policy to questions
of virtue and character. Republicans were thus able to argue, in the
words of William Henry Seward, that to make the United States "the
greatest of all the States" demanded "labor perfected by knowledge and
skill. . . . voluntary, enlightened labor, stimulated by interest, affection,
and ambition."[24] Moreover, the political leaders of antebellum southern
society had, in their defenses of slavery, decried work as a marker of
slavery rather than a virtue of free men. Manual work, in the formulation of South Carolina senator James H. Hammond, was "the drudgery
of life . . . requiring but a low order of intellect and but little skill," and
it stood in direct opposition with "that other class which leads progress,
civilization, and refinement."[25] Far from being a maker of a virtuous
citizenry, work in Hammond's view disqualified men from the qualities
of political participation. Confederates knew that such views had proved
central to the Republican critique of their region, and thus the commitment to work that the soldiers of the Confederacy identified as the
foundation of their postwar selves seemed an unlikely rhetoric.

Yet the very challenge of reshaping northern assumptions about
regional dispositions to labor also presented an opportunity, since it
created a clear metric for how defeat had reframed white southerners'
dispositions and attitudes—and, by extension, their capacity to act as

good citizens. Since one of the war's most significant consequences had been the overthrow of slavery as both a labor system and as the grounds for a political philosophy that held work in low esteem, former Confederates who embraced the dignity of work could demonstrate that they had discarded the assumptions of antebellum and wartime mastery and submitted to the triumph not only of Federal power, but of Republican ideals. When Congress convened the Joint Committee on Reconstruction to investigate conditions in the postwar South in December of 1865, it produced a visible public venue for former Confederates to stake their claims. Union occupation officials (both civil and military) and former Confederates appeared before the Committee to plead that Confederate veterans receive the trust of the Federal government as it sought to destroy the legacy of slavery and rebellion and build a productive, democratic replacement.

For those who wished to see governance in the postwar South taken out of the hands of former Confederate soldiers, the assertion that such men despised work and valued idleness carried the serious implication that Confederate soldiers, despite their own assertions to the contrary, both would not and could not choose to find purpose and direction in rebuilding their lives through honest toil. W. L. Chase, a United States Army officer stationed in northern Virginia, found "very few people there who are industrious" and heaped particular scorn upon former soldiers. He identified "a class of young men, returned from the army . . . who are very bitter against the government, and are lying around barrooms."[26] These men went out of their way to provoke conflicts, insult army officers (including Chase), and harass freedpeople because they supposedly would not engage themselves in any useful activity. Thomas M. Cook, a war correspondent from the New York *Herald* who established his own newspaper in Wilmington, North Carolina, took a more sympathetic view of southern whites generally than did Chase but still attributed discord and violence within his community to "hot heads" consisting chiefly of "boys and young men thrown upon the world and living upon the street corners."[27] Since in this formulation of white southern ideology the act and the actor were mutually constitutive—slaves performed manual labor and those who performed such work were slaves—witnesses expressed little surprise that former Confederates forced African Americans to work through coercive violence while showing no inclination to labor themselves. Brig. Gen. John Ely attributed "fiendish outrages" against former slaves to "white people, who are in many cases banded together under the cognomen of 'Regula-tors' 'Nigger Killers' &c." Ely identified the groups' members as "generally returned rebel soldiers of the lowest grade of white humanity, working at no respectable employment."[28]

The deliberations of the Joint Committee on Reconstruction tested whether Confederate veterans could convince the nation of their dedica-tion to work, rebuilding, and pursuit of a future that departed from the South's antebellum and wartime structures and ideals. The testimony of witnesses not only generally failed to translate Confederate claims of dedication to work from the personal and domestic realms to the terrain of national politics, but also fixed in the public mind a view of former Confederate soldiers as men incapable of shedding their predilections for violence and their commitment to white mastery. The resultant birth of Congressional Reconstruction is a well-studied subject. Congress, impelled by the outrage of its constituents at the intransigence of white southerners, passed the Civil Rights Act, confirmed it over President An-drew Johnson's veto, and passed the Fourteenth Amendment in the span of two months from April to June 1866. This legislation altered the defi-nition of citizenship more completely than any law of the United States before or since, save perhaps the Nineteenth Amendment, by declaring that former slaves were citizens, barring any former Confederate civil or military leaders who had previously taken an oath of allegiance to the United States from Federal office, and apportioning representation to the southern states according to the proportion of male citizens of all races entitled to vote in national elections. As legal scholar Taja-Nia Henderson has shown, even as the Fourteenth Amendment expanded the franchise to millions of black men, it "simultaneously imposed un-precedented limitations on the citizenship rights of white male South-erners."[29] When the legislatures of all of the former Confederate states except Tennessee refused to ratify the amendment, Congress passed the Reconstruction Act of 1867, which placed the South under military control until they had ratified new constitutions that enfranchised men regardless of previous condition of servitude and passed the Fourteenth Amendment.

In the wake of Military Reconstruction, former Confederates retained their attachment to the rhetoric of dignified work but refashioned it to paint electoral politics and the institutions of governance it controlled as illegitimate. Confederate veterans demonstrated the insidious pos-sibilities contained in deploying the rhetoric of work as a basis for citi-

zenship when they claimed that the freedpeople's collective laziness held
the South back from its potential as a land of plenty. They interpreted
Congress's actions not as a logical consequence of their own lawlessness
and violence, but rather as evidence that northerners were committed to
rebuilding southern political and civic life along the lines of corruption
and retribution. This led former Confederates to create a critique of representative democracy that posed an electorally disadvantaged populace
of "true citizens" against the corrupt, undeserving political alliance of
freed slaves, vengeful northerners, and bitter Unionists led by a cabal
of Republican schemers. The crucial fulcrum that former Confederates
relied on to draw distinctions between themselves and the "undeserving" men who controlled electoral politics was their disposition to work.
A standard of citizenship that enfranchised and empowered the lazy
and the idle at the expense of the diligent and the industrious could
only result from a combination of corruption and vindictiveness, and
it could never produce a government capable of building prosperity in
the devastated South. R. H. Allen thus typified the views of many white
southerners when he explicitly connected the illegitimacy of governance
in the aftermath of Military Reconstruction with the laziness of the African Americans whom it seemed to serve. "No work done today," his
diary read on December 16, 1867:

> All our Freedmen Laborers went hair [hare] hunting, indeed they are
> perfectly worthless, have not made expenses generally since the war, and
> there is no remedy, we are under the iron heel of a military negro despo-
> tism and the Labor system grows worse and less effective every day. The
> negroes dont work near so well now as they did the first year after the
> war, they seem to think that they can live without work at all, and they
> are stealing all the small stock, such as hogs and sheep in the country.[30]

By contrast, noted Allen's fellow Virginian Charles Morris, the men who
had fought for the Confederacy retained "the truer pride of independence & desire to make our way in any honest calling. Since the necessity has arisen many hands that once were soft & white are now hard
& rough with daily toil & yet they are uncomplaining & ask only to be
employed."[31] Newspapers kept their reading public focused on the contrast between virtuous white labor and black idleness, and critiqued
Reconstruction by suggesting that African American enfranchisement
came at the cost of the otherwise inevitable prosperity of the region.
"The people's money has been squandered without stint to keep up a

military despotism in the South, to enforce negro superiority there, and to feed and clothe the lazy negro population," the Nashville *Union and Dispatch* fumed in the aftermath of the Reconstruction Acts. "Radicalism prefers that the Negro should rule, rather than the country should flourish and prosper."[32] The juxtaposition was clear and its racial connotations explicit. Politics and power lay in the hands of former slaves whose aversion to work rendered them incapable of producing a just or effective government, and the former Confederates most inclined to diligence and effort had to suffer the results.

From this critique emerged the tenets of the various campaigns of white supremacist insurgency that would collectively carry the title of "Redemption." These campaigns relied on the contrast between deserving and undeserving citizens to justify both their need to seize power and the methods they used to secure it. In the eyes of the "Redeemers," those who supported a federally controlled Reconstruction that served the interests of the idle against the needs of the diligent cast themselves outside the community and needed to be driven from the field just as if they were the regiments, squadrons, and batteries of an invading army. "A majority of forty thousand negro voters has for the moment paralyzed" the white voting populace, warned the Charleston *Daily News,* "but they will be filled with a new strength when, true to the instincts of their race, they become alive to the application of the principle that by the colored man the white man cannot be ruled. The white race will guide the giant machine [of society]."[33] "Time and necessity will convince [the freedman] that freedom does not consist in idleness," the same paper promised a year later; if not, "the idle and dissolute will disappear."[34] A local Democratic political organizer in Alabama defined his party's goals as "to toil on with commendable ambition, & never, no never, be content until the last hated Radical & Scalywag has been driven [from] our borders. With a determined & united effort they can be made to flee from it like the grasshoppers in a mown meadow would flee from the strides of a giant."[35]

Stripped of the military rhetoric and the metaphors, these campaigns amounted to deliberate assaults on the persons, the rights, and the claims to power of all who pursued a vision of citizenship grounded in democratic equality. A northern-born witness living in New Orleans summed up Redemption campaigns as "acts of violence and murder [that] exist in nearly all the southern States, in States where there is no claim that the officers are not duly elected; the programme in all these States is to obtain *control* of the state goverments this the old rebel element determined to do."[36] In the eyes of those Confederates who participated in such campaigns, however, the character of the electorate as measured through its disposition to work more than justified such widespread disfranchisement. If black men did not value labor and accept it as fundamental to a man's civic character, then their claims before the law, upon the state, and for the elective franchise would amount to mere theft of governing authority from productive citizens—therefore subverting the purpose of government itself. In effect, Confederate veterans responded to charges of subverting democracy with the claim that democracy was only as good as the men who practiced it.

The tactics and the effects of the Ku Klux Klan, the Red Shirts, the White League, and similar groups organized to subvert democratic rule and deny civil rights to African Americans have received elaborate scholarly attention.[37] Yet in focusing on their methods, scholars have at times missed an important element in their motives. Thinking about Redemption as a product of a broader ideology crafted to meet the many needs that former Confederates faced helps scholars avoid conflating violent resistance to democracy with a kind of anticitizenship, which amounts to both a teleological view of citizenship and an analytical dead end. Citizenship in the post–Civil War period was not a fixed objective to be pursued or opposed; rather, it comprised a set of claims a person made about their relationships to the state, to their representatives, to their dependents, to their peers, and to those they deemed their inferiors. Confederate soldiers left their armies at the war's conclusion convinced that defeat required them to dispense with public engagement and to rebuild themselves and the basis for their claims to citizenship. The ideology of work held the promise of aligning a source of self-definition independent of national loyalty or military outcome with the domestic and political contributions that white men could leverage to justify their claims to postwar citizenship. Confederate veterans saw in Congressional Reconstruction and military rule the rejection of such claims, and from that rejection they created an alternative conception of political practice. Against definitions of citizenship that emphasized its categorical protections for all citizens, former Confederate soldiers proffered a contingent framework for citizenship that sought to distinguish the deserving categories of citizens from those who had not earned the right to claim such

status. They used the rhetoric of work not only to justify white supremacy, but also to explain their expansion of the battle to define citizenship
beyond competitions between candidates and parties for elective offices
and onto the dark, bloody fields of coordinated terror, repression, and
murder. Rather than a vision of citizenship in which the legitimacy of
government turned on how it reflected the will of the people, the politics
of postwar Redeemers operated in reverse. They began with the premise
that the deserving would control the state, and worked backward from
that envisioned result to determine who should constitute the electorate.

This contingency matters because it reveals how contests over citizenship in the Reconstruction era were not static battles between fixed
categories of identity or interest groups, but rather moments of definition and redefinition in which individuals fashioned, over and over
again, claims to belonging as well as justifications for exclusion across
multiple audiences at once. Framing Confederate veterans' views on
citizenship as simple resistance to the changes pursued by freedpeople,
Republicans, or the victorious North only reveals part of their attempts
to join their objectives in the arena of national and state politics with
their own internal needs and those of the people who made up the social
and cultural tapestry of their homes and communities. The result was
a claim to citizenship that blended dominance with subordination and
demands for power with pleas for inclusion, thus providing a consistent
ideological vision that could function in times and contexts of weakness
as well as those of strength.

The end of the Civil War produced a phenomenon of exceptional rar-
ity in the history of American democracy—a moment when discursive
arguments about the citizen's ideal character gave immediate definition
to the legal and structural boundaries of citizenship itself. This understanding of citizenship in which the rights of citizens derived from their
self-ascribed character shaped not only how former Confederates but
also how white northerners and African Americans understood inclusion in the body politic.[38] Rather than a contest between office-seekers to
appeal to a clearly delineated electorate, politics acquired a profoundly
reciprocal character in which victorious constellations of political interests possessed the power to reshape the electorate that chose them.
As Gregory Downs has so aptly characterized it, Reconstruction was,
at its core, "a war over which patrons would heed the cry of which subjects," in which the law's contents, its makers, and its applicants were
all simultaneously the terrain of political contestation.[39] In that mul-

tivalent nexus lay great opportunity, since who shaped the laws, what the laws said, and who could claim their benefits and protections moved almost simultaneously rather than in sequence. Yet precisely because the spoils of political victory were so substantial and the participants in lawmaking so malleable, liberal visions that linked civic inclusion to participation in governance proved exceptionally vulnerable to critiques that connected the character of citizens to the functions of government. An ideology of work, bound up in the thick context of race in a postslave society but ostensibly constructed as a marker of manhood independent of race or region, allowed former Confederates to critique the legitimacy of the government through attacks on the character of those in whose interest it governed. Their critique would shift the functional meaning of citizenship in the Reconstruction South from a relationship between citizens of a governing body and the rights they enjoyed to a much more dangerous and subjective battle between the deserving and the undeserving, in which the terrain of contestation was nearly unrestricted.

NOTES

The author wishes to acknowledge the help of several individuals whose reading of this essay substantially improved its contents, including Michael Blaakman, Paul Quigley, the attendees at the "Citizenship in the Era of the Civil War" symposium at Virginia Tech University, and the anonymous reader for Louisiana State University Press.

1. Charles E. Dabney to "Father," May 30, 1865, Saunders Family Papers, Virginia Historical Society.

2. For detailed examination of the process through which Confederates bound their individual selves to their would-be nation, see Stephen Berry, *All That Makes a Man: Love and Ambition in the Civil War South* (New York: Oxford University Press, 2003); Peter Carmichael, *The Last Generation: Young Virginians in Peace, War, and Reunion* (Chapel Hill: University of North Carolina Press, 2005); Gary Gallagher, *The Confederate War* (Cambridge, MA: Harvard University Press, 1999); Joseph Glatthaar, *General Lee's Army: From Victory to Collapse* (New York: Free Press, 2008); Lisa Laskin, "'The Army is Not Near So Much Demoralized as the Country Is': Soldiers in the Army of Northern Virginia and the Confederate Home Front," in *The View from the Ground: Experiences of Civil War Soldiers,* ed. Aaron Sheehan-Dean (Lexington: University Press of Kentucky, 2007), 91–120; Jason Phillips, *Diehard Rebels: The Confederate Culture of Invincibility* (Athens: University of Georgia Press, 2007); Paul Quigley, *Shifting Grounds: Nationalism and the American South, 1848–1865* (New York: Oxford University Press, 2012); George Rable, "Despair, Hope, and Delusion," in *The Collapse of the Confederacy,* ed. Mark Grimsley and Brooks D. Simpson (Lincoln: University of Nebraska Press, 2001), 129–67; Anne Sarah Rubin, *A Shattered Nation: The Rise and Fall of the Confederacy, 1861–1868* (Chapel Hill: University of North Carolina Press, 2005); and Aaron Sheehan-Dean, *Why Confederates Fought: Family and*

Nation in Civil War Virginia (Chapel Hill: University of North Carolina Press, 2009). For investigations of how Confederate veterans remade their private lives in the aftermath of defeat, see James J. Broomall, "Personal Reconstructions: Confederates as Citizens in the Post–Civil War South," in *Creating Citizenship in the Nineteenth Century South,* ed. William A. Link, David Brown, Brian Ward, and Martyn Bone (Gainesville: University Press of Florida, 2015), 111–33; James Marten, *Sing Not War: The Lives of Union and Confederate Veterans in Gilded Age America* (Chapel Hill: University of North Carolina Press, 2011); and Jeffrey McClurken, *Take Care of the Living: Reconstructing Confederate Veteran Families in Virginia* (Charlottesville: University of Virginia Press, 2009).

   3. Gaines Foster, *Ghosts of the Confederacy: Defeat, the Lost Cause, and the Emergence of the New South* (New York: Oxford University Press, 1988).

   4. Charles E. Dabney to "Father," May 30, 1865, Saunders Family Papers, VHS.

   5. Laura Edwards, *A Legal History of the Civil War and Reconstruction: A Nation of Rights* (New York: Cambridge University Press, 2015), 124–25. See also Laura Edwards, *The People and Their Peace: Legal Culture and the Transformation of Inequality in the Post-Revolutionary South* (Chapel Hill: University of North Carolina Press, 2009); Ariela Gross, *Double Character: Slavery and Mastery in the Antebellum Southern Courtroom* (Princeton, NJ: Princeton University Press, 2000); Stephanie McCurry, *Masters of Small Worlds: Yeoman Households, Gender Relations, and the Political Culture of the Antebellum South Carolina Low Country* (New York: Oxford University Press, 1995); and Stephanie McCurry, *Confederate Reckoning: Power and Politics in the Civil War South* (Cambridge, MA: Harvard University Press, 2010).

   6. This essay focuses on the rhetorical and ideological value of work as a tool for former Confederates to find coherence and levy claims for inclusion in post–Civil War considerations of citizenship and the nature of the body politic. It is not an attempt to assess the "New South" strain of political economy advocated by railroad interests, old-line Whigs, and industrialists in the aftermath of the Civil War, though the conceptual origins of each are likely interrelated. See Edward Ayers, *The Promise of the New South: Life After Reconstruction* (New York: Oxford University Press, 1992); Peter Carmichael, *The Last Generation: Young Virginians in Peace, War, and Reunion* (Chapel Hill: University of North Carolina Press, 2005); Dan T. Carter, *When the War Was Over: The Failure of Self-Reconstruction in the South* (Baton Rouge: Louisiana State University Press, 1985); and C. Vann Woodward, *Origins of the New South, 1877–1913* (Baton Rouge: Louisiana State University Press, 1951).

   7. Reuben E. Wilson to Julia Jones, May 13, 1865, Jones Family Papers, Southern Historical Collection, University of North Carolina.

   8. Diary of George Washington Finley Harper, May 8–May 31 and June 8, 1865, Southern Historical Collection, UNC.

   9. William L. Amonett to Rev. T. M. Ward, September 30, 1865, William L. Amonett Papers, Mississippi Division of Archives and History.

   10. M. Telfair to Isabella Caroline Hamilton, December 21, 1865, Isabella Caroline Hamilton Papers, Georgia Historical Society.

   11. Journal of Floride Clemson, June 26, 1865, in *A Rebel Came Home: The Diary and Letters of Floride Clemson, 1863–1866,* ed. Ernest Lander and Charles McGee (Columbia: University of South Carolina Press, 1989), 89.

   12. Eliza Carolina Middleton Huger Smith to Mrs. Edward L. Cottenet, July 12, 1865, in *Mason Smith Family Letters, 1860–1868,* ed. Daniel Elliott Huger Smith, Alice Ravenel

Huger Smith, and Arney Robinson Childs (Columbia: University of South Carolina Press, 1950), 221.

13. Eva B. Jones to Mary Jones, June 27, 1865, in Robert Manson Myers, *The Children of Pride* (New Haven: Yale University Press, 1984), 551–52.

14. "Education in the South," Columbia *Phoenix,* August 21, 1865.

15. "There is Plenty of Work Now Offering . . . ," *Western Democrat,* July 18, 1865.

16. Eva B. Jones to Mary Jones, June 27, 1865, in Myers, *The Children of Pride,* 551–52.

17. Charles F. Barnes to Rebecca Barnes, July 26, 1865, Barnes Family Papers, Small Special Collections Library, UVA.

18. Mark Bradley, *Bluecoats and Tar Heels: Soldiers and Civilians in Reconstruction North Carolina* (Lexington: University Press of Kentucky, 2009), 123–25. For a vitriolic but detailed account of proceedings before military courts in North Carolina during Presidential Reconstruction, see J. G. de Roulhac Hamilton, *Reconstruction in North Carolina* (New York: Columbia University Press, 1914), 163–69. For a perceptive interpretation of the persistence of military power and wartime conditions of governance after the surrender of the major Confederate armies and well into the postwar years, see Gregory P. Downs, *After Appomattox: Military Occupation and the Ends of War* (Cambridge, MA: Harvard University Press, 2015).

19. William Shultz and John Nissen to Jacob Cox, May 10, 1865, in "R. E. Wilson," Confederate Soldier Service Files, NARA 270, National Archives and Records Administration, Washington, DC.

20. William A. Hauser to Julia Jones, July 22, 1865, Jones Family Papers, Southern Historical Collection, UNC.

21. John Howard McCue to William Cabell Rives, Jr, April 21, 1865, Rives, Sears, and Rhinelander Family Papers, Small Special Collections Library, UVA.

22. Ezekiel John Ellis to Ezekiel John Ellis, Sr., April 25, 1865, Ezekiel John Ellis Family Papers, Louisiana and Lower Mississippi Valley Collections, LSU.

23. William G. Harrison to Samuel Barron, November 15, 1865, Barron Family Papers, Small Special Collections Library, UVA.

24. Speech of William Henry Seward, March 3, 1858, in United States Congress, *Congressional Globe,* Thirty-Fifth Congress, First Session (Washington, DC: John C. Rives, 1858), 944. See also Eric Foner, *Free Soil, Free Labor, Free Men: The Ideology of the Republican Party Before the Civil War* (New York: Oxford University Press, 1970), and William Gienapp, *The Origins of the Republican Party, 1852–1856* (New York: Oxford University Press, 1987).

25. Speech of James Henry Hammond, March 4, 1858, in *Congressional Globe,* 962.

26. *Report of the Joint Committee on Reconstruction,* Part II, 95.

27. *Report of the Joint Committee on Reconstruction,* Part I, 277.

28. Brevet Brigadier General John Ely to Captain H. S. Brown, April 9, 1866, in *Freedom: A Documentary History of Emancipation,* ed. Ira Berlin, Joseph F. Reidy, and Leslie Rowland, ser. 2: *The Black Military Experience* (Cambridge: Cambridge University Press, 1982), 762.

29. Taja-Nia Henderson, "The Lost History of the Fourteenth Amendment's Disqualification Clause," paper delivered at "Citizenship and the American Civil War" conference, Blacksburg, VA, April 2015.

30. Entry of December 16, 1867, Diary of R. H. Allen, Robert Henderson Allen Papers, Virginia Historical Society.

31. Charles Morris to William Cabell Rives, May 4, 1867, Rives, Sears, and Rhinelander Family Papers, Small Special Collections Library, UVA.

32. "The Cost of Reconstruction," Nashville *Union and Dispatch,* July 7, 1868.

33. "Stick!," Charleston *Daily News,* June 8, 1868.

34. "A Sea Islander Among the Hills," Charleston *Daily News,* July 27, 1869.

35. Undated transcript of political speech, Richard C. Ramsey Papers, Alabama Division of Archives and History.

36. Charles W. Boothby to George Boothby, September 15, 1874, Charles W. Boothby Papers, Louisiana and Lower Mississippi Valley Collections, LSU.

37. Among the excellent studies of the function of Reconstruction-era violence are Carole Emberton, *Beyond Redemption: Race, Violence, and the American South After the Civil War* (Chicago: University of Chicago Press, 2013); Steven Hahn, *A Nation Under Our Feet: Black Political Struggles in the Rural South from Slavery to the Great Migration* (Cambridge, MA: Belknap Press, 2003); James Hogue, *Uncivil War: Five New Orleans Street Battles and the Rise and Fall of Radical Reconstruction* (Baton Rouge: Louisiana State University Press, 2006); Nicolas Lemann, *Redemption: The Last Battle of the Civil War* (New York: Farrar, Strauss, & Giroux, 2006); Elaine Frantz Parsons, *Ku-Klux: The Birth of the Klan During Reconstruction* (Chapel Hill: University of North Carolina Press, 2016); Bradley Proctor, "The K.K. Alphabet: Secret Communication and Coordination of the Reconstruction-era Ku Klux Klan in the Carolinas," *Journal of the Civil War Era* (forthcoming); George Rable, *But There Was No Peace: The Role of Violence in the Politics of Reconstruction* (Athens: University of Georgia Press, 1984); Hannah Rosen, *Terror in the Heart of Freedom: Citizenship, Sexual Violence, and the Meaning of Race in the Postemancipation South* (Chapel Hill: University of North Carolina Press, 2009); and Richard Zuczek, *State of Rebellion: Reconstruction in South Carolina* (Columbia: University of South Carolina Press, 1996).

38. See Carole Emberton, "Only Murder Makes Men: Reconsidering the Black Military Experience," *Journal of the Civil War Era* 2, no. 3 (2012): 369–93; Emberton, *Beyond Redemption;* and Caitlin Verboon, "The 'Fire Fiend,' Black Firemen, and Citizenship in the Urban South," in this volume.

39. Gregory Downs, *Declarations of Dependence: The Long Reconstruction of Popular Politics in the South, 1861–1908* (Chapel Hill: University of North Carolina Press, 2011), 101.

To "Serve Both as a Light and as a Beacon to Our Noble Old State"

Southern Citizens in Latin America

CLAIRE WOLNISTY

On August 8, 1865, former Confederate States navy commander Matthew Fontaine Maury shared his thoughts about how to avoid humiliation at the hands of the Civil War's victors. Maury concluded in a letter to Robert E. Lee, "The best thing for us now is to aid in building up here in Mexico a good and stable Empire which in times that are coming may serve both as a light and as a beacon to our noble old state."[1] Even though Lee did not support Matthew Maury's colonization efforts in Mexico, he still wished Maury's fellow southern "citizens" in Mexico well in their endeavors.[2] Through their use of the word *citizen,* both Lee and Maury defined white southerners in Mexico as loyal to the South.[3]

Thousands of southerners who relocated to Latin America after the downfall of the Confederacy ask us to conceive of a citizenship in which transnational familial, social, and economic relationships took precedence over all other manifestations of citizenship.[4] As other essays in this volume illustrate, people debated the centrality of a person's place of residence, relationship to a national government, familial connections, and military service within definitions of citizenship and loyalty after the war. Southern emigrants to Latin America contributed to those debates when they pledged allegiance to a country that did not exist.[5]

Southern emigrants cultivated an ideological and cultural allegiance to an imagined South by rooting their understandings of citizenship in very real "meshworks" that stretched across national borders.[6] Familial, social, and economic "meshworks" drove understandings of southern identity throughout their efforts in Latin America.[7] Southerners measured their success in Latin America according to how well they could provide for family members through their connections to that part of the world. Because of these emphases, white southern emigrants declared themselves loyal southerners even as they appeared to abandon the South.[8]

To sustain my argument about the creation of a southern cultural citizenship, I organize this essay around four main problematics. First, I address the appeal of places like Brazil for southern emigrants. Second, I identify the types of people who fulfilled emigration boosters' definition of "acceptable" southern emigrants. Third, I outline some of the qualities of the southern colonies in Brazil. Finally, I analyze the ways in which southerners rationalized what many observers labeled as widespread failures among southern emigrants. Collectively, these discussions identify some of the transformations, continuations, and limitations of citizenship for southern emigrants in the wake of the Civil War.

Southerners migrated to a range of places in Latin America after the Civil War, including Mexico and British Honduras, but the most significant sources for this project focus on Brazil.[9] Private letters played such an important role in maintaining ties between emigrants and their acquaintances in the South that when the mail steamships fell behind predicted arrival dates in Rio de Janeiro, George Barnsley, a southern emigrant who founded a medical practice in that city, complained, "No letters! No monies! No nothing!"[10] Because emigrants viewed their own correspondence to be the main way in which they cultivated ties with the South, I prioritize it in this essay.

For southern emigrants, Brazil appeared to hold the solution for many of the South's difficulties after the war.[11] George Barnsley, who was a Georgia plantation owner before he practiced medicine in Brazil, wrote in his diary, "If it is political troubles that you would avoid, there is no escape except by [fast] emigration to other climes beyond the equator to Brazil, to which place many Texans are embarking."[12] Economic failures also troubled potential emigrants. The loss of slave labor especially devastated former slave owners. The notion that their newly freed slaves would actually demand a place in southern society horrified plantation owners more than losing their labor and economic base. On July 31, 1865, George Barnsley received a letter from the United States which bluntly stated, "The place is alive with Yankees and free negroes."[13] J. Marshall McCue of Mt. Solon, Virginia reported about the nature of race relations to Cyrus Hall McCormick of reaper fame when he wrote, "So Negroes and low whites are in ascendancy."[14] These political, economic, and social developments caused another southerner to write to George Barnsley on July 31, 1865, claiming, "Ah! What anguish it causes, when we assemble all the loved ones we have lost, and all for naught."[15] In 1867, J. D. Porter, one of the main boosters for emigration to Brazil, concluded that the idea that whites would have to abandon the country because blacks were taking it over "holds the minds of our people."[16] One of McCue's friends explained how he felt at the end of the war, "I go to Brazil because each day I loose [*sic*] some of the little self-respect remaining to me."[17] This correspondent determined about life in the postwar United States, "To live as we are now living is worse than death."[18] The results of the Civil War clearly created demoralization among these individuals. Brazil offered a means of alleviating that demoralization.

Southern emigrants who saw Brazil as a viable solution to the devastating consequences of losing a war rooted their assertions in historical precedence. Some southerners hailed Brazil as the logical partner of the South during the war. The *Charleston Mercury* claimed at the beginning of the Civil War, "The Confederate States desire the most cordial relations with Spanish America and Brazil. These are the peoples most identical with us in institutions—institutions which the rest of the world and the United States hate."[19] The newspaper article asserted, "It is for these to support and strengthen each other in practicing justice and exercising the comity and courtesy of nations."[20] The *Mercury* also claimed, "No people in the world, for example, have been freer from foreign aggressions and hostility than the slaveholding people of Brazil and Spain."[21] Robert Montague recognized southern interest in Brazil and emphasized parallels between Brazil and the South when he listed Brazil as a potential ally to the South in his April 1, 1861, speech advocating the secession of Virginia.[22] While Brazil never became an active partner of the South during the war, Brazil appealed to southern emigrants in the aftermath of the Civil War because the country had yet to officially abolish slavery.

Early emigration boosters highlighted the possibility of southerners bringing slaves into Brazil. Andrew McCollam of Louisiana concluded about migrants in Brazil, "And I can truly say if 100 families from Louisiana could be located here and the institution of slavery insured I should think I found a new land of promise."[23] Dr. James Gaston, an early explorer, made similar assertions in *Hunting a Home in Brazil* about southerners being able to bring slave labor with them when they moved. Even if Brazil was gradually abolishing slavery within its borders, Gaston claimed, Brazil's citizens would always recognize the "mastery of the white man."[24] Dr. Gaston described how the upper class of Brazilian society relied on a combination of slave and wage labor to get its work done, which meant that southern emigrants should not have much trouble setting up plantation systems and using slave labor in those systems. Authors succeeded in convincing many southerners that slavery was still safe in Brazil. As Andrew McCollam observed in his diary, "Among a few Brazil was desired because it was the last resting place of slavery."[25] Lucita Mardie Wait recalled in 1937 about the motivations of Capt. William Couasart, her great aunt's cousin in Brazil, "He thought they would buy slaves and get rich easily."[26]

Many potential emigrants and emigration boosters did not see a significant rupture between their lives in the South and their future lives in Brazil. The pervasiveness of slavery and family within definitions of self-identity allowed emigrants to transfer their slaveholder and familial identities across geographic and national spaces with relative conceptual ease. Citizenship, for southern emigrants, meant upholding the duty of rebuilding the slave society of their "noble old state" in Brazil because they did not believe they could re-create it under the auspices of the North.[27]

Southerners built a number of settlement sites in Brazil, centered in three main geographic regions.[28] Reverend Ballard Dunn, a former Episcopal minister in New Orleans, purchased a tract of land in the Jaquiá valley of the Ribiera de Iguape River Basin in the São Paulo Province in 1866.[29] During the mid-1860s, southerners such as James Gaston and Frank McMullan developed the Iguape and Cananéa settlements in that basin. Other southern settlements included a settlement on Lake Juparanã under the leadership of Charles Gunter just north of Rio de Janeiro and a settlement outside of Paraná. Five settlement clusters outside of Santa Bárbara, which developed during the 1860s and 1870s under the leadership of Col. William Norris of Alabama—Estação, Retiro, Campo, Funil, and Santa Bárbara—proved to be the most enduring series of southern settlements.[30]

Southern emigration boosters and leaders carefully selected people they believed to be worthy of creating and sustaining these southern settlements in Brazil. Frank McMullan, one of the emigration leaders, personally vouched for the characters of the people he brought to Brazil. McMullan claimed in an October 18, 1866, letter to Joaquim Maria Nascentes de Azambuja, the minister of Brazil to the United States: "The emigrants that will accompany me, will be first class citizens, the most of whom possessed fortunes before the war."[31] Frank's brother, James McMullan, declared in the *New Orleans Times* of January 24, 1867, that candidates for emigration to Brazil needed to be "Southern in feeling."[32] Lest the descriptor "southern in feeling" be too open to interpretation, James McMullan added "pro-slavery in sentiment" and "they have maintained the reputation of honorable men" to his list of emigrant qualifications.[33] The idealized southern emigrant citizen valued his familial connections and possessed significant social capital in his community, two qualities that could speak to his honor.

"Pro-slavery in sentiment" proved to be more important to establishing a citizenship of "southern in feeling" than actually owning slaves after the Civil War. Despite the efforts of emigration boosters to convince potential emigrants that they could bring their slaves with them to Brazil, the logistics of actually transporting slaves to Brazil and the near-impossible task of convincing former slaves to travel with former masters meant that the majority of southern emigrants resolved to try to find slaves in Brazil instead of bringing former slaves with them from the South. As George Barnsley concluded about the manifest of a ship carrying southern emigrants to Brazil, "The Commune with few exceptions had no slave in these statements [of the ship's baggage]."[34] For many southerners, this aspect of the ideal southern emigrant remained a fantasy with symbolic importance.[35]

Emigration boosters required southern emigrants to be "honorable men" as well as "pro-slavery in sentiment." Members of the upper class constituted the majority of southerners who moved to Brazil. On a practical level, upper-class emigrants could likely afford the initial emigration costs of moving to Brazil more than their lower-class counterparts.[36] Upper-class emigrants also possessed the resources to protect their familial interests.[37] Most importantly for the emigration boosters who defined acceptable emigrants, upper-class emigrants could participate in the compilation of public displays and often purse-taxing rituals that established oneself as honorable and a person with social capital.[38]

Upper-class potential southern emigrants funded emigration companies. The founding members of one southern emigration company resolved "to make all necessary arrangements for the procurement of lands, and for the establishment of a good and permanent settlement there [Brazil]."[39] According to the *New Orleans Daily True Delta* of February 15, 1866, upper-class community leaders formed approximately two dozen emigration societies and organizations in states such as Mis-

sissippi and Louisiana. The Southern Colonization Society, centered at
the Edgefield Court House in South Carolina, became the largest of these
emigration companies.[40] The society equipped and funded Dr. Hugh
Shaw and Maj. Robert Meriwether to travel to Rio de Janeiro and printed
their reports about sites suitable for colonization with the *Edgefield Ad-
vertiser* in an attempt to recruit southern colonists. At least twenty other
agents, in addition to Shaw and Meriwether, organized exploratory expeditions to Brazil for the purposes of identifying future settlement sites
during the mid-1800s.[41]

The relatively upper-class status of emigrants allowed them to protect their familial interests. Familial ties of loyalty defined the nature of
emigration and colony establishment in Brazil. James Gaston explained
his emigration goals in a letter dated September 28, 1865: "My object is
to determine or locate a suitable location for a colonization by our families from South Carolina and [England] who are desirous of coming to
live in this country."[42] Before Gaston actually brought people to Brazil,
he predicted that those people would move primarily in familial units.
Gaston's prediction that ties of loyalty between individual southern families would be stronger than any regional ties between larger groups of
people proved correct.

The Barnsley Family of Woodlands Plantation in Cass County, Georgia
demonstrates how familial ties drove southern emigration to Brazil.
George Barnsley, the family's eldest son, served as an assistant surgeon
in the Civil War after starting as a private in the Eighth Georgia Regiment.
He joined a group of emigrants following Frank McMullan to Brazil
in 1866. He moved to Brazil and his brother, Lucien, followed shortly
after. Apart from the years 1890 to 1896, George lived with his family in
Brazil until his death in 1919. While George initially traveled to Brazil
with a group of approximately 240 people under the leadership of Frank
McMullan, connections to his family proved to be his primary ties.[43]
Lucien and George relied on each other for business connections and
investment opportunities while in Brazil. Their father, Godfrey, never
did join them in Brazil, but it was not for lack of the brothers trying to
convince him to join them. George Barnsley offered Godfrey a home
with him in Brazil in 1870, indicating that while not all of the Barnsley
brothers' business ventures enjoyed success, they were profitable enough
to allow the brothers to remain in the country.[44]

Upper-class status relied on the testimony of friends and neighbors. James A. Marchant of Louisiana fully understood the importance

of character witnesses before he moved to Rio de Janeiro. In fact, he equipped himself with a list of twenty-two signatures from men who approved the following statement:

> We, the undersigned citizens of the above named town, Parish and State, and comrades of James A. Marchant, Esq., in the "Lost Cause, do hereby take pleasure in recommending him to the people of Brazile [*sic*] to which country he intend(s) to emigrate. Mr. Marchant is an excellent farmer, a good controller of hands, an[d] of the people. A slave holder previous to the war, reduced thereby, to toil, in a new country a path he has chosen for the future. May his realizations be as bright as his anticipations.[45]

Marchant's neighbors publicly vouched for his honorable character and his proslavery credentials before he left for Brazil.

Some southern emigrants proved they were upper-class "honorable men" by joining Masonic lodges. Upper-class men reaffirmed their status and belonging through their Masonic membership.[46] The physician Russell McCord made sure that he diligently paid his Masonic dues and maintained his Masonic credentials for over twenty-five years, despite moving to Brazil during that time span.[47] James Gaston also continued his Masonic membership while he was in Brazil.[48] When Mr. Rogers, George Barnsley's and Lucien Barnsley's mutual friend, died in 1871, Charles Nathan went to the funeral primarily because Rogers was a fellow Mason. As far as George and Lucien Barnsley could determine, not much else connected Rogers and Nathan together when they were both alive.[49] Social connections that bolstered character such as membership in societies, companies, and genteel culture often sustained emigrants through the settlement process.

In ways that echoed Early Republic–era economic qualifications on political participation, southern emigrants placed limitations on citizenship when they laced their definitions of it with upper-class connotations. A person's status as an acceptable, honorable southern individual whom emigration contract holders could deem as an emigrant worthy of southern citizenship in Brazil depended on "southern in feeling." Proslavery sentiment and personal connections aided in measuring something as abstract as a feeling. Because nineteenth-century concepts of honor depended on character evaluations from other people, upper-class associations such as emigration societies and Masonic lodges, and knowledge of cultural rules of behavior, identified southern emigrants to each other. This personal knowledge of other individuals would not have

been possible without these associations' capacities to build networks
or foster "meshworks" which blended social relationships. While these
meshworks allowed some southerners to recommend other potential emigrants to emigration boosters and contract holders, they also excluded
people who did not belong to emigration clubs or Masonic lodges, or
did not have knowledge about the upper-class rules of proper behavior.

Personal connections between southern emigrants replaced other
traditional methods of claiming citizenship. The majority of men who
left the South as emigrants fought as soldiers in the war. They did not
employ their military service as a reason to claim they were proper
citizens, however. Instead, they called on their neighbors and friends
to vouch for their honorable character. Southern emigrants also did
not highlight their Confederate political service if they possessed it, but
preferred to publicize their social and proslavery credentials in their
efforts to prove worthy of emigration. In short, they created a citizenship
of belonging.

Southern emigrants in settlements such as Iguape and Campo attempted to cultivate an identity separate from that of their Brazilian
neighbors.[50] The *Galveston Daily News* claimed about southern emigrants in Brazil, "They seem to be proud that they are American, and
in only one or two instances have they become naturalized to the Brazilian empire."[51] While the newspaper somewhat exaggerated its claims
about naturalization, the article did highlight widespread attempts at
a distinct, southern existence.[52] Instead of assimilating into local communities as Brazilian citizens, southerners cultivated their familial connections to the South through correspondence and movement and highlighted what they saw to be uniquely southern contributions to Brazil.

Southern emigrants often separated themselves from their Brazilian
neighbors by returning to the South for visits or extended stays when
possible. According to a reporter for *The Daily Picayune* of July 16, 1888,
"They [southern emigrants] frequently visit their friends in the United
States, but as yet, as far as I can learn, not one of them has left Brazil
to try his fortune in the states."[53] Because people often focused on supporting individual families, they maintained ties with their property,
friends, and kin in the South when possible.

The Barnsley family exemplifies how southern emigrants within the
same family lived in multiple physical locations, both within Brazil itself
and between the South and Brazil. Initially, George Barnsley traveled
to Brazil on his own and maintained a steady correspondence with his

brother and father as long as steamships would carry his letters back home.[54] While the three Barnsley men lived in two physical locations, they approached their financial problems as a familial unit. This understanding of finances communicated through correspondence meant that George Barnsley returned to Georgia for six years to see to his father's financial affairs before living in Brazil again.[55] There was not a sudden disconnect between living in the South and then living a separate life as a southern emigrant in Brazil; family members often traveled across national borders to visit each other and on occasion they relocated for varying amounts of time. George Barnsley's children adopted similar patterns of mobility during the 1870s and 1880s. Two of George Barnsley's sons, Charles and George Barnsley, returned to live in the United States permanently while their father remained in Brazil with their brother, Godfrey, and their sister, Adelaide, or "Addie."[56] Addie herself continuously wrote to her father, George Barnsley, while different family members were in Georgia and she was in Brazil.[57] As a result of these multiple relocations, the members of the Barnsley family learned to share in the life of two communities, their physical surroundings in Brazil or Georgia and the imagined community of loyal southerners they created through their constant letter-writing.[58]

Southern emigrants created a familial citizenship of belonging that bridged two physical communities. Southern emigrants remained involved in their family members' lives through written correspondence and would, at times, cross national boundaries back into the South in order to address familial needs.[59] Their ability to seamlessly travel between the South and Brazil indicates that while they often returned to Brazil, southern emigrants also harbored no ill will towards southerners who remained in the South, especially if they were related to those southerners by blood.[60] Furthermore, this obligation to family became multigenerational.

Southern emigrants also identified each other as southern citizens by highlighting the ways in which they believed they were separate from Brazilians. They saw superior technical knowledge and slave management practices as distinctly southern attributes. In particular, southerners living in Brazil often emphasized their Protestant upbringing as one of the characteristics that ideologically if not physically separated them from Catholic Brazilians and united southern emigrants as a community.

A Protestant background often served as an initial point of similarity for southern emigrants and continued to serve as a connective tissue between various southern communities in Brazil after initial settlement. Most of the 150 people who followed Reverend Ballard Dunn to Lizzieland, Dunn's 614,000-acre claim in the Ribiera de Iguape River Basin, belonged to Dunn's congregation in New Orleans.[61] In fact, many of the emigrant leaders and initial explorers, including James Cooley Fletcher and W. C. Emerson, claimed an official role in a church.[62]

Traveling Protestant preachers, much like Masonic brothers, remained important links between different southern families settled in Brazil. James McFadden possessed a church on his property that served as a way to bring disparate southern families together, because they would travel to the church when he housed a preacher or reverend willing to speak at the church for several nights in a row.[63] Lucita Mardie Wait, the daughter of southern emigrants, remembered that her father would let different travelers preach at their house for a time to whatever congregation would come listen to them before the preachers moved on to the next church.[64]

Southern emigrants fashioned an exclusive citizenship rooted in characteristics they believed separated themselves from Brazilians.[65] They performed shared religious backgrounds through their Protestant meetings to differentiate themselves from their Catholic Brazilian neighbors.[66] Meshworks in lived daily lives, such as the transnational family matters of the Barnsley family or the religious ties between people, defined belonging more than national identities or political concerns.[67]

Southern emigrants in Brazil did not often succeed at creating self-sustaining, independent southern settlements, despite the best efforts of emigration boosters and the emigrants themselves. Southerners experienced widespread failure at each stage of the settlement process when emigrants could not make ends meet. Southerners heard stories that dissuaded them from leaving the South in the first place, they were often unable to support themselves in Brazil, and they despaired of creating extensive southern settlements in that country.

Southerners who gave up creating new lives in Latin America criticized such enterprises the most. The grumbling of failed migrants did not abate after the initial years of settlement because "the croaking of disappointed and disgusted Americans" still met recently arrived southerners in 1868.[68] As J. D. Porter acknowledged, many failed migrants had good reason to complain. They needed sufficient funds to move, they did not always find an adequate source of income in Brazil, and at times they needed to adapt to foreign languages and customs.[69]

The general failure of southern settlements in Brazil as a whole to develop into independent entities shaped how individually successful southerners rationalized southern settlement shortcomings. The majority of southern emigrants who remained in Brazil with their families and who left records of their experiences actually conceptualized southern settlement shortcomings in terms of individual southern strengths. As George Barnsley claimed years after he came to Brazil, "American life in the south had for its effects a certain *individualism* utterly opposed to any concentrated common action."[70] Julia Hentz Keyes, the daughter of novelist Caroline Lee Hentz and a former Alabama resident, also focused on what she believed to be innate human characteristics when she mused about failed large-scale southern settlement plans, "We cannot but regret, even at this late day, that a spirit of restlessness should have ruled the Emigrants and scattered once more, a happy band of friend[s]."[71] Barnsley and Hentz Keyes removed human agency, and thus blame, when they concluded that innate characteristics that were not necessarily negative in and of themselves, like individualism and restlessness, became reasons why southerners failed to establish extensive settlements in Brazil.

Southerners who remained in Brazil through the 1870s defined their success and continued southern citizenship in terms of meeting individual and familial economic goals. They acknowledged that large-scale southern settlement efforts were no longer possible but still characterized their lives in Brazil as successful southern ones. Providing for a family in Brazil became a reason to stay there. James Gaston reached this conclusion about his goals in Brazil. He explained, "If I seek the good things of this life, it is that my family may share them with me. If I seek exemption from the cares and vexations of life, it is to shield them from annoyance."[72] Gaston joined many emigrants who defined themselves as loyal, successful southerners in Brazil because they could provide for their families despite the economic devastations many families sustained in the wake of the Civil War.

Several published periodicals centered in southern settlements around Santa Bárbara identified attributes that newspaper editors thought brought successful southerners together in Brazil. Instead of emphasizing ideas about nationalism, appealing for recognition from sovereign powers, or employing theories about creating a separate, southern nation internal to Brazil, newspaper editors honed in on agricultural pursuits to unite southerners into a larger shared identity of independent agriculturalists.[73] Colonel Censir and Rev. W. C. Emerson ran a newspaper exclusively for southern emigrants, the *Brazilian Immigrant and Agriculturalist*. They envisioned the newspaper as a forum that would allow emigrants to offer each other farming advice and to identify how to exchange goods. Planters with successful watermelon and tomato crops could offer advice to other aspiring planters.[74] These newspaper editors rightfully identified successful agricultural pursuits as a measure of southern citizenship because many of the initial emigration contracts brokered between emigration leaders and Brazilian government officials equated southern emigrants to farmers.[75] "Farmers" became the emigrants' primary identification; thus, if southerners were successful farmers who fed their families, they could then claim to be successful southern emigrants and citizens as well.[76]

Southern emigrants emphasized innate characteristics of citizenship. They rationalized general southern settlement failures in Brazil by maintaining that innate southern strengths prevented southerners from being able to work extensively with each other. Qualities of citizenship, in this particular conceptualization of citizenship, could not be learned or policed through contracts with political and sovereign entities.[77]

When citizens could not create large, southern settlements together, southern citizenship also entailed successful economic practices by families living within Brazil. Not all southerners became farmers in Brazil, but the majority did. As a result of the predominance of this occupation, successful farming became especially important to defining who was a successful southern emigrant citizen who could be a model of citizenship to other southerners in forums such as newspaper articles. Given the extensive economic ties southern emigrants maintained with their relatives and friends who remained in the US South, this conceptualization of the successful southern citizen in Brazil is not surprising.

Southern emigrants to Brazil in the wake of the Civil War offer a window into the ways in which southerners claimed allegiance to an entity—the Confederacy—that for most people ceased to exist. Southern emigrants detached ideas about southern loyalty from place of residence, sovereignty, military service, and civic education but clung to class, social status, the ideal of slave ownership, and providing for family as markers of southern citizenship. Southern emigrants defined this particular citizenship through familial and economic meshworks cultivated across national borders. They relegated slavery to the theoretical realm but emphasized the need for southern citizens to be honorable, upper-class men. In their attempts to create a distinct cultural citizenship in Brazil, southern emigrants also highlighted their contributions to Brazil and sought fulfillment in hard, agricultural work.

The practical aspects of actualizing all of these principles of citizenship did not always come to fruition, but the strength of these ideals remained strong. To some degree, first-generation southern emigrants imparted their values to many of their children. Second- and third-generation southern emigrants to Latin America responded to their surroundings in different ways, but a cohort of these emigrant descendants still conceptualized themselves as southern citizens. As second-generation emigrant Lily Page de Schultz wrote in 1941, "I was born during the Confederate war and grew up clinging to my dear father with his ideas and love of Virginia and old family traditions, but all my life I have been too poor to ever have gone to my father's country, yet I am [a] Southerner and Virginian!!!"[78] In some ways, Matthew Maury's dream of illuminating his noble old state in Latin America survived.[79]

NOTES

1. August 8, 1865, letter from Matthew Maury to Robert E. Lee, "Letterbook, 1865 April 2–1866 November 27 of Robert Edward Lee," Mss1 L51 g 70–205, Lee Family Papers, Virginia Historical Society. A very early version of this project appeared in the Spring 2014 edition of the *Madison Historical Review*. The author thanks the editors of this periodical for their permission to include some of that research here.

2. September 8, 1865, letter from Robert E. Lee to Capt. M. F. Maury, Mss1 L51 g 70–205, Lee Family Papers, Virginia Historical Society.

3. In order to recognize the plurality of souths, I opt not to capitalize "southerner."

4. Exact numbers of emigrants are difficult to pinpoint since travelers often did not leave records of their travels. Numbers of southern emigrants who moved to Brazil in particular during the years immediately following the Civil War range from 2,000 to 5,000. For example, "Document #8" of the Calceçao Tavares Bastos Collection at the Biblioteca Nacional do Brasil, #I 28,15,005 m. 031–043, claims that Carlos (Charles) Nathan brokered a contract for 5,000 emigrants in 1867. This contract is no guarantee that all 5,000 people moved to Rio de Janeiro, but it is a good benchmark. "Document #2" in the same collection reports that 1,839 "American" emigrants came to Brazil between December 1866 and May 1867. For additional number documentation, see Cyrus B. Dawsey and James M. Dawsey, eds., *The Confederados: Old South Immigrants in Brazil* (Tuscaloosa: University of Alabama Press, 1995), 5.

5. The literature discussing whether or not southerners espoused nationalism is long and extensive. I generally adhere to a classic, Drew Faust, *The Creation of Confederate Nationalism: Ideology and Identity in the Civil War South* (The Walter Lynwood Fleming Lectures in Southern History) (Baton Rouge: Louisiana State University Press, 1990), while using terms such as *loyalty* and *nationalism*.

6. For examples of recent conversations that situate the Civil War era in global, comparative, and hemispheric contexts, see the forum "Teaching the Civil War Era in Global Context," *The Journal of the Civil War Era* 5, no. 1 (March 2015): 126–53, with David M. Prior, Robert E. Bonner, Sarah E. Cornell, Don H. Doyle, Niels Eichhorn, and Andre M. Fleche; Sven Beckert, *Empire of Cotton: A Global History* (New York: Knopf, 2014); Andrew Torget, *Seeds of Empire: Cotton, Slavery, and the Transformation of the Texas Borderlands, 1800–1840* (Chapel Hill: University of North Carolina Press, 2015); and Don Doyle, *The Cause of All Nations: An International History of the American Civil War* (New York: Basic Books, 2015).

7. Anthropologist Lynn Stephen's use of "meshworks" is helpful to consider when asking how these southern emigrants still considered themselves members of a South that no longer existed in the eyes of their enemies. As Stephen explains, networks often do not exclude each other. Social networks are often also economic, religious, and political networks. Because Steven studied indigenous Oaxacans in Mexico, California, and Oregon, I make no claims about similarities between indigenous Oaxacans and southern emigrants. I simply adopt a similar methodology to studying how groups of people might form one community with members in various geographical locations. "Meshworks" helps capture the multifaceted nature of social networks that develop between people living in multiple localities. Lynn Stephen, *Transborder Lives: Indigenous Oaxacans in Mexico, California and Oregon* (Durham, NC: Duke University Press, 2007), 6, 19.

8. David Eltis, "Introduction: Migration and Agency in Global History," in *Coerced and Free Migration: Global Perspectives* (Stanford, CA: Stanford University Press, 2002), 31.

9. For an extensive study of the Confederate exodus to Mexico, see Todd Wahlstrom, *The Southern Exodus to Mexico: Migration across the Borderlands after the American Civil War* (Lincoln: University of Nebraska Press, 2015).

10. Diary of George in the George Scarborough Barnsley Papers, #1521, Southern Historical Collection, The Wilson Library, University of North Carolina at Chapel Hill.

11. Southern emigration to Latin America also demonstrates that people emigrated out of the United States as well as to and within the United States during the mid-nineteenth century. Southern emigration *out* of the United States in the wake of the Civil War adds an understudied dimension to hemispheric migration patterns across the American continents during the mid-nineteenth century.

12. Diary of George in the George Scarborough Barnsley Papers. Several emigrants stayed a while in Texas before moving further south.

13. July 31, 1865, letter from an unknown individual to George Scarborough Barnsley in the George Scarborough Barnsley Papers.

14. June 22, 1867, letter from J. Marshall McCue to Cyrus Hall McCormick in the J. Marshall McCue Paper, #454-z, Southern Historical Collection, The Wilson Library, University of North Carolina at Chapel Hill.

15. July 31, 1865, letter from unknown individual to George Scarborough Barnsley in the George Scarborough Barnsley Papers.

16. October 14, 1867, letter from J. D. Porter to Charles Nathan in the J. D. Porter Letters, #892-z, Southern Historical Collection, The Wilson Library, University of North Carolina at Chapel Hill.

17. June 22, 1867, letter from McCue to McCormick in the J. Marshall McCue Paper.

18. Diary of George in the George Scarborough Barnsley Papers.

19. *Charleston Mercury,* September 12, 1861, 1.

20. Ibid.

21. *Charleston Mercury,* April 10, 1861, 1.

22. Quoted in Edward L. Ayers, ed., *America's War: Talking About the Civil War and Emancipation on their 150th Anniversaries* (Washington, DC: American Library Association and the National Endowment for the Humanities, 2011), 65.

23. Andrew McCollam Diary in the Andrew McCollam Papers, #449, Southern Historical Collection, The Wilson Library, University of North Carolina at Chapel Hill. Significantly, McCollam identifies families, not individuals, as the primary emigrant unit.

24. J. McFadden Gaston, *Hunting a Home in Brazil: The Agricultural Resources and Other Characteristics of the Inhabitants* (Philadelphia: King and Baird, 1867), 374.

25. Andrew McCollam Diary in the Andrew McCollam Papers.

26. "Memories of a Childhood Spent in Brasil" by Lucita Mardie Wait in the Hardie Family Papers, #1879-z, Southern Historical Collection, The Wilson Library, University of North Carolina at Chapel Hill.

27. Interestingly, there is more mention of re-creating a unified and uniform southern society than of re-creating the society of a particular state. Matthew Maury only regularly mentioned "state" instead of "society" in his correspondence to General Lee.

28. Many southerners were well aware of the potential economic and ideological benefits of engaging in enterprises in Latin America, be they commercial investments or filibustering expeditions, before southern emigrants moved there after the Civil War.

29. Dawsey and Dawsey, eds., *The Confederados,* 19.

30. Ibid., 34, 142–43. Today, the municipalities Santa Bárbara and Americana house approximately 178,596 and 212,791 residents, respectively.

31. October 18, 1866, letter from Frank McMullan to Minister of Brazil to the United States, Rockwell Hall Smith Collection, Mss1 Sm645 a, Virginia Historical Society.

32. *New Orleans Times,* January 24, 1867.

33. Douglas Audenreid Grier, *Confederate Emigration to Brazil, 1865–1870* (Ann Arbor, MI: University Microfilms, 1969), 89, 91.

34. Ibid.

35. Some southern emigrants did bring slaves into Brazil, but such examples are rare. As Adam Rothman explores, slave owners also tried to bring slaves to Cuba after the Civil War. *Beyond Freedom's Reach: A Kidnapping in the Twilight of Slavery* (Cambridge, MA: Harvard University Press, 2015).

36. Many individuals urged their friends and family members to come join them in Brazil, but those family members and friends could not always come due to the "want of money sufficient for traveling expenses." For example, see January 17, 1866, letter from Mrs. C. V. Berrien to George Scarborough Barnsley in the George Scarborough Barnsley Papers #1521, Southern Historical Collection, The Wilson Library, University of North Carolina at Chapel Hill. H. Hall took economic shortages in the South into consideration when he wrote about his experiences in Brazil for the *Sun and Times* in Columbus, Georgia. He advised people considering making the move to Brazil, "No single man (unless a mechanic) should come with the expectation of setting up himself without money enough to buy a farm and purchase his subsistence for one year, say two thousand dollars ($2,000)." Quoted in Lawrence Hill, *Diplomatic Relations between the United States and Brazil* (Durham, NC: Duke University Press, 1932), 48.

37. George Scarborough Barnsley reported that many of the people who followed Frank McMullan "had been large planters in the Southern States before the civil war and other officers of high rank during the same." Notes on Brazil during the years of 1867 to 1880 in the George Scarborough Barnsley Papers #1521, Southern Historical Collection, The Wilson Library, University of North Carolina at Chapel Hill. While many of the upper-class travelers to Brazil had been planters in the South, not all of them were. Many emigrants were planters, doctors, lawyers, or military officers in the South before they traveled to Brazil. *Mobile Daily Register*, February 21, 1870.

38. Bertram Wyatt-Brown, *Honor and Violence in the Old South* (New York: Oxford University Press, 1986).

39. *Daily Courier,* March 7, 1866.

40. *New Orleans Daily True Delta,* February 15, 1866.

41. Dawsey and Dawsey, eds., *The Confederados.*

42. Journal of Trip to Brazil, June 10 1865–November 9 1865 in the James McFadden Gaston Papers, #1470, Southern Historical Collection, Wilson Library, University of North Carolina at Chapel Hill.

43. A *Diario do Rio* newspaper clipping from May 18, 1867, in "Document #2" of the Calceçao Tavares Bastos Collection claims that McMullan led 278 people, but this claim is no guarantee that George Barnsley was among that particular group.

44. The Barnsley family was not the only one to travel to Brazil en masse. For example, William H. Norris and his son, Robert C. Norris, became the leaders of another southern colony, Dixieland, near Campo in São Paulo.

45. April 4, 1868, letter, "La Recommendation For James A. Marchant," E: 112, Box 1, Folder 5, Marchant (James Alexander) Family Papers, Hill Memorial Library, Louisiana State University.

46. Descendants of southern emigrants living in the 1950s still commented on the frequency of Mason membership as evidenced by tombstones. See October 9, 1955, letter, p. 6, September 5, 1955, letter, Smith, Rockwell Hall Collection, #Meg15m645aFA1, Virginia Historical Society.

47. Masonic certificates from 1872, 1873, 1875, and 1897, in the Ann Eliza McCord Papers, #1594-z, Southern Historical Collection, The Wilson Library, University of North Carolina at Chapel Hill.

48. February 10, 1878, letter in the James McFadden Gaston Papers.

49. March 12, 1871, letter in the Andrew McCollam Papers, #449.

50. This is, of course, not to claim that southerners considered all Brazilians to be the same. Many southerners made clear distinctions between Brazilians of Portuguese ancestry and those with African ancestry.

51. *Galveston Daily News,* June 11, 1886.

52. Southern responses to Brazilian naturalization appear to be rather mixed. Julia Louisa Hentz Keyes claimed that southerners could be naturalized after two years of residence on a piece of property. If they took an oath to the "empire and constitution," then the process would take less time. Despite this option, she concluded that foreigners had all of the civil rights granted to natives (Keyes, "Our Life in Brazil," in the Julia Louisa Hentz Keyes Reminiscence #1672-z, pp. 13–14, Southern Historical Collection, Wilson Library, University of North Carolina at Chapel Hill. Paperwork promoting emigration to Brazil

lays out several qualifications for southern emigrants, including a preference for "farmers," people between ten and fifteen years of age, and people of northern European descent, but does not specify that these emigrants need to become legal citizens of Brazil before obtaining their land. "Document #19," Calceçao Tavares Bastos Collection at the Biblioteca Nacional do Brasil, #I 28,15,005 m. 031–043. According to Matthew Maury, a similar situation existed in Mexico. "It is important for emigrants to Mexico from England, and the Continent, as well as from the Southern States, to know that they are not required to bring passports. Arriving at Vera Cruz, they will find the colonization agent, Mr. Y. P. Oropesa, who will pass them and their effects free through the Custom house, and give them gratis such certificates, information, and assistance, as they may require to speed them on their way." Minor Family Papers, Mss1M663c 4247 Section 72, Virginia Historical Society.

53. *The Daily Picayune,* July 16, 1988, 6.

54. March 7, 1890, letter from Robert Rogers to George Barnsley in the George Scarborough Barnsley Papers.

55. "Original of Reply to a Circular asking for information of the Ex-confederates emigrants April 1915 by Dr. George Scarborough Barnsley," p. 76, Folder #25, George Scarborough Barnsley Papers.

56. Ibid., pp. 27, 35.

57. For example, August 2, 1881, letter from Addie to George Barnsley, Folder #17 in ibid.

58. For other examples of families with members living in both Brazil and the South, see the *Confederate Veteran* of March 1921 (referenced in Notes, ca. 1865–1980, concerning Confederate expatriates outside the United States, #159187, Virginia Historical Society) and "Our Life in Brazil," in Julia Louisa Hentz Keyes Reminiscence, 1874, p. 80.

59. Both of these conclusions are further supported by the fact that George Barnsley visited friends as well as family in the United States and agreed to write up some memoirs for the Daughters of the Confederacy. "Original of reply to a Circular asking for information of the Ex-confederates emigrants April 1915 by Dr. George Scarborough Barnsley," folder #25 in The George Scarborough Barnsley Papers.

60. Improved transportation technology, such as the steam engine, also greatly overcame the obstacles of traveling over very long distances.

61. Hill, *Diplomatic Relations between the United States and Brazil,* 42.

62. Journal July 1 1882–April 1, 1883, March 10, 1929–September 3, 1935, in the James McFadden Gaston Papers.

63. Ibid.

64. The Methodist American College in Rio de Janeiro continued to be a strong Protestant center in 1891. Ida Mason Dorsey Brown Papers, Mss1 B8134 a 36–37, Virginia Historical Society.

65. Such ideological separating constructs rarely withstood the practical aspects of living in a foreign country. George Barnsley, for example, needed to attend a medical school in Rio de Janeiro before he obtained a license to practice medicine in Brazil. Relação do Rio de Janeiro, Curador Geral dos Órfãos, Cobrança judicial, Honorários medicos, Número 643, Apelação 0, Caixa 560, Maço 0, Gal C, Local Resende Apelação cível—ACI, Ficha 163888, p. 9, Archivo Nacional do Brasil. Other emigrants needed help with learning Portuguese. "Brazilian Travel Diary," # 05235-z, pp. 24, 143, Southern Historical Collection, Wilson Library, University of North Carolina at Chapel Hill.

66. A classic work on creating imagined communities remains Benedict Anderson, *Imagined Communities: Reflections on the Origin and Spread of Nationalism* (London: Verso, 1983).

67. Micol Seigel provides a useful framework for these connections when she calls network nodes, such as letters or physical places of intense transnational interactions and entities, "touchpoints." She posits, "Sometimes people gazed out at each other to understand themselves as national beings, using their viewfinders to locate useful touchpoints. . . . The communities they imagined in that process (to paraphrase Benedict Anderson) were odd-shaped beasts, neither fully within nor simply larger than their nation-states." *Uneven Encounters: Making Race and Nation in Brazil and the United States* (Durham, NC: Duke University Press, 2009), xii.

68. September 28, 1868, letter from J. D. Porter to Charles Nathan.

69. Ibid.

70. "Notes on Brazil during the years of 1867 to 1880 by George Scarborough Barnsley M. D." in the George Scarborough Barnsley Papers. Underlining in original.

71. "Our Life in Brazil" in the Julia Louisa Hentz Keyes Reminiscence.

72. Journal of Trip to Brazil June 10 1865–November 9 1865, in the James McFadden Gaston Papers #1470, Southern Historical Collection, Wilson Library, University of North Carolina at Chapel Hill.

73. Such a vision is not unlike elements of Thomas Jefferson's agrarian society.

74. Joseph L. McGee, *Brazilian Reflector*, August 1868 in "Document #10" of the Calceçao Tavares Bastos Collection at the Biblioteca Nacional do Brasil, #I 28,15,005 m. 031–043.

75. For example, see "Document #19" in ibid.

76. For a more extensive study of the relationship between types of work and citizenship, see David Williard, "An Ideology beyond Defeat: Confederate Visions of Work and Citizenship in the Reconstruction South," in this volume.

77. Porter claimed that "Brazil offers the Southern political enfranchisement," but southern political involvement in Brazil appears to be quite rare. July 5, 1867, James D. Porter Letter to Mr. John D. Templeton, p. 9, Virginia Historical Society. The fact that George Barnsley knew a man whose son actually dabbled in Brazilian political parties was worthy of mention in Barnsley's list of southern acquaintances in Brazil. "Notes on Brazil during the years of 1867 to 1880 by George Scarborough Barnsley M. D." in the George Scarborough Barnsley Papers, folder #23.

78. July 1, 1941, letter from Lily Page de Shultz Page to Mrs. J. Houston, Page Family Papers, Virginia Historical Society.

79. Some emigrant descendants in Brazil still celebrate their ancestry with annual festivals.

Afterword

LAURA F. EDWARDS

Questions about citizenship necessarily involve questions about governance. That connection, however, is not always apparent in the current historiography, particularly in US history, where the scholarship tends to construe citizenship as a legal status that establishes an individual's attachment to an already constituted nation. As a result, the literature focuses on one side of citizenship: on the rights and privileges of citizens, not the governing institutions that confer citizenship. As Paul Quigley points out in his brilliant introduction to this volume, citizenship is a relatively recent concept, one that was ill-defined and fluid in the first half of the nineteenth century. But nation-states are also relatively new. In fact, conceptions of citizenship predated the formation of a modern nation-state in the United States. Citizenship's history is thus bound up with a broader history of governance, a history that involves multiple, often overlapping governing institutions.

While the focus of *The Civil War and the Transformation of Citizenship* is not governance, its history looms large in the volume's essays. As they show, the Civil War placed incredible pressure on government at all levels, imposing new responsibilities while making existing ones more difficult to fulfill—a situation that raised questions about the meaning of citizenship. At the same time, the war also opened up spaces for a wide variety of Americans to act on their own ideas about what government should be and do—ideas that were expressed in terms of citizenship. In this afterword, I want to linger on the history of governance to underscore the volume's significance to our understanding of citizenship: that changes in Americans' relationship to government—the essence of citizenship—were far more profound than the current scholarship suggests.[1]

Governance refers to the wide range of institutions and practices that exercised legal authority in the nineteenth-century United States and on which Americans relied to resolve their conflicts and maintain order. Governance obviously included the state—that is, state governments and the Federal government, the institutions that comprise the state and that share governing authority within it according to the US Constitution. But governance was not limited to the state, particularly in the early nineteenth century. Local government, which included county and municipal courts where a great deal of daily business was done, shared authority with governing institutions at the state and Federal levels. Governing authority, moreover, also resided in institutions that were relatively private, such as churches, voluntary organizations, neighborhoods, and households. To complicate matters, the line between the categories of private and public forms of governance often blurred.[2]

Conceptions of citizenship grew out of this context of multiple, overlapping governing jurisdictions. In the first half of the nineteenth century, Americans were as likely to identify themselves as citizens of their states or even their hometowns as they were as citizens of the United States. The meaning of citizenship, moreover, depended on the particular governing body. The 1817 New York City Ordinances, for instance, required municipal officials to be "citizens of the State of New-York, and inhabitants and householders of the City of New-York." State citizenship was essential for officials who had to uphold state as well as municipal laws. So it was important in that context. But that definition of citizenship disappeared in ordinances dealing with matters relating to governance within the city, such as the regulation of markets, assembly in public areas, and fire prevention and control. Those referred to the citizens of New York City, a category that seemed more like "inhabitants," because everyone was obligated to abide by those regulations. Nowhere did the New York City ordinances refer to US citizenship. There was little need, since that status had a negligible effect on governance within the city, as described in the municipal ordinances.[3]

The fact that Americans had more experience with some governing jurisdictions than with others also shaped conceptions of citizenship. The Federal government figured prominently in the territories, which lacked the institutional apparatus of state government. It also dealt with the rights of those individuals who were not within a state's jurisdiction: not just in the territories, but also in relation to Indian nations, in the District of Columbia, and in Federal cases. Native Americans, in particular, felt the full weight of Federal authority because of their status as members of foreign nations. So did free blacks, although it was because of their tenuous legal status within the United States. In fact, free blacks not only claimed birthright citizenship long before it was written into Federal law, but also connected civil rights, which lay within the jurisdiction of states and localities, to citizenship—a combination that moved such cases into Federal courts. But for most white Americans who lived within the jurisdiction of existing states, the Federal government was a distant entity. Generally, they encountered Federal authority in only a few ways: through the military, the campaigns of aspirants to Federal office, or the postal service. As such, their status as US citizens did not really affect the course of their daily lives.[4]

People were more likely to encounter the authority of states, which had jurisdiction over most of the work of governance, through their responsibilities to protect the rights of individuals and to maintain the public order. Nowhere is the relative power of states more evident than in the question of US citizenship. States exercised considerable authority over all those people deemed citizens of the United States before passage of the Fourteenth Amendment, which not only provided a definitive statement about who qualified for US citizenship and clarified the meaning of that status, but also solidified Federal control over citizenship. The Federal government remained surprisingly silent on questions involving US citizens before that. The 1790 Naturalization Act did limit citizenship to those who were free and white. But that act and subsequent legislation addressed the situation of new immigrants who sought application for naturalization. Their provisions did not extend to those who resided in the United States at its inception and never applied for citizenship. Nor did Federal law define the rights and obligations that came with US citizenship.[5]

To the extent that the substance of US citizenship was spelled out at all, it was at the state level. States also had their own definitions of state citizenship, which did establish rights and obligations, but which varied among states. To complicate matters, those two concepts—US citizenship and state citizenship—emerged in an ad hoc way, through statutes and case law, with no clear distinction between the two. States did not usually question the citizenship status (be it US or state) of those who lived in their boundaries, although there was considerable discussion about the rights and citizenship status of free blacks in the decades immediately preceding the Civil War, which culminated in the US Supreme

Court's decision in *Dred Scott*, with its denial of US citizenship to all people of African descent. But *Dred Scott* was controversial precisely because it upset the status quo and encroached on the jurisdiction of states. In fact, the controversy surrounding *Dred Scott* made its implications ambiguous. Indeed, it is no coincidence that states' jurisdiction over matters involving individual rights—an area where states' and the Federal government's legal authority overlapped—constituted a central point of tension in the conflicts leading up to the Civil War, particularly in the 1850s when the Federal government increasingly involved itself in matters relating to the status of African Americans.[6]

State governments' authority and their presence in Americans' lives, however, extended only so far, because states defined rights and the public order so narrowly. In the first half of the nineteenth century, only a small minority of Americans could claim the full range of rights, a situation that excluded the vast majority of Americans from one of the primary roles of state government. In this period, the term *individual rights*—or *rights* for short—referred to those rights that, at the time, were thought to be conferred by government, namely civil rights and, increasingly, political rights, which were available to those people recognized as legal individuals (namely free white men, particularly those with property). Secondarily, the term referred to natural rights, which belonged to everyone and could not be abridged by government, at least in theory. In practice, what constituted a natural right was contested and ultimately dependent on government recognition and enforcement. Natural rights—even life and liberty—were also connected to civil and political rights, in the sense that those who could claim civil and political rights (free white men) had stronger claims to natural rights than those who did not (such as married women, the enslaved, and even the working poor). Property ownership was inseparable from individual rights in the early nineteenth century. Property requirements for suffrage had only recently been eliminated for white men by the time of the Civil War. Even then, universal white manhood suffrage was not quite universal: elections for some offices in some states were still restricted on the basis of property. And most civil rights involved the ownership, accumulation, and exchange of property or access to those jurisdictions with authority over that body of law. Not all citizens—be they citizens of a state or the United States—could claim the rights that states were charged with protecting.[7]

In practice, moreover, rights tended to uphold existing inequalities, a situation that tended to distance the state even further from the interests and needs of most Americans. Nineteenth-century political leaders, regardless of party affiliation, invoked rights in expansive terms, often in connection to liberty, freedom, and equality, with the implication that they could accomplish those ends. To be sure, rights were necessary for individuals to function independently in American society. Without them, it was impossible to claim legal ownership of property, enter into contracts, or defend one's interests in state or Federal courts. But in the legal system, rights did not do the kind of work that the political rhetoric of the time implied. They resolved competing claims among individuals by identifying winners and losers, a situation that undercut the connection between rights and equality posited in political rhetoric. State courts, moreover, were committed to the preservation of rights as such, not to the concerns of the individuals who brought their problems for adjudication. As such, the legal framework of rights produced outcomes of questionable justice, according to the standards of many Americans: a conviction overturned because of an improperly framed indictment, for instance, or the seizure of property because of a faulty bill of sale. More often than not, the application of rights tended to preserve existing inequalities, because lawmakers concerned themselves with the rights that governed property ownership and economic exchange, a body of law concerned with the interests of those who owned property, not those without. That situation explains the popular stereotype of lawyers as parasites who exploited arcane rules to profit from the misfortune of others.[8]

States' broad powers to regulate in the name of the public health and welfare also restricted people's access to state government, further limiting the meaning of citizenship. State constitutions did have bills of rights, but the rights they enumerated were not absolute. In fact, state and local governments exercised wide latitude in limiting or suspending rights and citizenship status in the name of the public good. That legal logic sanctioned not just slavery, but also the range of restrictions placed on free blacks, all women, and many white men without property in states without slavery.[9]

States then further removed themselves from Americans' lives by delegating significant power to counties and municipalities in matters involving the public order, making local areas, not the states, the juris-

dictions most closely associated with those duties. That situation dates
to the Revolution, when lawmakers turned their colonies into states and
then decentralized the most important functions of state government—
all in the name of bringing law closer to the people. Much of the daily
business of governance was done in local legal venues: the circuit courts
and even more localized proceedings, such as magistrates' hearings and
trials. Their locations made the law part of the fabric of people's lives.
They convened wherever there was sufficient space—in a house, a barn,
a mill, or a yard. That was true even for circuit courts in the first decades
of the nineteenth century, when many counties lacked the formal court-
houses that would later house circuit courts. Local courts were the legal
jurisdictions that would have been the most familiar to most Americans,
given the wide range of issues handled in these venues and the wide
variety of people who were involved in the process adjudicating them.[10]

Local jurisdictions were the ones with which most Americans were
the most familiar. Not only were they the most accessible, but they also
dealt with the issues that affected most people's lives, which was why it
was possible for Americans to think of themselves as citizens of counties, cities, and towns. Local jurisdictions had authority over a broad,
ambiguous area of public law, which included all crimes as well as a
range of ill-defined offenses that disrupted "the peace" of the social order. The peace was a well-established, highly gendered concept in Anglo-
American law that expressed the ideal order of the metaphorical public
body, subordinating everyone (in varying ways) within a hierarchical
system. It was inclusive, but only in the sense that it enclosed everyone
in its patriarchal embrace, raising its collective interests over those of
any given individual. Keeping the peace meant keeping everyone—from
the lowest to the highest—in their appropriate places, as defined by rigid
inequalities of the early nineteenth century.[11]

While this localized system did not recognize the rights of free
women, children, enslaved people, or free blacks, it still incorporated
them into its basic workings, because they were part of the social order
that it was charged with overseeing. The system maintained their subordination and regulated their behavior. But it also relied on information
they supplied about community disorder. Take, for example, two cases
in North Carolina initiated by slaves: one slave complained to a magistrate that a free black man had been playing cards with other slaves on a
Sunday; another complained that the same free black man assaulted one
of those slaves after the card game. (One suspects that a third complaint

could have been filed about the consumption of "spirituous liquors," another common morals charge.) Technically, these slaves gave "information," because laws prohibited all slaves from filing a complaint; the magistrate then proceeded with the case based on that information. These two enslaved men had their own reasons for what they did, reasons distinct from the magistrate's likely concerns about disorder among slaves and free blacks. As such, the cases illustrate central elements of this part of the legal system. Different people pursued different ends within it, sometimes at the same time. Masters filed charges against slaves they could not control. Wives filed charges against husbands. Children informed on their parents. Families regularly brought their feuds to court for resolution, with wives, husbands, parents, children, siblings, aunts, uncles, and cousins all lining up to air their dirty laundry. Even enslaved people tried to mobilize local courts to address their concerns. That was possible because the system *depended* on the participation of everyone in the local community so as to maintain order.[12]

The "law" in this part of the system was capacious and uncontrolled by legal professionals. In most legal matters, the interested parties collected evidence, gathered witnesses, and represented themselves. Local courts did follow state laws regarding rights in procedural respects, particularly in determining who could prosecute cases in their own names. But determinations about the merits of the claims—righting the wrongs in question—relied on common law in its traditional sense as a flexible collection of principles rooted in local custom, but which also included an array of texts and principles, in addition to statutes and state appellate law, as potential sources for authoritative legal principles. The information provided by those with an interest in the case also mattered, because the expectation was that outcomes should preserve the social order as it existed in particular localities. Of course, the definition of "order" was broad and varied, reflecting the interpersonal conflicts that characterized even the most tightly knit communities. So it was not unusual for witness after witness to come forward to tell what they knew, a situation that magistrates bore patiently, knowing that the resolution of the legal conflict was also about healing a rift in the community. Preservation of the social order was also why court officials took evidence and even prosecuted cases on behalf of individuals without the legal right to testify or prosecute—enslaved people, married women, and minors.[13]

This level of government existed in the lived context of people's lives and existing social relationships. While the scholarship tends to identify those dynamics as the stuff of social history, they were also the means of connecting people to local government and, hence, the stuff of citizenship. Still, citizenship was a nebulous concept at the local level, because there was no clear definition of it. In formal terms, citizenship was less important than the notion of a settlement or residence in an area, which established an individual's claim to poor relief and other local services. But in popular usage, citizenship at the local level meant belonging—a concept that scholars use to define citizenship more generally, but which is particularly applicable in the context of localities. Citizenship meant ties to a place and a commitment to the people there. It was about actions: the observation of the local customs and regulations as well as attention to the work necessary to keep families and communities together. It was also about emotions: an individual's feeling that a particular place was home and others' recognition of those feelings.[14]

This open-ended sense of citizenship, however, created conflict, because it allowed so many people to feel that they did belong—or should belong—and that they should have a say in how the public order was constituted. But all these people regularly disagreed. Local governing processes acknowledged that situation and provided a means for arriving at an outcome that would allow people to put conflicts behind them and move on. Consensus, however, was more apparent than real. In the slave South, it rested on a social order that subordinated the vast majority of the population—all African Americans, free white women, and propertyless white men. These groups experienced different levels of subordination, with enslaved African Americans enduring the most extreme forms. But none of these people could redefine the structural dynamics of the social order, even though they participated in the system and occasionally bent it to their interests. To the extent they had credibility, it was because of the social ties that also defined their subordination. They were insiders, not outsiders: enslaved people who had the support of their masters and other whites; married women who were known as good wives and neighbors; poor white men known for their work ethic and amiability. Positive outcomes of cases involving those insiders did not result in favorable treatment for anyone else. To the contrary, local communities in the slave South inflicted horrific punishments on those, particularly enslaved African Americans, who did not fulfill their subordinate roles. Those outcomes seemed just plain wrong to those who did not have the status to receive favorable treatment. Still, the culture of local governance was deeply engrained within American society, and it carried considerable power at the time of the Civil War, framing expectations about what government should be and do, even for those on the margins.[15]

The Civil War upended this governing structure. Before the Civil War, the United States and the Federal government formed just one piece of Americans' identities as citizens in the first half of the nineteenth century. They spoke of *these* United States, referring to an entity that was less a coherent nation than it was a coalition of separate states. By the end of the Civil War era, the rhetorical constructions of citizenship had become more singular and definitive: Americans were, primarily, citizens of *the* United States. That conception of citizenship was most clearly articulated by Lincoln in the Gettysburg Address, with its powerful image of a newly consecrated nation, one built on the past but remade in the crucible of war: "It is rather for us to be here dedicated to the great task remaining before us—that from these honored dead we take increased devotion to that cause for which they gave the last full measure of devotion—that we here highly resolve that these dead shall not have died in vain, that this nation under God shall have a new birth of freedom, and that government of the people, by the people, for the people shall not perish from the earth."[16]

Citizenship could be expressed in this way because of the changes in the institutions of government, particularly in the expansion of the Federal government's authority and reach, which brought it into the lives and concerns of more Americans. The Civil War and Reconstruction rank among the most dramatic events in the history of state formation. It is widely acknowledged that change in this period concentrated more legal authority at the Federal level, creating a government with a truly national reach for the first time in American history and initiating a process that turned the United States into a nation-state. Secession challenged the traditional balance of power between the Federal government and the state governments. The exigencies of war then forced the United States and even the Confederacy to locate more power at the Federal level. Many wartime measures proved temporary, especially in the Confederacy. But the policies of Reconstruction—particularly the three new constitutional amendments—permanently enhanced the power of the Federal government in the reconstituted United States.

Essays in *The Civil War and the Transformation of Citizenship* reveal new aspects of that transformation by exploring Americans' changing relationship to the Federal government, as it existed on the ground. The existing historiography has covered the upheaval of war and its devastating implications for civilians as well as soldiers. But essays in this volume shift the focus away from the military conflict to civil authority, analyzing the difficulties of Americans who were suspended between two competing Federal governments.[17]

The creation of the Confederacy did not redefine the citizenship of all white southerners. The United States never acknowledged the legitimacy of the Confederate nation and continued to characterize whites there in terms of their relationship to the United States. They were either traitors or loyalists. The Confederacy did recognize the legitimacy of the United States, but that led it to define whites within its territory in similar terms: as traitors or loyalists. To be sure, loyalty to the nation and its government was always expected of citizens and, before that, of subjects. But, as essays in *The Civil War and the Transformation of Citizenship* suggest, the volatile governing dynamics of the Civil War era fundamentally altered the standards of loyalty and, by extension, of citizenship.[18]

People living in the Confederacy, particularly areas occupied by the United States Army, had to choose the nation to which they were loyal. They also had to prove their loyalty, directly and personally, to Federal officials. That was no easy task. Neither actions nor documentation were definitive. For that matter, documentation, in the form of passports or birth certificates, did not always exist. Instead, proof of loyalty lay more in the authenticity of feelings, which were highly subjective and extremely difficult to discern. The dilemma is particularly apparent for the men forced into the Confederate army through conscription and then captured by the United States Army, as Angela Zombek shows in her essay, "Citizenship—Compulsory or Convenient: Federal Officials, Confederate Prisoners, and the Oath of Allegiance." Imprisoned Confederate soldiers found it virtually impossible to establish their loyalty to the United States. Regardless of what they said, the obvious incentives to escape imprisonment suggested that they were lying about their true feelings for the sake of convenience.

Other white southerners struggled with their feelings of allegiance, as Jonathan Berkey's and Lucius Wedge's explorations of loyalty oaths show. Loyalty oaths were particularly consequential at this time because of their religious meanings. The words were more than mere words: to swear falsely was to endanger one's soul. Conflicts over loyalty oaths, as Lucius Wedge argues in "'I am a citizen of Heaven!': William H. Wharton, Andrew Johnson, and Citizenship in Occupied Nashville," exposed different connections to the nation. Andrew Johnson, who understood his loyalty to the civil authority of the United States in religious terms, used oaths as a way to coerce support for the United States. But others in his home state of Tennessee refused the oaths and the question of national loyalty by asserting the primacy of a "higher government." Loyalty to the Federal government, moreover, had material consequences that it did not before the Civil War, as underscored in Jonathan Berkey's essay, "Swallowing the Oath: The Battle over Citizenship in Occupied Winchester." In order to cross into US territory, Confederates in the Winchester area "swallowed" the loyalty oath, compromising their religious faith, their personal integrity, and their standing in the community, but knowing that it was the only way to see family and friends and to obtain needed supplies.

This conception of loyalty also posed problems for Confederate veterans and Confederates unwilling to accept defeat. According to David Williard in "An Ideology beyond Defeat: Confederate Visions of Work and Citizenship in the Reconstruction South," Confederate defeat had profound personal and political implications for soldiers because they had bound their selfhood so completely to the fate of the Confederacy. To reestablish a connection to themselves, their communities, and the nation that they had fought against, they pursued an "ideology of work." That effort, however, ran counter to their continued connections to the Confederate cause, expressed as violent racism. As Claire Wolnisty shows in "To 'Serve Both as a Light and as a Beacon to Our Noble Old State': Southern Citizens in Latin America," some Confederates fled the United States altogether and moved to Latin America. They still maintained loyalty to the Confederacy there, despite the defeat of that nation and the fact that they were outside its former jurisdiction. The emotional ties were what mattered.

The expectations of loyalty described in these essays dovetail with the findings of recent scholarship on nationalism, which also emphasizes the importance of deeply personal connections to the nation in the Civil War era.[19] As *The Civil War and the Transformation of Citizenship* also suggests, those expectations found their way into policies that, ultimately, remade the governing structure of the United States. During the Civil War, leaders of the Confederacy reached deep into the daily lives of everyone within its jurisdiction, appropriating their labor, property, and lives for the nation, and leaving little for anything else. In the United States, lawmakers never extended Federal authority to the extent that Confederates did, but they also asked Americans for their labor, their earnings, and their lives to support the war effort. More than that, Republican leaders justified the expansion of Federal authority in terms of the government's essential relationship to "the people." That rhetoric fueled expectations that the Federal government would do—and should do—more for all the people than it had in the past. As a result, Americans began looking to the Federal government, not just state or local governments, to protect, support, and further their interests. They began to expect more out of US citizenship.[20]

It was that context that encouraged and supported claims like those of the enslaved women in Tamika Y. Nunley's essay, "'By Stealth' or Dispute: Freedwomen and the Contestation of American Citizenship." Nunley explores the efforts of these women to secure their freedom under Federal legislation that emancipated slaves in the District of Columbia in 1862. Enslaved women negotiated directly with Federal officials, forcing them to recognize their interests and concerns. As Nunley argues, those strategies transformed the meaning of citizenship, stretching it to include a much wider range of people and issues.

The cases that Nunley explores were part of a larger effort on the part of African Americans to use the institutions of government, particularly at the Federal level, during and after the Civil War. Although contemporary observers and later historians have taken such actions for granted, it is remarkable that people who had been enslaved would look for redress in the governing institutions that had maintained their enslavement. But they did. Historians usually attribute such faith to the promise of rights. But formerly enslaved African Americans also were acting on other expectations, deeply rooted in their experiences with the areas of government with which they were most familiar, namely local government. Drawing on that knowledge, they demanded that the Federal government should maintain a just public order. This time, though, they insisted on *their* vision of justice.[21]

Those expectations about the duties of government explain why enslaved African Americans, like the women in Nunley's essay, began bringing their complaints to Federal officials during the Civil War, when their claims to freedom, let alone to rights, were still tenuous. African Americans sought out military officials and military courts to adjudicate their conflicts as soon as they could during the Civil War. They continued to do so after Confederate surrender, but before passage of the Fourteenth Amendment—a time when states of the former Confederacy limited the rights of all African Americans through the notorious Black Codes. African Americans came to these venues with rights claims. But they also expected Federal officials to address the kinds of issues that would have fallen to local courts and that had been handled within the framework of doing what was right: interpersonal conflicts, often involving violence and including domestic issues, as well as matters involving broader questions of social justice, such as the treatment of refugees, payment of wages, and reunification of families. In those cases, they expected Federal venues to do what was right, not just to uphold rights. The various courts under Federal jurisdiction, which lacked an established body of law to handle this diverse array of claims, struggled to keep up. Reading the records, the consternation of some officials is so palpable that you can almost see their furrowed brows and their heads in their hands, trying to figure out how to handle the conflicts in front of them. Needless to say, most of the issues were not of the kind that had fallen within Federal purview before. But African Americans persisted, pushing past jurisdictional boundaries in the pursuit of justice and, in the process, forging a direct relationship to the US government.[22]

The exercise of Federal authority in cases of this kind might have been temporary, if not for the passage of the Reconstruction Amendments, particularly the Fourteenth Amendment, which gave the Federal government authority over the states' handling of rights—something that the Federal government did not have before. To be sure, those powers were limited and largely negative. The Fourteenth Amendment placed restrictions on states, prohibiting them from making or enforcing "any law which shall abridge the privileges or immunities of citizens of the United States" or depriving any person "of life, liberty, or property, without due process of law." It also prohibited the denial "to any person within its jurisdiction the equal protection of the laws." The Federal government could regulate the administration of rights, as defined by the states; but it could not create or distribute rights. Later Civil Rights Acts extended Federal authority in ways that brought it into state law more actively. But given political opposition and the limited resources of Federal enforcement agencies, that authority was never fully utilized in the late nineteenth century.[23]

That negative power was, nonetheless, profound, particularly in the states of the former Confederacy. The Fourteenth Amendment forced states to extend rights to African Americans, which made it possible for them to bring cases to state and local courts. What happened in those local courts then altered Federal authority. Specifically, the Fourteenth Amendment opened up paths for ordinary Americans' conceptions about a just public order to migrate out of local venues through claims to rights that the Federal government was now bound to protect. So did the Fifteenth Amendment, which did for voting rights what the Fourteenth did for civil rights. Not only did these amendments bring the Federal government closer to the lives of Americans, but they also transformed the kinds of issues that the Federal government handled. Where it had once dealt with the mail and the military, it now regularly handled conflicts over the public order that were formerly the province of local and state courts.[24]

Earl Maltz's essay, "Rethinking the Racial Boundaries of Citizenship: Native Americans and People of Chinese Descent," underscores how profound the change in Federal authority was in this period. Much of the historiography focuses on the Federal government's handling of the civil rights of African Americans. But, as Maltz shows, "Republicans and Democrats were also well aware that Federal action might affect the status and rights of other racial minorities as well." The Federal government's claims to authority over the status and rights of citizenship challenged states' handling of Chinese immigrants. They also forced the question of Native Americans' relationship to the United States. As Maltz shows, Federal lawmakers wrote in provisions that kept both groups outside the bounds of the national community.

Federal officials ultimately failed to protect the civil and political rights of African Americans in the South. But African Americans did not necessarily see citizenship only in terms of the civil and political rights protected, at least in theory, by the Federal government through the Fourteenth and Fifteenth Amendments. As Caitlin Verboon demonstrates in her essay, "The 'Fire Fiend,' Black Firemen, and Citizenship in the Postwar Urban South," African Americans continued to assert connections to their communities through service. African American firefighters in Columbia, South Carolina, organized their own voluntary associations to assist the larger community. "Firemen," writes Verboon, "acted out what citizenship meant on that local, everyday level." As such, they "helped to mold what postwar society would look like just as surely as jurists or legislators did." In so doing, they joined the different levels of citizenship—local, state, and Federal—that had existed before the Civil War.

The Federal government's enhanced authority, however, remained and continued to expand. The Reconstruction Amendments provided the foundations for an elaborate Federal bureaucracy that made its appearance in the twentieth century, with a proliferation of agencies charged with securing Americans' rights and promoting their health and welfare. The Pension Bureau was one of those agencies. Although it existed before the Civil War and is not usually connected to the major legal or political changes of that era, the Bureau's duties expanded exponentially during the Civil War. That growth resulted, in part, from the sheer number of Civil War veterans. But it also resulted from the increase in and extension of benefits, which came with new regulations to determine eligibility.[25]

Increasingly, Americans experienced Federal power through their relationships to bureaucracies like the Pension Bureau. Elizabeth Regosin's exploration of Huldah Gordon's efforts to obtain a pension, in her essay "Toward the Temple of American Liberty: Huldah Gordon and the Question of Former Slaves' Citizenship," suggests the nature of these relationships. They were immediate, intimate, and ongoing. They were also freighted with expectations—expectations on the part of Federal officials about what Americans should be and do as well as expectations on the part of Americans about what government should be and do. Bureau officials probed deeply into the lives of Gordon and her family repeatedly before finally approving her pension. That pension came at a high cost to Gordon. But it provided her with economic security, a rare and valuable thing for a single, African American mother in the late nineteenth century. It also allowed her to affirm her ties, as a free person, to the United States.

The process of obtaining a pension, which Regosin describes so eloquently, encapsulates the transformation captured and explored in *The Civil War and the Transformation of Citizenship*. Citizenship was a relationship between Americans and their government. Americans made new claims on their government during the Civil War era, but those claims took on the meanings that they did because of changes in government. Perhaps the most profound change was in expectations of what the Federal government should do for its citizens. The policy changes of the Reconstruction era allowed the aspirations of diverse groups of Americans to move into the realm of Federal government. Those aspirations expressed the unique values of particular groups of Americans;

they were also deeply rooted in existing governing practices—practices outside the realm of state and Federal government. The results remade the relationship between Americans and the nation, raising expectations about the Federal government's role in maintaining a just social order. Those expectations could only result in conflict, since there was no consensus among the American people about what constituted a just society. Yet those aspirations guided the nation's development and, ultimately, our own expectations about what citizenship should mean.

The essays in this volume also suggest new avenues for future research. In general, the essays' keenest historical insights come from archival research that focuses on dynamics close to the ground. That focus allows for the exploration of the American people's relationship to their governing institutions in concrete, material ways. Just as important, it also includes a consideration of Americans' relationship to government at all levels—local, state, and national. The authors take this approach because they are following the sources. In listening so carefully to sources, however, they are creating a more historically grounded view of citizenship, one that moves outside teleological narratives that deal primarily with the Federal government, where questions of citizenship ultimately ended up, but which played a far less authoritative role in the decades between the American Revolution and the Civil War. The authors have pointed us all in a new, historically productive direction, one that we hope will inspire further work and additional insights.

NOTES

1. This article draws on several other publications by the author: Laura F. Edwards, "Status without Rights: African Americans and the Tangled History of Law and Governance in the Nineteenth-Century U.S. South," *American Historical Review* 112 (April 2007): 365–93; Edwards, *The People and Their Peace: Legal Culture and the Transformation of Inequality in the Post-Revolutionary South* (Chapel Hill: University of North Carolina Press, 2009); Edwards, "Reconstruction and the History of Governance," in *The World the Civil War Made,* ed. Gregory P. Downs and Kate Masur (Chapel Hill: University of North Carolina Press, 2015), 30–44; Edwards, *A Legal History of the Civil War and Reconstruction: A Nation of Rights* (New York: Cambridge University Press, 2015); and Edwards, "The Reconstruction of Rights: The Fourteenth Amendment and Popular Conceptions of Governance," *Journal of Supreme Court History* 42 (November 2016): 310–28.

2. Edwards, *The People and Their Peace* and "Reconstruction and the History of Governance." Such a perspective is common in scholarship that focuses on the colonial period. See Christopher L. Tomlins and Bruce H. Mann, eds., *The Many Legalities of Early America* (Chapel Hill: University of North Carolina Press, 2001); Lauren Benton, *A Search for*

Sovereignty: Law and Geography in European Empires, 1400–1900 (New York: Cambridge University Press, 2011); Philip J. Stern, *The Company-State: Corporate Sovereignty and the Early Modern Foundation of the British Empire in India* (New York: Oxford University Press, 2011). But the idea of "many legalities" and overlapping legal arenas tends to drop out of the scholarship focused on the nineteenth century, where the presumption is that the new nation secured a monopoly on legal authority with its founding. Recent work, however, suggests otherwise. See, for instance, Brian Balogh, *A Government Out of Sight: The Mystery of National Authority in Nineteenth-Century America* (New York: Cambridge University Press, 2009); William J. Novak, "The Legal Transformation of Citizenship in Nineteenth-Century America," in *The Democratic Experiment: New Directions in American Political History*, ed. Meg Jacobs, William J. Novak, and Julian Zelizer (Princeton, NJ: Princeton University Press, 2003), 85–119; Novak, "The American Law of Association: The Legal-Political Construction of Civil Society," *Studies in American Political Development* 15 (Fall 2001): 163–88; Christopher Tomlins and Michael Grossberg, eds., *The Cambridge History of Law in America*, vol. 2, *The Long Nineteenth Century, 1789–1920* (New York: Cambridge University Press, 2008); Barbara Young Welke, *Law and the Borders of Belonging in the Long Nineteenth Century United States* (New York: Cambridge University Press, 2010); Kevin Butterfield, *The Making of Tocqueville's America: Law and Association in the Early Nineteenth Century United States* (Chicago: University of Chicago Press, 2015).

3. *Laws and Ordinances . . . of the City of New York* (New York: T. and J. Swords, 1817).

4. For the meaning of citizenship, see Novak, "The Legal Transformation of Citizenship in Nineteenth-Century America." While scholars continue to debate the strength and reach of Federal authority in the nineteenth century, it is generally agreed that the Federal government was less powerful and less visible in the lives of Americans in this century than it would be in the twentieth century. See, for instance, Balogh, *A Government Out of Sight*; Novak, "The Myth of the Weak American State," *American Historical Review* 113 (June 2008): 752–72.

5. Naturalization Act, 1 U.S. *Statutes at Large* 103 (1790); Novak, "The Legal Transformation of Citizenship"; James H. Kettner, *The Development of American Citizenship, 1608–1870* (Chapel Hill: University of North Carolina Press, 1978).

6. *Dred Scott v. Sandford* 60 U.S. 393 (1857). In the 1830s and 1840s, northern courts had adopted the position that slave law from southern states could not reach into their states; see Leonard W. Levy, *The Law of the Commonwealth and Chief Justice Shaw* (Cambridge, MA: Harvard University Press, 1957); Paul Finkelman, *An Imperfect Union: Slavery, Federalism, and Comity* (Chapel Hill: University of North Carolina Press, 1981). That was why both the Fugitive Slave Act, 9 U.S. *Statutes at Large* 462 (1850), and the decision in *Dred Scott* proved so controversial. Literature on African Americans' attempts to sue for freedom suggests how legally ambiguous the distinction between slavery and freedom was for African Americans in the decades between the Revolution and the Civil War: Martha S. Jones, "Time, Space, and Jurisdiction in Atlantic World Slavery: The Volunbrun Household in Gradual Emancipation New York," *Law and History Review* 29 (November 2011): 1031–60; Kelly Kennington, *In the Shadow of Dred Scott: St. Louis Freedom Suits and the Legal Culture of Slavery in Antebellum America* (Athens: University of Georgia Press, forthcoming 2017); Edlie L. Wong, *Neither Fugitive nor Free: Atlantic Slavery, Freedom Suits, and the Legal Culture of Travel* (New York: New York University Press, 2009). Questions about freedom were tied to questions about racial identity, which were not easy to resolve

either; see Ariela J. Gross, *What Blood Won't Tell: A History of Race on Trial in America* (Cambridge, MA: Harvard University Press, 2008).

7. Edwards, *A Legal History of the Civil War and Reconstruction*, particularly 90–119; Edwards, "The Reconstruction of Rights."

8. Edwards, *The People and Their Peace*, particularly 205–98. For an especially compelling account of the limits of rights in the early nineteenth century, see Christopher L. Tomlins, *Law, Labor, and Ideology in the Early American Republic* (New York: Cambridge University Press, 1993).

9. For states' regulatory power, see William J. Novak, *The People's Welfare: Law and Regulation in Nineteenth-Century America* (Chapel Hill: University of North Carolina Press, 1996). For states' regulatory power and the limitations on rights, see Edwards, *The People and Their Peace.*

10. Edwards, *The People and Their Peace*, particularly 26–53, 256–85. Also see Martha S. Jones, "*Hughes v. Jackson*: Race and Rights beyond *Dred Scott*," *North Carolina Law Review* 91 (June 2013): 1757–83; Kimberly Welch, "Black Litigiousness and White Accountability: Free Blacks and the Rhetoric of Reputation in the Antebellum Natchez District," *Journal of the Civil War Era* 5 (September 2015): 372–98; Kelly Kennington, *In the Shadow of* Dred Scott; Felicity Turner, "Rights and the Ambiguities of Law: Infanticide in the Nineteenth-Century U.S. South," *Journal of the Civil War Era* 4 (September 2014): 350–72.

11. Edwards, *The People and Their Peace*, particularly 64–99.

12. *State v. Woodson Chavis*, 1851, Criminal Actions Concerning Slaves and Free Persons of Color, Granville County, NCSA; Edwards, *The People and Their Peace*, 64–132.

13. Edwards, *The People and Their Peace*, 64–132.

14. Welke, *Law and the Borders of Belonging*; Cornelia H. Dayton and Sharon V. Salinger, *Robert Love's Warnings: Searching for Strangers in Colonial Boston* (Philadelphia: University of Pennsylvania Press, 2014); Kunal Parker, *Making Foreigners: Immigration and Citizenship Law in America, 1600–2000* (New York: Cambridge University Press, 2015). Also see Meggan Farish's forthcoming dissertation, "Rethinking Violence, Legal Culture, and Community in New York City, 1785–1826."

15. Edwards, *The People and Their Peace*, 169–201; Edwards, "Status without Rights"; Edwards, "The Reconstruction of Rights."

16. Gettysburg Address, 9 November 1863, available at The Avalon Project: Documents in Law, History, and Diplomacy, avalon.law.yale.edu/19th_century/gettyb.asp, accessed August 24, 2016; Priscilla Wald, *Constituting Americans: Cultural Anxiety and Narrative Form* (Durham, NC: Duke University Press, 1995). Of course, people referred to "the United States" before the Civil War, just as they continued to refer to "these United States" after the Civil War. But, as Wald's work suggests, the shift is at the level of conceptualization: in many Americans' perception of their connection to United States as a unified, national entity.

17. The essays build on the work of Gregory P. Downs, *After Appomattox: Military Occupation and the Ends of War* (Cambridge, MA: Harvard University Press, 2015), which emphasizes the role of the Federal government, through military occupation, on the ground in the states of the former Confederacy during Reconstruction.

18. These essays build on recent scholarship, including William A. Blair, *With Malice toward Some: Treason and Loyalty in the Civil War Era* (Chapel Hill: University of North Carolina Press, 2014); Paul Quigley, "State, Nation, and Citizen in the Confederate Crucible

of War," in *State and Citizen: British America and the Early United States*, ed. Peter Onuf and Peter Thompson (Charlottesville: University of Virginia Press, 2013), 242–70; Paul Quigley, "Civil War Conscription and the International Boundaries of Citizenship," *Journal of the Civil War Era* 4 (September 2014): 373–97.

19. For recent scholarship, see Gary Gallagher, *The Union War* (Cambridge, MA: Harvard University Press, 2011); Gallagher, *Becoming Confederates: Paths to a New National Identity* (Athens: University of Georgia Press, 2013); Paul Quigley, *Shifting Grounds: Nationalism and the American South, 1848–1865* (New York: Oxford University Press, 2012); Anne Sarah Rubin, *A Shattered Nation: The Rise and Fall of the Confederacy, 1861–1868* (Chapel Hill: University of North Carolina Press, 2005).

20. Edwards, *A Legal History of the Civil War and Reconstruction.*

21. Edwards, "Status without Rights"; Edwards, "The Reconstruction of Rights."

22. Edwards, "Status without Rights"; Edwards, "The Reconstruction of Rights." Downs, *After Appomattox,* emphasizes the pervasiveness and importance of Federal legal venues, which often took over for local courts in the years following Confederate surrender. Recent scholarship on African Americans' experiences during the Civil War and Reconstruction often uses government documents, particularly legal records, and underscores the fact that African Americans made every effort to use various levels of the legal system. Generally, however, such work does not link those sources or the resulting cases to broader changes in law and legal institutions. The work associated with the Freedmen and Southern Society Project, which pioneered in the use of Federal records that had been largely overlooked, provided the framework for subsequent scholarship. See, for instance, Ira Berlin, Joseph P. Reidy, and Leslie S. Rowland, eds., *The Black Military Experience*, ser. 2 of *Freedom: A Documentary History of Emancipation, 1861–1867* (New York: Cambridge University Press, 1982); Ira Berlin, Barbara J. Fields, Thavolia Glymph, Joseph P. Reidy, and Leslie S. Rowland, eds., *The Destruction of Slavery*, ser. 1, vol. 1 of *Freedom: A Documentary History of Emancipation, 1861–1867* (New York: Cambridge University Press, 1985); and Ira Berlin, Stephen F. Miller, and Leslie S. Rowland, "Afro-American Families in the Transition from Slavery to Freedom," *Radical History Review* 42 (1988): 89–121. For other work on the period that makes extensive use of legal sources, see Laura F. Edwards, *Gendered Strife and Confusion: The Political Culture of Reconstruction* (Urbana: University of Illinois Press, 1997); Mary Farmer-Kaiser, *Freedwomen and the Freedmen's Bureau: Race, Gender, and Public Policy in the Age of Emancipation* (New York: Fordham University Press, 2010); Crystal N. Feimster, "'What If I Am a Woman': Black Women's Campaigns for Sexual Justice and Citizenship," in *The World the Civil War Made*, ed. Downs and Masur; Barbara J. Fields, *Slavery and Freedom on the Middle Ground: Maryland during the Nineteenth Century* (New Haven, CT: Yale University Press, 1985); Kate Masur, *An Example for All the Land: Emancipation and the Struggle Over Equality in Washington, D.C.* (Chapel Hill: University of North Carolina Press, 2010); Susan E. O'Donovan, *Becoming Free in the Cotton South* (Cambridge, MA: Harvard University Press, 2007); John C. Rodrigue, *Reconstruction in the Cane Fields: From Slavery to Free Labor in Louisiana's Sugar Parishes, 1862–1880* (Baton Rouge: Louisiana State University Press, 2001); Julie Saville, *The Work of Reconstruction: From Slave to Wage Laborer in South Carolina, 1860–1870* (New York: Cambridge University Press, 1994); Leslie A. Schwalm, *A Hard Fight for We: Women's Transition from Slavery to Freedom in South Carolina* (Urbana: University of Illinois Press, 1997).

23. Edwards, *A Legal History of the Civil War and Reconstruction*, 90–119.

24. Edwards, "Reconstruction and the History of Governance"; Edwards, "The Reconstruction of Rights."

25. Scholarship on the Pension Bureau suggests the importance of this process. See, for instance, Elizabeth Ann Regosin, *Freedom's Promise: Ex-Slave Families and Citizenship in the Age of Emancipation* (Charlotte: University Press of Virginia, 2002); Brandi C. Brimmer, "Black Women's Politics, Narratives of Sexual Immorality, and Pension Bureaucracy in Mary Lee's North Carolina Neighborhood," *Journal of Southern History* 80 (November 2014): 827–58.

CONTRIBUTORS

Jonathan M. Berkey is associate professor of history at Concord University, Athens, West Virginia. He received his PhD and MA from Pennsylvania State University and his BA from Gettysburg College. He has contributed scholarship on the Civil War's impact on Shenandoah Valley civilians to a number of publications, including *The Shenandoah Valley Campaign of 1862,* edited by Gary Gallagher, and *Enemies of the Country,* edited by John Inscoe and Robert Kenzer. He is completing a study examining how civilians waged war in Virginia's lower Shenandoah Valley.

Laura F. Edwards is the Peabody Family Professor of History at Duke University. She is most recently author of *A Legal History of the Civil War and Reconstruction: A Nation of Rights,* published in 2015.

Earl M. Maltz is distinguished professor at Rutgers University School of Law in Camden, New Jersey. He is the author of nine books and many articles on constitutional law and constitutional history. His most recent book, entitled *The Coming of the Nixon Court: The 1972 Term and the Transformation of Constitutional Law,* was published in 2016.

Tamika Y. Nunley is assistant professor of history at Oberlin College. Her book manuscript *At the Threshold of Liberty* examines how enslaved African Americans interacted with the social, geographical, and legal demarcations of slavery and freedom in Washington, D.C. At Oberlin, she teaches courses about slavery, the American Civil War, women and gender, and digital humanities.

Paul Quigley is director of the Virginia Center for Civil War Studies and the James I. Robertson, Jr., Associate Professor of Civil War History in the history department at Virginia Tech. He is the author of *Shifting Grounds: Nationalism and the American South, 1848–1865,* which won the British Association for American Studies Book Prize and the Jefferson Davis Award from the Museum of the Confederacy.

Elizabeth Regosin is Charles A. Dana Professor of History at St. Lawrence University. She is the author of *Freedom's Promise: Ex-Slave Families and Citizenship in the Age of Emancipation* and coeditor, with Donald R. Shaffer, of *Voices of Emancipation: Understanding Slavery, the Civil War, and Reconstruction through the U.S. Pension Bureau Files.*

Caitlin Verboon earned her PhD from Yale University in 2015 and is an assistant editor at the Freedmen and Southern Society Project, where her research focuses on black family and kinship after the Civil War. She is also currently revising her manuscript on the uses of public space in defining citizenship in the Reconstruction-era urban South.

Lucius Wedge received his PhD from the University of Akron in 2013. He formerly taught as an adjunct professor at Walsh University, the University of Akron, and Notre Dame College. Currently he is revising his dissertation, *Andrew Johnson and the Ministers of Nashville: A Study in the Relationship between War, Politics, and Morality,* for publication.

David C. Williard is assistant professor of history at the University of St. Thomas in St. Paul, Minnesota, where he studies the transformative effects of war on the meaning of citizenship in the eras of the Civil War and Reconstruction. He is currently at work on a book titled *Confederate Legacy: The Problem of Soldierhood in the Post–Civil War South.* His study of war crimes and their consequences in North Carolina, "Executions, Justice, and Reconciliation in North Carolina's Western Piedmont, 1865–1867," appeared in the *Journal of the Civil War Era* in March 2012.

Claire Wolnisty is assistant professor of history at Angelo State University. Her research interests include the Civil War Era South, migration, and nineteenth-century networks between the South and Latin America.

Angela M. Zombek earned her PhD at the University of Florida and is assistant professor of history at St. Petersburg College in Clearwater, Florida. Her book manuscript, *Penitentiaries, Punishment, and Military Prisons: Familiar Responses to an Extraordinary Crisis during the American Civil War,* will be published in 2018.

INDEX

Note: page numbers followed by "n" indicate endnotes.